BEST Practices, BEST Thinking,

and Emerging Issues in School Leadership

WILLIAM OWINGS  LESLIE KAPLAN

EDITORS

CORWIN PRESS, INC.
A Sage Publications Company
Thousand Oaks, California

For information:

Corwin Press, Inc.
A Sage Publications Company
2455 Teller Road
Thousand Oaks, California 91320
www.corwinpress.com

Sage Publications Ltd.
6 Bonhill Street
London EC2A 4PU
United Kingdom

Sage Publications India Pvt. Ltd.
B-42 Panchsheel Enclave
Post Box 4109
New Delhi 110 017 India

Printed in the United States of America

Library of Congress Cataloging-in-Publication Data

Best practices, best thinking, and emerging issues in school leadership/
edited by William A. Owings and Leslie S. Kaplan.
    p. cm.
Includes bibliographical references and index.
ISBN 0-7619-7862-3 © — ISBN 0-7619-7863-1 (p)
  1. Educational leadership-United States. 2. School management and
organization-United States. I. Owings, William A., 1952- II. Kaplan, Leslie S.
LB2805 .B47 2003
371.2—dc211
                       2002151957

This book is printed on acid-free paper.

03   04   05   06   10 9 8 7 6 5 4 3 2

Acquisitions Editor:	Robert D. Clouse
Editorial Assistant:	Erin Clow
Production Editor:	Diana E. Axelsen
Copy Editor:	Teresa Herlinger
Typesetter:	C&M Digitals (P) Ltd.
Cover Designer:	Tracy E. Miller
Production Artist:	Janet Foulger
Indexer:	Jeanne Busemeyer

Contents

Prologue

It isn't your father's school anymore, to paraphrase a commercial.

If Principal R. Van Winkle had fallen asleep in 1950 and awakened in 2000, few physical changes in the school building itself would be apparent, other than whiteboards and computers. If, however, he were to step into the principal's office, he would find the role vastly changed.

First, the relationship of principal with faculty has been transformed. The autocratic or benevolent dictator role has become one of building vision and consensus, developing teacher leadership, and implementing and sustaining change. Principals model, not mandate, best instructional practices. Principals are responsible for orchestrating a community of learners in which all educators continually strengthen their performance for the benefit of student achievement.

Next, Van Winkle would face federal, state, and local politics to a degree never encountered before. *A Nation At Risk* (1983) initiated education reform as a highly visible political agenda. Since the 1989 Governors' Conference in Charlottesville, Virginia, and the adoption of Goals 2000, virtually every state has enacted education reform. Unfortunately, many media and political depictions misrepresent current education's effectiveness, as Gerald Bracey states. These distortions have undermined public confidence and good will in spite of the fact that public schools have never been more successful. Subsequently, this misleading portrayal has diminished teachers' and the educations community's standing. Today, even local school boards' election and governance are politically driven.

In addition, Van Winkle would find a rather well-researched body of literature on best practices in teaching, learning, and leadership. Teaching would remain an "art" but increasingly would rely on the science of brain-based learning. He would find the issue of teacher quality paramount for his professional survival, and he would discover the critical role of principal leadership in raising student achievement. Van Winkle would find technology in the classroom has changed from chalk to computers. He would have to learn quickly how to use technology to enhance the school's learning culture.

Van Winkle would also take one look at the student body and find radical demographic shifts. He would hear many languages spoken as students passed in the hallways. He would see various ethnic cultures with significant changes from his day in attitude and dress. Since Van Winkle's long nap began, public schools are again the social and learning engine of our democratic society. As Bud Hodgkinson and Gene Carter write, our nation's diversity will only increase, and the role of public schools in building a common American culture while respecting individual and group diversity will continue.

Similarly, Van Winkle would find newly included groups of students in the school—those identified with special needs. New acrostics—IEP, LD, SED, IDEA, LEP—would confuse and perplex the newly awakened principal. Preparing these students for effectiveness in a complex world beyond the small and sheltered community Van Winkle knows brings another major challenge.

Moreover, Van Winkle would find a level of accountability that never existed before he fell asleep. He would discover that assessments of student progress had evolved into high-stakes testing for students, principals, and schools. He would find the new ESEA (Elementary and Secondary Education Act, 2001, "No Child Left Behind")—schools not making "satisfactory progress" toward goals must allow students to attend other schools at the "failing" school's expense. Should this lack of progress continue, Van Winkle would find his school closed.

Likewise, virtually all case law and legislation that guide school operations' legalities have come into effect since 1950. *Brown, Tinker, Lemon,* the Civil Rights Act, and Public Law 94-142 have significantly impacted the practice of education. Van Winkle can no longer rely solely on his past experience or personal judgment when making decisions about his school, his staff, and his students.

In short, Van Winkle would be hopelessly lost in today's principalship with yesterday's knowledge and skills. If he is to survive in his new role, he must cope with the changes and become aware of the issues facing education today. If he is to be truly effective, he must take a proactive and perhaps even an activist role in influencing politics and legislation affecting education. This book will make students of educational leadership aware of these critical and emerging issues facing our profession.

AWARENESS OF CRITICAL AND EMERGING EDUCATIONAL ISSUES

Perhaps most importantly, school administrators need to be aware of media misrepresentation of school effectiveness. Bracey's book, *Setting The Record Straight* (Association for Supervision and Curriculum Development [ASCD], 1997) identifies commonly held yet erroneous beliefs about our profession. If administrators are to be effective, they must know the truth about these myths-stated-as-fact. By knowing the realities, principals can counter the myths with logical and factual arguments rather than with defensive apologies.

These misrepresented issues include declining test scores, poor international comparisons of student achievement, the high cost of education, dismal graduation rates, the differences in results between public and private schools, and the inability of American public school graduates to compete in the global marketplace. All these issues resulted in and fuel the modern standards movement.

Accountability for student achievement has never been higher. Forty-nine states have enacted or are in the process of enacting high-stakes, standards-based testing. Ronald Brandt and Linda Nathan address the issues of high-stakes testing for students and communities. Standards have undoubtedly increased student achievement. The issue for many states is whether the standards and their assessments are appropriate. The consequences for students and schools are only now becoming clear.

Teacher quality is another issue. Research now quantifies what we have known intuitively. Since Principal Van Winkle's initial practice, we know now, as Robert Marzano reports, that having an effective teacher accounts for at least 26 percentile points on academic achievement tests. Principals need to know how to enhance teacher and teaching quality so every student will benefit from having an excellent teacher. Teacher quality is the fundamental equity issue for all students.

A related topic is for principals to know and be able to use the growing body of scientific knowledge about how students learn and which teaching practices accelerate and support diverse students' achievement. Much of the synthesis on brain-based learning is reported by Robert Sylwester (see *A Celebration of Neurons: An Educator's Guide to the Human Brain*, 1995). Van Winkle saw instruction as content-driven teacher performance. Teachers disseminated knowledge; students received it. They may or may not have learned it. Today, when students have access to more information than teachers can ever "deliver," the teacher-student relationship changes, as does the students' involvement with the subject. Teachers must understand, for example, the relationship of stress and learning, and of practice and transfer, and they must provide differentiated instruction, have students establish sense and personal meaning, and foster a positive and supportive climate. Van Winkle initially saw students "parrot" information; today, he must see students apply, analyze, synthesize, and evaluate what they learn. He saw students working independently; today, they must often work effectively in teams. Increasingly, as Alan November states, technology is a means to foster this heightened student involvement in learning.

We can apply these insights and strategies to assist those who learn differently. We now expect all students to learn to a common high standard, and frequently, in the same classrooms. Principals face many challenges enlarging their school communities to accept and support students who learn differently, as Phyllis Milne writes. These traditionally disenfranchised students now have knowledgeable parents and advocates who represent their interests. Kathy Mehfoud notes the safeguarded legal procedures that direct special education students' programs. Van Winkle, who never saw a special needs student in his school, would be over-whelmed.

THE IMPORTANCE OF BEING PROACTIVE

Awareness of where the accountability movement is taking education is critical. High-stakes testing reveals what some consider to be weaknesses in the schooling process. In addition, in a time of critical teacher shortages, state lawmakers are enacting provisions to decrease teacher and principal licensure requirements. Raising standards for students while decreasing standards for teachers and school leaders makes no sense unless lawmakers want public schools to fail and open the door for privatization of education. As Linda Darling-Hammond and Gordon Cawelti point out, research clearly connects teacher quality and principal leadership with student achievement. Educators need to be proactive in demanding research-based licensure requirements that enhance educator quality for their students. Many "quick-fix" alternative licensure routes do not prepare individuals to be effective in the classroom or the main office.

Increasingly, it will become critical for all educators to take a proactive and sometimes activist stance for our profession. Principals must be able to articulate the issues that impact student learning and well-being within their own school community. Principals must press for issues related to teacher quality for the sake of student achievement. Likewise, educational leaders must communicate the "big picture" that education requires meeting desired and measured standards but goes far beyond test scores. Influence, therefore, begins at home but must extend to the state capitol where legislation that impacts local practice begins.

Professional organizations have the ability to influence state and federal legislation through their member representatives. Members within the organization are also citizen voters who share a responsibility in shaping society. Influence involves developing position statements on important topics and educating legislators about various issues. In addition, collaborating with related educational organizations compounds their effectiveness as they work together toward common goals.

Principals practice in a crisis-filled environment. As Paul Houston illustrates, the Chinese symbol for crisis is made up of two sub-symbols: danger and opportunity. If we do not become proactive, our profession faces grave danger. When we actively influence policy at the political level, we can see great opportunity for enhancing public education. We must work in the political arena to benefit all our students. The choice to influence is ours.

—*William A. Owings*
—*Leslie S. Kaplan*

REFERENCE

Sylwester, R. (1995). *A celebration of neurons: An educator's guide to the human brain*. Alexandria, VA: Association for Supervision and Curriculum Development.

A Brief Look at the ISSLC Standards

The high expectations for student safety and achievement placed on today's school leadership are unprecedented. As these critical and emerging issues and the public accountability for results impact the schoolhouse, the principal's role is changing. School leaders need a way to make sense of the varying and often conflicting pressures placed upon them as they work to improve their schools.

During the past decade, the Council of Chief State School Officers (CCSSO) has led a national initiative to create a common vision to ensure effective school leadership. Through the CCSSO-sponsored Interstate School Leaders Licensure Consortium (ISLLC), a set of unified standards has been developed and a corresponding professional development process has been recommended to ensure use of research-based practices in preparing principals for their roles. These standards provide a coherent philosophical and practical lens that principals can use to assess and act on these factors. A quality school leader promotes the success of all students by doing the following things:

1. *Developing a vision of learning shared and supported by the school community.* The school leader identifies and removes barriers to the shared vision and invites, recognizes, and celebrates all school community members' contributions.

2. *Advocating, nurturing, and sustaining a school culture and instructional program conducive to student learning and professional growth.* The principal treats all individuals with dignity and respect; gets more data from stakeholders before making decisions; values conflict resolution and consensus building; maintains a culture of high expectations; understands human growth and development and the principles of effective instruction; and provides multiple opportunities to learn.

3. *Ensuring effective and efficient management of the learning environment.* The principal addresses health and safety issues first; uses operations procedures that maximize learning; uses effective problem framing, problem-solving skills, and conflict-resolution skills; practices sound fiscal management, valuing both price and service; avoids appearance of conflicts of interest; and shows flexibility in dealing with students' learning needs.

4. *Responding to diverse community interests and needs and mobilizing community resources.* The principal builds family partnerships to support learning; respects parents' information and insight about students' learning needs; recognizes parents' and students' religious and civil rights; gives credence to individuals with conflicting opinions; suggests alternative plans of action; nurtures relationships with community leaders; and accesses community resources to solve problems.

5. *Acting with integrity, fairness, and in an ethical manner.* The principal develops and uses written policies to ensure fairness in resource use.

6. *Understanding and responding to the larger political, social, economic, legal, and cultural context.* The principal understands and responds appropriately to changes in the larger society in ways that enhance student safety and learning.

These standards provide clear guidance for principals as they navigate the critical and emerging issues raised here. Each issue requires leaders to understand and enact these standards as guides for planning and decision making, often using several standards at the same time. The standards provide a clear blueprint for principals to effectively meet the many critical and emerging issues in educational leadership.

REFERENCES

Council of Chief State School Officers (1998). *Propositions for quality professional development for school administrators.* Washington, DC: Author.
Council of Chief State School Officers (2000). *Collaborative development process for school leaders.* Washington, DC: Author.

About the Editors

**William A. Owings, Ed.D.,** is Associate Professor of Education at Old Dominion University in Norfolk, Virginia, where he chairs the Educational Leadership program. Formerly, he held a similar position at Longwood University in Farmville, Virginia, where he was also Founder and Director of the Longwood University Principals' Institute and Longwood Center for School Improvement. He has worked as a public school teacher, an elementary school principal, a high school principal, an assistant superintendent, and a division superintendent of schools. In addition, his scholarly publications appear in *Educational Leadership*, the *NASSP* (National Association of Secondary School Principals) *Bulletin*, *NASSP Principal Leadership*, *NASSP Schools in the Middle*, and *Phi Delta Kappa Fastback Series*. His book, *Teacher Quality, Teaching Quality, and School Improvement*, coauthored with Dr. Leslie S. Kaplan, is scheduled for Winter 2003 publication. Dr. Owings also serves on the Board of the Association for Supervision and Curriculum Development (ASCD) and the Virginia affiliate's Board of Directors and ASCD Issues Committee. In addition, he is a frequent presenter at many state and national conferences and a consultant to school divisions on educational leadership and instructional improvement.

Leslie S. Kaplan, Ed.D, is Assistant Principal for Instruction at Warwick High School in Newport News, Virginia. She has worked as an assistant principal in high school and middle schools and has been a middle school and high school guidance counselor and English teacher. In addition to school-based leadership, she also served in the central office as a director of program development. She has received recognition as both 1988 Virginia Counselor of the Year and 1998 Virginia Assistant Principal of the Year, and she is a popular speaker at state and national conferences on the issues of instructional leadership and improvement. She is the former founding co-director of the Longwood University Principals' Institute and Longwood Center for School Improvement. Her scholarly publications appear in *The School Counselor, NASSP Bulletin, NASSP Principal Leadership, NASSP Schools in the Middle,* and *Phi Delta Kappa Fastback Series.* Her book, *Teacher Quality, Teaching Quality, and School Improvement,* coauthored with Dr. Owings, is scheduled for Winter 2003 publication. She also serves on the *NASSP Bulletin* Advisory Committee and is the immediate past president of the Virginia Association for Supervision and Curriculum Development.

About the Contributors

M. David Alexander, Ed.D., is Department Chair and Professor in the Department of Educational Leadership and Policy Studies at Virginia Polytechnic Institute and State University. He has been a teacher, coach, school board member, professor, regional laboratory administrator, and university administrator. He has consulted with national, state, and local organizations. He has given more than 150 international, national, regional, and state presentations on school law, school finance, and educational administration of public schools, and has authored or coauthored seven books. He has also published more than 60 chapters, journal articles, and research reports. Among his books are *American Public School Law* and *The Law of Schools, Teachers, and Students in a Nutshell.*

Sandra L. Berger is the Gifted Education Information Specialist at the ERIC Clearinghouse on Disabilities and Gifted Education in Arlington, Virginia. She has been involved with technology for 12 years, has written numerous textbook chapters and articles, and writes a regular periodical column on technology. Major publications include *College Planning for Gifted Students, 1998 Revised Edition.*

Frank M. Betts, Ed.D., is a former university teacher, school superintendent, Director of ASCD's Education and Technology Resource Center, and ASCD Deputy Executive Director for Operations. He developed the *ASCD Curriculum Handbook* and the *Curriculum/Technology Newsletter* and was instrumental in ASCD's publication of professional development resources on the Internet. After a short retirement, he returned to education to lead the community-based Computers for Kids Foundation on Colorado's western slope.

Gerald W. Bracey, Ph.D., is an independent researcher and writer in Alexandria, Virginia. He is also an Associate with the High/Scope Educational Research Foundation in Ypsilanti, Michigan and an Associate Professor in the Graduate School of Education at George Mason University, Fairfax, Virginia. Each October since 1991, he has produced

"The Bracey Report on the Condition of Public Education" in *Phi Delta Kappan*. His most recent books are *What You Should Know About the War on America's Public Schools* (2002) and *Put to the Test: An Educator's and Consumer's Guide to Standardized Testing* (revised edition, 2002).

Ronald S. Brandt, Ed.D., is Executive Editor Emeritus of *Educational Leadership* and other publications of the Association for Supervision and Curriculum Development (ASCD) and holds an adjunct appointment as Senior Research Associate at the National Study of School Evaluation, Schaumburg, Illinois. He is the author of *Powerful Learning* (1998), and editor of *Assessing Student Learning* (1998) and *Education in a New Era* (2000). More recently he has written articles appearing in *Principal, Phi Delta Kappan, Education Week*, and *Educational Leadership*. He is a member of the board of directors of McREL, a regional education laboratory in Aurora, Colorado. In 1996, he was named to the EdPress Hall of Fame for his contributions to education publishing, and, in 1997, was honored by the National Staff Development Council for lifetime contributions to staff development for educators. In the 1960s, he taught at a teacher training college in Nigeria, West Africa, in a University of Wisconsin project. He was a junior high school principal, staff member of the Upper Midwest Regional Educational Laboratory, director of staff development for the Minneapolis public schools, and associate superintendent in Lincoln, Nebraska.

Gene R. Carter, Ed.D., is Executive Director of the Association for Supervision and Curriculum Development (ASCD). Previously, he served for nine years as the superintendent of schools in Norfolk, Virginia, where he succeeded in reducing the dropout rate, built a partnership program with the private sector, implemented a districtwide school improvement program, established an early childhood education center for 3-year-olds and their parents, and implemented a regional scholarship foundation for public school students. He has written numerous articles and book chapters concentrating on educational issues and topics. He is the coauthor of *The American School Superintendent: Leading in an Age of Pressure* (1997).

Gordon Cawelti, Ph.D., is Senior Research Associate for the Educational Research Service in Arlington, Virginia, and also serves as Director of the Achievement Consortium, which is sponsored by the Mid-Atlantic Regional Educational Lab in Philadelphia. From 1969 to 1973, he served as superintendent of the 80,000-student Tulsa Public Schools where he was involved in developing several innovative schools and provided leadership in the school desegregation process. He served for 19 years as Executive Director of the Association for Supervision and Curriculum Development. During this time, ASCD grew from 12,000 to 155,000 members, established affiliates in all 50 states and in Germany, the Netherlands, the United Kingdom, Singapore, Japan, Canada, and in the Caribbean. He has published over 150 articles and books on school leadership and curriculum, including *Effects of High School Restructuring: Ten Schools at Work*. He was also editor of the *Handbook of Research on Improving Student Achievement*. His more recent research has focused on high- performing school districts whose substantial gains in student achievement were reported in *High Student Achievements: How Six School Districts Changed Into High-Performance Systems*.

Kelly Clark/Keefe, Ed.D., is Research Assistant Professor at the University of Vermont. She teaches qualitative research methods courses and is engaged in applied educational inquiry to assess the policy outcomes associated with Vermont legislation for reforming special and general education. Other scholarly interests include studying and practicing arts-based approaches to educational research, embodied conceptualizations of identity development, and the relationship of socioeconomic status and gender to educational experiences.

Linda Darling-Hammond, Ed.D., is the Charles E. Ducommun Professor of Education at Stanford University and was Founding Executive Director of the National Commission on Teaching and America's Future. Her research, teaching, and policy interests are focused on teacher quality, school restructuring, and educational equity. Among her 9 books and more than 200 journal articles is *The Right to Learn: A Blueprint for Schools that Work*, which received the AERA Outstanding Book Award in 2000.

Michael F. DiPaola, Ed.D., is a member of the faculty of the Educational Policy, Planning and Leadership Program of the School of Education at William & Mary. His career in public education spanned three decades, including a decade of classroom teaching. He also served as an assistant principal in a 7-12 building and as principal of a grade 10-12 senior high school. Prior to joining the faculty at the college, he was the Superintendent of the Public Schools in Pitman, New Jersey, for six years. His teaching and research interests include the interactions of professionals in school organizations, performance evaluation, intra-organizational conflict, professional preparation of administrators, and the superintendency.

Kenneth A. Engebretson is Executive Director for Technology Information Services in the Newport News Public Schools, Virginia. In that role, he oversees the operation of the division's technology information services department to include management information systems, library media services, network and computer support services, and instructional technology. He provides project leadership and management control for significant business information and instructional technology initiatives funded by the school division. Formerly, he was CIO for the Tidewater Physicians Multispecialty Group in Newport News and Senior Systems Analyst for Betac Corporation in Hampton, and he served in the U.S. Air Force for 26 years.

Nora G. Friedman, Ed.D., is principal of the South Grove Elementary School in the Syosset School District, New York, and mentor to a team of enrichment specialists, district-wide. She has worked in schools as a classroom teacher, enrichment specialist and building administrator implementing or considering the implementation of the Schoolwide Enrichment Model. She earned a doctorate in education at Hofstra University, focusing her work on the policy implications for the implementation of this model. She is a nationally certified Talents Unlimited Trainer and has many years of experience as a teacher and an administrator working with colleagues and parents to bring academic challenge and school satisfaction to a broad range of students.

Michael Fullan, Ph.D., is Dean of the Ontario Institute for Studies in Education of the University of Toronto. An innovator and leader in teacher education, he has developed a number of partnerships designed to bring about major school improvement and educational reform. He participates as researcher, consultant, trainer, and policy advisor on a wide range of educational change projects with school systems, teachers' federations, research and development institutes, and government agencies in Canada and internationally. He has published widely on the topic of educational change. His most recent books are *The New Meaning of Educational Change, 3rd Edition* and *Leading in a Culture of Change.* He has also published *Change Forces: The Sequel*, *Change Forces: Probing the Depths of Educational Reform*, and the *What's Worth Fighting For* series. He is currently leading the evaluation team conducting a four-year assessment of the National Literacy and Numeracy Strategy in England. With colleagues, he is conducting training, research, and evaluation of literacy initiatives in several school districts, including the Toronto School District Board, York Region, Peel and Edmonton Catholic School District.

Susan Brody Hasazi, Ed.D., is Professor in the Department of Education and Director of the Doctoral Program in Education Leadership and Policy Studies at the University of Vermont. She has directed numerous USDE personnel preparation projects for training special and general educators and human services professionals in the skills necessary to meet the transitional and postsecondary needs of youth considered at risk of academic failure. She is the author or coauthor of more than 50 professional publications.

Her work has appeared in many publications, including *Exceptional Children*, *Journal of Disability Policy Studies*, *Journal of Vocational Rehabilitation*, and *Mental Retardation*.

Harold L. ("Bud") Hodgkinson, Ph.D., is Director of the Center for Demographic Policy at the Institute for Educational Leadership, Inc., in Washington, D.C. He is widely known as a lecturer and analyst of demographic and educational issues. His consulting assignments have included over 600 colleges and universities, numerous public and private schools and school systems, state and federal agencies, and many corporations, including Bank of America, South Trust, 3M, Federal Express, IBM, and General Motors. He is the author of 12 books, three of which have won national awards, and more than 200 articles, for which he has been honored by the American Education Press Association. His recent publications include *Bringing Tomorrow Into Focus; Hispanic Americans: A Look Back, A Look Ahead; Immigration to America: The Asian Experience* (with Anita M. Obarapor); and *A Demographic Look at Tomorrow*. He has been editor of several journals, including the *Harvard Educational Review* and the *Journal of Higher Education*. In 1989, he was one of three Americans awarded the title of Distinguished Lecturer by the National Science Foundation.

Paul D. Houston, Ed.D., has served as a teacher and building administrator in North Carolina and New Jersey, as well as assistant superintendent in Birmingham, Alabama, and superintendent of schools in Princeton, New Jersey; Tucson, Arizona; and Riverside, California. He has also served in an adjunct capacity for the University of North Carolina, Harvard University, Brigham Young University and Princeton University. He has served as a consultant and speaker throughout the United States and abroad, and he has published more than 100 articles in professional journals. In 1991, he received the Richard R. Green Leadership Award from the Council of Great City Schools, for his leadership in urban education. He coauthored the book *Exploding the Myths* (1993), and in 1997 published *Articles of Faith and Hope for Public Education*.

Robert J. Marzano, Ph.D., is a Senior Fellow at the Mid-Continent Regional Laboratory (McREL) in Aurora, Colorado. Previously, he was Associate Professor at the University of Colorado and a high school English teacher and department chair. An internationally known trainer and speaker, he has written 15 books and more than 100 articles and chapters in books on such topics as reading and writing instruction, thinking skills, school effectiveness, restructuring, assessment, cognition, and standards implementation.

Thomas S. Mawhinney, Ed.D., has been an educator for 31 years and the principal of Rhinebeck High School for the past 9. He is the author of several articles on teaching and learning. He also is on the faculty of the weeklong International Learning Styles Institute held yearly in New York City.

Kathleen S. Mehfoud, J.D., is a partner in the Richmond, Virginia office of the law firm of Reed Smith LLP. She has practiced law for 24 years and has concentrated her practice in education law and special education law. She provides consultation services on a national basis and represents over half of the school boards in Virginia. She also serves as chair on the School Attorneys Special Education Advisory Council, providing consultative services to LRP Publications, and she serves on the Foundation Board for Mary Washington College.

Phyllis Milne, Ed.D., is principal of Tabb Elementary School in York County, Virginia. She has also served as a reading specialist and as a first- and fourth-grade teacher. In addition, she is a professorial lecturer for The George Washington University.

Patricia Morgan, M.Ed., is the state coordinator for the Higher Education Collaborative in Vermont, a field-based, multi-institutional special education teacher preparation program. She has been a faculty member at the University of Vermont for fifteen years, and is currently a student in the doctoral program in educational leadership and policy studies at the University of Vermont. Her work on numerous grants has focused primarily on school reform and transition issues in secondary schools.

Linda Nathan, Ed.D., is Headmaster at the Boston Arts Academy in Boston, Massachusetts. She was instrumental in starting Boston's first performing arts middle school and in creating the city's first middle college high school, Fenway High School, which is recognized nationally for its innovative educational strategies and school-to-work programs. She is co-founder and a board member of the Center for Collaborative Education–Metro Boston, an education reform organization. From 1995-1998, she served on the National Academy of Science's Commission on the Science of Learning, and she was honored as a 1990 Massachusetts Teacher of the Year. In addition to her achievements as an educator, she has worked as an actor, director, and playwright, and has recently worked on uses of school reform in Puerto Rico, Brazil, and Argentina.

Alan November is an internationally respected consultant in integrating technology across the curriculum. He has given numerous keynote addresses and has worked in forty-seven states as well as Canada, Scotland, England, Ireland, France, and Russia. He has also published articles and is the author of *Computer Literacy Through Applications* (1985).

A former science teacher and technology coordinator, he worked for three decades in the education field and was honored as the first Christa McAuliffe Educator by the National Foundation for Improvement in Education.

William Patterson, Ed.D, is the Director of the University of Denver High School and teaches graduate and undergraduate courses on school reform at the University of Denver. He may be contacted at wpatters@du.edu.

Marguerite A. Pittman has been a principal for 11 years, working in three elementary schools. She has also served as an instructional specialist, administrative assistant, assistant principal, and teacher. She taught self-contained primary educable mentally disabled students and kindergarten in Hampton City Schools, Virginia, and kindergarten in Newport News Public Schools, Virginia.

Patricia Jordan Rea, Ed.D., is Assistant Professor of Educational Leadership at The George Washington University and Visiting Scholar at Eastern Virginia Medical School. Her research interests include outcomes for students with disabilities, and professional collaboration and its impact on student performance.

Laura L. Sagan is an eighth-grade social studies teacher at Bulkeley Middle School in Rhinebeck, New York. She is a doctoral candidate in Instructional Leadership at St. John's University. She also is an adjunct instructor at the State University of New York at New Paltz.

Richard W. Shelly, Ed.D., is Resident Practitioner for Testing and Assessment at the National Association of Secondary School Principals. He was the founding director of the Roanoke Valley (Virginia) Governor's School for Science and Technology. He may be contacted at shellyr @principals.org.

Jennifer A. Sughrue, Ph.D., is Assistant Professor at Virginia Tech in the Department of Educational Leadership and Policy Studies, where she teaches public school law, finance, history of American schooling, and comparative international education. She has 20 years of experience in K-12 education, primarily as a teacher and administrator in international schools in Africa and South America. Her research interests are primarily in the area of educational law, finance, and policy.

Gerald N. Tirozzi, Ph.D., is Executive Director of the National Association of Secondary School Principals (NASSP). Previously, he has served as Assistant Secretary of Elementary and Secondary Education at the U.S. Department of Education (1996-1999), professor at the University of

Connecticut's Department of Educational Leadership (1993-95), president of Wheelock College (1991-93), Connecticut's Commissioner of Education (1983-1991), and superintendent in the New Haven (CT) Public Schools (1977-1983), where he previously worked as a principal, guidance counselor, and teacher. He serves on a number of national advisory boards and professional organizations, including: the International Baccalaureate, the National Council for Corporate and School Partnerships (founded by Coca Cola Corporation), the Learning First Alliance, and the *USA Today* Education Advisory Panel.

Chriss Walther-Thomas, Ph.D., is Professor in the Educational Policy, Planning, and Leadership Program at the College of William & Mary in Williamsburg, Virginia. Previously, she was clinical instructor for eight years at the University of Utah in Salt Lake City. She completed her doctoral work at the University of Kansas, and she taught elementary and middle school students with learning and behavior disorders in Salt Lake City. She is coauthor of a textbook on inclusive schools, *Collaboration for effective inclusive education: Developing successful programs* (2000). A recipient of numerous competitive federal and state grants, she has authored or coauthored more than 30 articles and chapters, presented at numerous national conferences, and has served as a field editor for a number of education journals. She recently completed a term as President of the Council for Learning Disabilities.

Part I

Understanding Schools and Leadership

1

Changing Demographics—
A Call for Leadership

Bud Hodgkinson

Overview

Demographics, the study of cohorts, provide certain "givens" with which all educational leaders work. Today, most schools must address issues of racial and economic diversity. Poverty has a pervasive relationship with school performance; if you know the household income and educational level of the parents, you can predict about half of the variance in scores on the NAEP, as well as most IQ tests. Likewise, transience, or the movement of students in and out of different schools, creates severe educational and community problems. High-transience states have the lowest percentage of high school graduates admitted to college and also have the nation's highest crime rates. States' differences in educational achievement are far greater than any

AUTHOR'S NOTE: Unless otherwise cited, all data are from *Statistical Abstract of the United States*, 2001.

test score differences between American students and those of other nations. Race also impacts educational leadership in complex ways. The complexity of school districts across many categories makes school leadership exponentially more difficult. If a leader plays a different role in a stable community than in one with high student turnover, schools of education are challenged to adequately prepare educational leaders for these new realities that vary from state to state.

"Leadership" is one of those words we assume we know. Nevertheless, it is almost impossible to predict that a particular person will become a leader in a particular situation. From Shakespeare's Henry V to Winston Churchill, the world is full of people who were assumed to have no leadership qualities, yet at the right time turned in spectacular performances. The opposite can also be true. Many new superintendents who would have been magnificent in a posh suburb ended up in an inner city as a mediocre practitioner. Indeed, part of life's fun is the surprise at how often some people can rise above their talents and background in a particular setting.

However, in education the leader must work with certain "givens." Many, if not most, of these givens fall under the category of demographics. Basically, psychology studies individuals, sociology studies groups, and demography studies cohorts. Black citizens of Wisconsin who are between 21 and 40 years of age are not a group but a cohort. Cohort behavior can be predicted with great precision without predicting the behavior of any individual within the cohort. Therefore, in this chapter, we will present a series of demographic developments that will demand a response from educational leaders, then conclude with some summary comments about leadership and demographic environments.

GLOBAL ISSUES—THE HUMAN SPECIES

Our species numbers a little over 6 billion at present, but everywhere in the world, females are having fewer children than their ancestors did. In 100 years, our species will have fewer youth and more elderly, and is predicted to stabilize at 11 billion. Our population will then begin a decline as 11 billion people cannot be maintained with the lower birth rate in 2100, and a large number of humans will have aged out of the child bearing years. We can feed 11 billion people and provide clean air and drinking water, but there is no way 11 billion of us can have flush toilets.

Few people live well. Of our current 6 billion, one-third live in only two nations—India and China at one billion each. When we think of the "developed" nations, we are talking about 11% of the population. When we discuss "globalization," we are talking about only a handful of the more than 200 nations containing our species—almost 2 billion people in the world today have never made a phone call. The computer the U.S. worker can buy with one month's wages would require eight years of work for the Bangladeshi worker. Our species is either very rich or very poor. Bill Gates's assets equal the total earnings of 42% of the U.S. population; the richest 200 people in the world represent about 40% of the world's prosperity. Currently, almost 200 million children have no education/schooling available to them at all and virtually no health care.

It is probably time for American students and teachers to understand what life is like for over a billion people who live in utter poverty. If we can teach children about the plight of the snail darter, it should be possible to convey the life of over 1.5 billion "endangered" members of our own species. The international protests against globalization, from Seattle to DC, suggest that the developed nations are proceeding to improve their own economies with complete disregard for a majority of the human species living in undeveloped nations.

It is vital that Americans understand this critical issue, and it will require the most courageous kind of educational leadership, from boards, superintendents, principals, and teachers. It will be crucial to present these facts without framing all the answers for our students, many of whom will live part of their lives in another nation, and many more of whom will have to adapt to an increasingly diverse United States. Our geography has made it all too easy to be isolationist, and the schools have aided in creating this mindset. If September 11 has truly changed our feelings about involvement in the world, and about our vulnerability to angry members of societies that resent our values, the schools will have to foster understanding through leadership in every public school in the nation.

CENSUS 2000—IMPLICATIONS FOR SCHOOLS

The nation reached a population of 281 million in 2000, but half of these people lived in only 10 states. (In fact, over a third lived in only nine metro areas!) *Nothing is distributed evenly across the United States*, not sex, race, religion, wealth, or educational level. In the year 2000, almost 40% of public school students were "minority," and there were more Hispanics (not a race but an "ethnic group") than there were blacks. People were allowed, for the first time, to choose as many racial categories as they wished (which we will consider later). At the time of the 2000 census, blacks had moved to the suburbs in record numbers, owned their own homes, and could afford to have their children attend college. In addition, many blacks migrated back to the "New South," especially the Coastal South, after their parents and grandparents had moved to the big cities in the Midwest and secured manufacturing jobs. Blacks, especially with college degrees, were welcomed "back" to the South; in 2000, none of the 10 most segregated cities in the nation were in the South. As of this writing, the black high school graduation rate is roughly equal to that of whites; access to college is also much improved for blacks, but the college graduation rate is not. Hispanics are still working on improving their high school graduation rate, although they have done very well in small business starts and in home ownership.

As residential patterns change, so do demographics in school populations. By 2000, approximately 80,000 schools were spread across 15,000 school districts in 3,068 counties, with almost 50 million students taught by 2.4 million teachers. (For every teacher there was one additional paid nonteaching adult.) Compared with the Baby Boom (1946-1954) and Boomlet (1977-1983) years, school enrollments in 2000 had increased very little across the nation, but again nothing is distributed evenly. Five states had considerable increases; ten states posted declines; and large numbers of states grew only a couple of percentage points in enrollments.

In addition, about half the population lived in suburbs, a quarter in big cities, and a quarter in small towns and rural areas. However, because of the local control tradition, our 80,000 schools are systematically skewed toward the small towns and rural areas. Nineteen thousand schools are in big cities, 22,000 in suburbs, and 39,000 in small towns and rural areas. Moreover, in 1990, the inner rings of big cities contained impoverished families, immigrants, elderly persons, and singles, while the outer rings teemed with children and young middle-class parents, all demanding a variety of youth services. By 2000, however, differences in economic status between inner and outer rings were decreasing; wealthy counties like Fairfax, Virginia, had over 30% of its students eligible for free federal lunch programs. Immigrants are increasing in the distant suburban rings, and singles are moving into every ring. Everything in the cities in 1990 has "come to a suburb near you," and vice versa. While national racial diversity has increased, over 70% of our 3,068 counties remain over 80% white. On the other hand, a few large places in the nation remain 100% white: most suburbs are now racially and economically diverse to some degree. While an incredible 43 million Americans move every year, this transience, unfortunately, creates one of the most severe educational problems. During a 5-year period, almost half of us move to a different house/apartment. No other nation's people move that often, nor would they want to! The vast majority of moves are within the same state, almost half within the same county; ten million people move to a different address (attend a different school) every year. Some estimate that a million young people in the United States have no fixed address or phone number.

Moreover, transience has a major impact on the community. Transience has a very direct link to crime. As a police chief told this author, "If you don't know your neighbor, you might just as well steal his lawnmower." In addition, a teacher in a transient area may begin and end the year with

24 students, but 22 of the 24 may be different students from the ones he/she started the year with! To be a principal in a school with a 35% yearly turnover is much more difficult than being principal in a school where almost all the students remain for years. The states with the highest percentage of 19-year-olds who have graduated from high school and been admitted to college (55-60%) are stable states with little transience, while the bottom states, with only 25 to 30% of 19-year-olds graduated from high school and admitted to college, are the nation's six most transient states with the six highest crime rates! These states' differences in educational achievement are far greater than any test score differences between American students and those of other nations. This greater complexity of school districts along many categories makes the issue of school leader-ship exponentially more difficult. By 2015, in schools in states like California, Texas, Florida, and New York, minority students will become the majority, while minorities in Maine schools will only account for 9% of the student body. A successful superintendent or principal from Maine, therefore, will not necessarily possess the qualities or experience to be a "leader" in Florida. While about 2,000 of our 3,068 counties have a white majority, and students might relocate to a more diverse part of the nation, what kind of diversity training should leaders receive? As one principal asked, "they need diversity training, but whom do they practice on?" How should school leaders be trained (if that's not an oxymoron) to deal with transient students and faculty, while also handling increased diversity of those who stay? If a leader plays a different role in a stable community than in one with a constant stream of people moving in and out, how do leadership training programs in schools of education prepare prospective principals and superintendents?

POVERTY AND LEADERSHIP

Although the United States is the richest nation in terms of Gross National Product, the family at the 90th percentile makes almost 6 times as much as the family at the 10th percentile of income, the biggest gap of any "devel-oped" nation in the Luxemburg Income Study (see www.lisproject.org). It is also clear that the gap between rich and poor in the United States is increasing. While it is seldom mentioned, when we look at the more than 17 million youth in the United States who live in poverty (20% of all children), about 9 million of them are white, 4 million are black, and almost 4 million are Hispanic. What the newspapers and TV cover is the fact that poor black children are 37% of all black youth, Hispanics about the same, while the 9 million poor white children are only 16% of all white children. While it is true that black and Hispanic communities have severe poverty problems, poor white children also have major economic issues, in Appalachia as well as in other areas. Given the large number of middle-class blacks, now college graduates and living in the suburbs with good jobs, being born black is no longer a universally handicapping condition. However, being born poor is—no one ever benefited from being born into poverty.

It is also clear that racial desegregation has not led to economic equality. Some examples of working on the issue of youth poverty can be seen— the San Francisco Schools are adding a few low-income students to a number of middle-income schools with excellent results. If the numbers of low-income kids are small, the middle-income majority does not suffer score declines. At the same time, the low-income students placed into this new environment often show surprising score and attitude gains. The Kentucky Schools decided about a decade ago to build an income "floor" under every student in low-income rural areas, to assure an equal investment with those students in more affluent suburban schools. Over the last 20 years, the rate of youth poverty in America has been steady at 20%. Poverty has a dramatic relationship to school performance. As noted above, the household income and educational level of parents can predict about half of the variance in scores on the NAEP, as well as most IQ tests. It is true that an occasional brilliant, charismatic school leader, usually a principal, has been able to inspire low-income students and teachers to very high performance levels. But such examples are so rare, they are the exception that proves the rule.

Environments do have a pervasive impact on behavior; studies show that a criminal, released back into the same environment that made him/her a criminal in the first place, will be back in jail within four years of release. Similarly, some environments clearly make it more difficult for the educational system to achieve success. The San Francisco experiment works by taking children out of difficult environments and putting them into productive ones, at least part-time. We also are trying to increase the number of parents who have the literacy skills needed to read to their children at home, thus improving the environment for learning in another way. Head Start, never fully funded, has shown pervasive and positive results through time. The shift from "day care" (hours of TV and naps) to "preschool" (children learn their letters and numbers, learn English when needed, and how to behave with other youngsters) is one of today's most promising efforts at equalizing opportunity. Nevertheless, poverty rates don't decline, and more efforts are needed in this direction.

Many of these changes will take years before they improve young people's school performances, and a real test of school leaders will be to make everyone—business, government, parent, and even teacher leadership—"stay the course" for the decade or more that will be necessary for improvement to take hold. "High-stakes" tests have a role to play, but it should be limited to assessing what curriculum innovations are working, and how they could be improved. Otherwise, it's like asking a thermometer to cure a fever. School leaders will have to make sure that what is taught in the classroom is of primary importance, well-aligned with state content standards, and that the tests not only assess how well the curriculum is learned, but also are demonstrably useful in improving performance.

THE TRANSFORMATION OF "RACE" IN CENSUS 2000

Ever since Thomas Jefferson directed the first U.S. census, we have used it to adjust the government to fit changes in the people by changing the number of U.S. House of Representatives' members from each state. No census has ever used exactly the same racial criteria as the previous census. However, we have never been able to describe ourselves as a combination of races and ethnic groups—until Census 2000. For a century, anthropologists have said that no scientific basis exists for racial categories; and other nations that have a census almost never use the U.S. definitions of race (at least as they were used in the last census—there are no "Hispanics" anywhere in the world except in the United States, and none listed there until the 1980 census).

Census 2000 has brought two major shifts in our thinking about race. First, racial lines are blurring. Seven million people said that they were of mixed racial ancestry in Census 2000, the first time the census has ever allowed this answer. Tiger Woods is indeed a "Cablinasian": Caucasian, black, Indian, and Asian. But is he *fully* black? Or is he exactly one quarter black, and who figured that out? If one adds Native Americans who are mixed to the Native American pool, one doubles the size of the American Indian population. Children of Asian and Hispanic immigrants are marrying out of their "race" in more than a third of the cases. The politics of race will cause some minority leaders to argue that "one percent of black blood makes you *fully* black" but then Tiger would have to be *fully* each of the categories that are actually only a quarter of who he is. Tiger could be considered four "total" people under this logic. In addition, all of the longitudinal studies of racial groups would be invalid, as the 7 million people of "mixed ancestry" could not be considered in any sample of progress in economics, education, housing, or on any measure of racial change in America, like the National Longitudinal Study. In order to qualify for federal funds, every superintendent would have to fill out, not the 5 racial categories for each student, but all the combinations as well (64 boxes to describe "race," another 64 if you add "Hispanics," who are not a race but an "ethnic group" very poorly defined in the census forms). Many court cases have already held that a school system may not force a student to choose between the mother and father's racial/ethnic heritage, thus supporting multiracial answers to school records questions on students' racial qualifications. The unmanageability of racial "labeling" in educational systems makes "poverty" a more useful variable—you're either eligible for free/reduced price federal lunches or you're not. Poverty may become the major criterion for inequity, which would make some sense, given the increased ambiguity of race.

The second major racial shift is the increased preference for national origin over race, even among blacks. For years we have known that Asians do not cluster in America; Chinese do, Koreans do, Japanese do. Even if Hispanics are not a "race," it's still true that Mexicans cluster in Texas, Cubans in Florida. American Indians are another obvious example. As early as 1900, "Euro-Americans" clustered separately, for instance, in groups of Germans, Italians, and Poles. In fact, if an Italian woman married a German man in 1900, the event would be called "miscegenation," and the two families might never speak to each other. Today, only 15% of "European-Americans" are German/German, Italian/Italian, and so on. The "melting pot" came to be through Americans marrying people who came from other nations, as we are now seeing with Hispanic and Asian immigrants.

However, the situation for blacks has been different. Since the 1960s, it has been essential for the civil rights agenda's establishment that all blacks be seen as identical—brothers and sisters of the same lineage. Any splintering would have drastically reduced the impact of the national campaign, from *Brown v. Board of Education* in Topeka to King's "I Have a Dream" speech in Washington. Ignoring differences within the black community was a political necessity, even though it was common knowledge that Martin Luther King Jr. had an Irish grandmother and that many black leaders, like Malcolm X, were of mixed white and black ancestry.

Yet in 2002, due in part to Census 2000's provision for people of mixed ancestry, even the black community is beginning to see national origin as more important than race. Although some civil rights activists and community leaders still emphasize black solidarity, blacks are no longer a monolithic group but are as varied as the Asian and Hispanic communities. For example, almost half of Miami's black community is West Indian, while a third of New York City's black population were born in another nation such as Haiti, Nigeria, Senegal, or Jamaica. In Boston, large numbers of blacks are Cape Verdean, and "brown blacks" are from Ethiopia and Somalia. Many U.S. Haitians are as worried about being seen as "all white" as they are about being seen as "all black." It is also becoming clear that many U.S. blacks actually know very little about their African origins. Will Smith, the actor, made his first trip to Africa in 2000 and reported that "everything I knew about Africa was 80% false" ("Nationality Trumps Skin Color," 2002).

Taking into account the nation's complex racial, ethnic, and national origins presents a challenge for educational leaders whose own diversity is thin and getting thinner. At present almost 40% of our students are "nonwhite," compared with 10% of secondary teachers, 14% of K-6 teachers, 16% of principals, and only 4% of superintendents (*Schools and Staffing in the United States*, 1996). It isn't just the schools—of our 3,000 counties, about 2,000 are more than 85% white. With 43 million of us moving every year, many students will move from virtually all-white schools into more diverse schools and communities, without much previous experience of knowing students from different backgrounds and cultures, because they were simply not present in any quantity in the school from which they moved.

It is of course true that American schools reflect the nation far more than they change it, but the complex issues involving the blurring of racial lines, the new preference for national origin, and the interaction of race and poverty create major challenges for educational leadership. Because each major metro area in the country has its own unique "fingerprint" of diversity, tradition, local/political leadership, and economic development, future educational leaders may have to be either "home grown" or an almost perfect fit from outside. Given the recent decline in black college students who choose to major in education, plus the widespread tendency to politicize the appointment of superintendents to the state level, it appears that local control (and leadership) of public schools is in for a difficult decade, especially in light of the new issues that surround race.

CONCLUSION

In this short piece, I have endeavored to present some major demographic trends that will require leadership from responsible educators, local and state governments, and school board members. Although we hear the mantras, "We're for Children," and "Leave No Child Behind," with one of every five youngsters in the world's richest nation growing up in poverty, it's hard to take the slogans as policy. There is no "silver bullet" providing a quick solution to any of the issues raised.

Educational leaders must understand how states differ from each other. If one looks at the percentage of 19-year-olds by state who have both graduated from high school and been admitted to college, the range, according to the Mortenson Institute (1996), is from 55-60% in North Dakota, Massachusetts, New Jersey, Iowa, Nebraska, and South Dakota, to only 25-30% in Texas, Georgia, Florida, Arizona, and Alaska. (Those states whose population is stable do well; the transient states do not.) These are huge differences in the educational fulfillment of the American dream of having one's children graduate from high school and be admitted to college. Before we become preoccupied with testing as the solution to educational problems, we might ask why the differences between the states are so great, far greater than the differences between the United States and other nations. What would it take for Texas, Georgia, and Florida to do as well as Iowa, Nebraska, and the Dakotas? We might also ask, are we content with the fact that about twice the youth are high school graduates and college students in some states than in others? Do we assume that students are simply smarter in Iowa than in Florida?

It is very difficult to keep our eye on equality and quality at the same time. In the 1960s, if one said that high scores on standardized tests were the only things that mattered, one would be criticized for ignoring issues of race and class. Today, if one speaks of class and race differences in schools and states, one is automatically assumed to be against high standards. Furthermore, a major question from the 1950s—"What knowledge is of most worth?"— is barely asked today. Certainly, school leaders must help the American public understand that diversity and high-performing schools are not at odds with each other. Demographics can be very helpful in defining the paths each state and each school must take on its own to achieve commonly accepted goals.

ISLLC QUESTIONS

Standard 1

- What does Hodgkinson suggest are several demographic issues that educators might see as barriers to the school's vision that must be identified and removed?

Standard 2

- How might a school's transient rate for students and faculty impact how educational leaders advocate, nurture, and sustain a school culture and instructional program conducive to all students' learning and staff professional growth?

Standard 3

- Which demographic issues might affect an educational leader's effective management of the organization, operations, and resources for a safe, efficient, and effective learning environment?

Standard 4

- Which of Hodgkinson's demographic issues provide additional challenges to educational leaders' collaboration with families and community members with diverse needs and mobilization of community resources?

Standard 5

- In what situations and in what ways do educational leaders need to consider demographic realities when attempting to act with integrity, fairness, and in an ethical manner?

Standard 6

- In what ways can educational leadership promote the success of all students while considering the demographic realities of the local community and the larger society?

REFERENCES

Condition of Education. (2001). Washington, DC: U.S. Department of Education, National Center for Education Statistics.

Hodgkinson, H. (2000). *Secondary schools in the new millennium*. Reston, VA: National Association of Secondary School Principals.

Hodgkinson, H., & Montenegro, X. (1999). *The U.S. school superintendent: The invisible CEO*. Washington, DC: Institute for Educational Leadership.

Luxemburg Income Study. (2002). Syracuse, NY: Syracuse University [available online at www.lisproject.org].

Nationality Trumps Skin Color. (2002, February 24). *The Washington Post*, p. A8.

Postsecondary Education Opportunity, #49. (1996). Washington, DC: Mortenson Institute.

Schools and Staffing in the United States: A Statistical Profile. (1996). Washington, DC: U.S. Department of Education, National Center for Education Statistics.

Statistical Abstract of the United States. (2001). Washington, DC: U.S. Census Bureau.

2

Media and Political Misrepresentation of Public Education

Gerald W. Bracey

Overview

Bracey provides substantial evidence that the American media are not providing readers with fair and accurate reporting about American public schools. The shallowness, lack of objective analysis, and occasional distortion of data about U.S. public schools, combined with the media's appetite for the negative, form a potent one-two punch against schools. Too frequently, the media uncritically reports information given by politicians and corporations who want to advance their political or ideological purposes: sow distrust of American schools and instead, support school vouchers, public funding for private schools, and other educational enterprises. Unfortunately, the general public appears to want to believe the worst about American education. The "landmark" study, *A Nation at Risk*, was specifically designed to promote distrust of U.S. public schools by citing selected, spun, and distorted statistics, and simplistic interpretations.

As part of the research that went into this chapter, I perused *The TRUTH About America's Public Schools: The Bracey Reports 1991-1997* (Bracey, 1997), and rediscovered that most of those reports had a section called "The Media." I came away both depressed and cheered—depressed because many of the problems discussed in those reports still exist, cheered because at least a few things have gotten better.

On the up side, we now have the thoughtful, reasoned columns from Richard Rothstein appearing every Wednesday in the *New York Times*. We also have a Houston antiques dealer putting up large numbers of newspaper articles on the Internet every day (www.educationnews.org; subscriptions are free). And we have Doug Oplinger and Dennis Willard at the *Akron Beacon Journal* conducting top-notch investigative studies of various topics in education. The Oplinger-Willard combo first described the political and fiscal machinations behind Ohio's charter school movement (Willard & Oplinger, 1999a, 1999b, 1999c; Oplinger & Willard, 1999a, 1999b, 1999c). More recently, they revealed how tax abatements for business and industry were costing Ohio public schools $115 million a year (Oplinger & Willard, 2002). The Oplinger-Willard team is depressing as well as elating. While they provide a model of what education reporting should look like, they also show the contrast between that model and most of the rest of what's out there.

Most reporting remains shallow and lacking in analysis. A recent article by Joseph Reaves at Arizona State University showed that editorials in the *New York Times, Atlanta Journal Constitution, St Louis Post-Dispatch* and *Los Angeles Times* dealt with the "No Child Left Behind" legislation very much as it was presented by the Bush Administration. The title of Reaves's piece says a lot: "Falling in Line" (Reaves, 2002). It reminded me of one commentator's criticism of the coverage of the war in Afghanistan. The commentator pointed out that the cable television channels brought on former generals, former security specialists, and others who on occasion criticized some specific tactic or strategy in the war. They produced no one who would question the Bush administration's policies or the war itself. If four of the leading newspapers in the nation aren't exercising their critical faculties (another failure of American public schools?), what can we expect from the rest of the media?

This problem is ongoing. A few years ago, Richard Harwood, former *Washington Post* ombudsman, noted that "for twenty years content analysis studies have shown that 70 to 90% of our content is at heart the voice of officials and their experts, translated by reporters into supposedly 'objective' news" (Harwood, 1994). Of course, if those officials are spinning information with a political or ideological purpose, objectivity is impossible unless the reporters go beyond the information given. Tamara Henry of *USA Today* wrote an article about a Western Michigan University evaluation of Pennsylvania charter schools. Alas, Henry did not actually read the report—her article was taken almost verbatim from a press release written by charter enthusiast, then-governor Tom Ridge (Henry, 2001).

The media's analysis deficit combined with the media's appetite for the negative form a potent one-two punch against schools. If it bleeds, it leads, goes the old saw. To confirm this in education, one need only examine the placement of stories each year when the College Board releases SAT scores. Downturns get Page One treatment, while gains are either ignored, buried deep in Section A, or relegated to the Metro section—a matter of only local interest.

This is not just my reading of the situation. U.S. Department of Education staffers Laurence Ogle and Patricia Dabbs experienced this feature of the media (Ogle & Dabbs, 1996) and were puzzled by it. Ogle and Dabbs helped issue the 1996 NAEP geography and history assessments. The geography results were generally positive. "The geography press conference was attended by the president of the National Geographic Society and the mood of almost all of the speakers was clearly upbeat. . . . The reporting in the press, however, was lackluster and negative at best. Few agencies picked up the story."

The history release was another matter. *The Washington Post's* Rene Sanchez called the results dismal. Lewis Lapham of *Harper's* called them a "coroner's report." Reporters beat down the doors to get to Ogle and Dabbs:

> Returning to our offices after the press conference, we found our voice mail jam-packed with media requests for additional information. News accounts were on the radio and reports were even spotted on the Internet [this was 1996, remember, the Net's infancy]. Requests for additional information flooded in from radio and television stations, newspapers, and a few talk-show hosts. . . . Even television's late-night comedy king, Jay Leno, spoke about (and ridiculed) the results. Clearly, the coverage of the negative news eclipsed the relatively good news about geography.

Ogle and Dabbs's experience just reinforced my conclusions expressed two years earlier in an article titled, "The Media's Myth of School Failure" (Bracey, 1994). Naturally, the mainstream media wouldn't publish it. The *Columbia Journalism Review* turned it down on the grounds that, "sadly," the sentiments were too familiar. I came to realize, though, that it wasn't just the media's myth. The media had help. More about that in a moment.

While the media engage in what I call WPSS, "Worst Possible Spin Syndrome," the general public manifests what I have deemed "The Neurotic Need to Believe the Worst." This is perhaps best seen in the general acceptance of "The Lists." I first encountered "The Lists" on my first day on the job in Cherry Creek, Colorado, Schools in August of 1986.

Outside my office was a green sheet of paper containing two lists. The first provided the worst problems in the schools in the 1940s. The second was the same list for the 1980s. The 1940s list contained things like chewing gum, talking out of turn, and cutting in line. The 1980s list was full of violence, gangs, drugs, alcohol, and teen pregnancy.

I recall thinking at the time that I was glad I was in a school district where those problems weren't so great. Fortunately, Barry O'Neill at Yale was thinking, "These lists don't look right to me." He decided to track down their origins. In the process, he found the lists widely accepted by people of all political stripes. Among the political rainbow of people who had cited them were William J. Bennett, Rush Limbaugh, Phyllis Schlafly, George Will, Herb Caen, Carl Rowan, and Anna Quindlen. They were variously attributed to CBS News, CQ Researcher, and the Heritage Foundation. They issued in fact from a single person, T. Cullen Davis in Fort Worth. Acquitted of murdering his wife's lover, Davis had become a born-again Christian. He had taken a hammer to his collection of jade and ivory statues, smashing them as idols of false religion. He had also used his new religious fervor to launch a crusade against the public schools. O'Neill asked Davis how he had constructed the list. Davis readily provided his methodology: "How did I know what the offenses in the schools were in 1940? I was there. How do I know what they are now? I read the paper" (O'Neill, 1994).

The media also have a proclivity for adopting certain words and phrases that are used over and over again. "Failing schools" is no doubt the most common of these, appearing in dozens, probably hundreds of stories about school reform, privatization, and so on, but always appearing without further explanation, as if no explanation is needed because we all know about them. Another catchword is "dismal," used to describe the performance of failing schools or American students in general—even if, to the objective eye, the performance looks better. In fact, American students scored at slightly above the international average in reading, mathematics, and science among the 32 nations that participated in the study. This is "dismal"?

The media, left to their own proclivities, would have enough of a negative emphasis, but, unfortunately, they get help from politicians and corporate America. The distortions were particularly rampant during the Reagan and Bush I administrations, but even the Clinton years saw a bias toward the negative. As a "liberal," Clinton sought not to destroy public schools but to seek more resources for them. To this end, he took the common tack (common, too, among professors at large research universities) of emphasizing problems. For instance, he more than once said that only 40% of American third graders can read independently. Yet, these same third graders had finished second among 27 nations in an international study of reading. Reagan entered the White House with an educational agenda of tuition tax credits, school vouchers, restoring prayer to the schools, and abolishing the U.S. Department of Education. One strategy to put this agenda into place was to hype the negative and ignore or suppress the positive. The first instance of this was a glorious treasury of selected, spun, and distorted statistics called *A Nation at Risk*.

Terrell Bell, Reagan's Secretary of Education, did not want to form a commission or issue a report. As recounted in his memoir, *The Thirteenth Man*, he sought a "Sputnik-like event" that would galvanize Americans into retooling their schools. Unable to find or produce a crisis, he resorted to the commission-and-report route (Bell, 1988). *A Nation at Risk* was, and in some quarters still is, hailed as a "landmark" study. In fact, the commissioners simply selected and spun the statistics, and gave some simplistic interpretations. Some statistics used probably didn't even exist. When, about a decade after the event, I tried to track down two of them, no one on the commission or on the commission's staff could remember where they came from. The two statistics indicated that half of gifted and talented students never match their ability with achievement in school and that college graduates score lower on tests. The document did not say lower on what tests, but in any case, we do not test college seniors—the report clearly was not referring to the small minority of seniors who take the GRE.

The most notorious instance of suppression occurred in the case of *The Sandia Report*, formally known as *Perspectives on Education in America*—a 176-page compilation of data about the condition of public education, including dropout rates, high school completion rates, SAT trends, NAEP trends, and international comparisons. Its summary conclusion was that "There are many problems in American education, but there is no system-wide crisis." This was too positive for the Bush administration. When the *Sandia* engineers came to Washington to present their findings, David Kearns, former Xerox CEO and then Deputy Secretary of Energy told them, "You bury this or I'll bury you." This I got from one of the engineers. An *Education Week* article account said only that "Administration officials, particularly Mr. Kearns, reacted angrily at the meeting" (Miller, 1991).

The report was suppressed. The official reason for nonpublication was that the report was undergoing "peer review," and it is to the eternal shame of Peter House of the National Science Foundation and Emerson Elliott of the U.S. Department of Education that they signed blatantly political critiques of the report. In 2001, I contacted Lee Bray, the first *Sandia* official to get in touch with me about the report in 1990. Bray had retired several years earlier and didn't want to open old wounds, but did affirm absolutely that the report was suppressed. It finally saw daylight in 1993 as the entirety of the May/June issue of the *Journal of Educational Research* (Carson, Huelskamp, & Woodall, 1993).

More typical of efforts to slant the public's view on education was the very different handling of two international studies. One showed

Americans not doing so well in math and science; the other showed Americans almost at the top of the heap in reading. The first study appeared in February 1992 (Lapointe, Askew, & Mead, 1992; Lapointe, Mead, & Askew, 1992). Secretary of Education Lamar Alexander and Assistant Secretary Diane Ravitch orchestrated a large press conference, and the study received wide coverage in both print and electronic media. The study found that U.S. students ranked low in most subjects (although their actual scores were near the international averages). "An 'F' in World Competition" was the headline over *Newsweek*'s story (Kantrowitz & Wingert, 1992).

The second study was published five months later in July 1992 (Elley, 1992). This time no press conference occurred. It took *Education Week* over two months to learn of the story and then it was only by accident. A friend of then *Education Week* reporter, Robert Rothman, sent him a copy from Europe. *Education Week* gave the study front-page coverage, as did *USA Today*, which played off the *Education Week* story (Rothman, 1992; Manning, 1992). The *USA Today* story carried a curious quote from Francie Alexander, then a deputy assistant secretary of education. She dismissed the study as irrelevant to the 1990s.

Why the different treatment of the two international reports? The math and science study would have made U.S. schools look bad; the reading study would not. Nine-year-olds in the United States ranked second in reading among 27 nations, and 14-year-olds ranked eighth among 31 nations. Only one country, Finland, had a significantly higher score than American 14-year-olds. And at both ages, America's best readers outscored even the Finns (although the differences were so small they did not approach statistical significance).

The Bush II administration has acknowledged that low socioeconomic students are not achieving well, but has put in place a testing program that will likely increase, not decrease the gap. The resources to assist schools are meager and, indeed, some argue that it will cost twice as much to put the testing requirements in place as the states will receive for implementing them. No doubt this is why the governor of Vermont has asked for an analysis of what would happen fiscally if the state surrendered its $25 million from the federal government.

While politicians and ideologists have helped foster the falsely negative image of education, they have teamed with the business community to multiply the impact. Business is mounting a coordinated effort through the National Alliance of Businesses, the Business Roundtable, and their by-product, Achieve, Inc. IBM CEO Louis V. Gerstner, Jr. has spearheaded the attacks, bringing governors and businessmen into collusion through his "summits." He is hardly alone. Intel CEO Craig Barrett, State Farm CEO Edward Rust, Texas Instruments CEO Thomas Engibus, as well as then Wisconsin Governor Tommy Thompson and former secretary of education William J. Bennett, have all taken to the op-ed pages of the *New York Times, Washington Post,* and *USA Today* in 2000, 2001, and 2002 to decry the threat that our "failing" schools pose to our competitiveness in the global marketplace (Barrett, 2001; Bennett, 2000; Engibus & Rust, 2000; Gerstner, 2002; Gerstner & Thompson, 2000).

In late 2000, a commission headed by former Senator John Glenn released a report claiming we had to improve math and science teaching *Before It's Too Late.* In the body of the text, the phrase "before it's too late" appears not only in italics, but also in red ink (National Commission on Mathematics and Science Teaching for the 21st Century, 2000). CEOs Barrett and Rust were on the commission. Rust, heading up the Business Roundtable's education taskforce, has been ubiquitous in criticizing America's schools in print and on the podium.

In fact, there is no correlation between achievement, as measured with test scores, and international market competitiveness, as defined by the World Economic Forum (WEF). The Forum, a high-powered group in Geneva with close links to economic think tanks at Harvard, ranks 75 nations annually on what it calls its Current Competitiveness Index (CCI). Of the 75 nations, 38 also had scores on the Third International Math and Science Study (TIMSS). The United States is second on the CCI and 29th on TIMSS; Korea is second on TIMSS but 27th on competitiveness; and so forth. Overall, the rank-order correlation coefficient between the CCI and TIMSS is .23. And even this overstates the correlation: The bottom seven nations are low on both variables that contribute to the relationship. If these seven nations are removed, the correlation actually becomes *negative* (although quite small) (Bracey, 2002b, 2002c).

The complete TIMSS study has given rise to a new cliché—and distortion. Gerstner used it in his keynote address to the most recent education summit, and Bill Clinton mouthed a version of it. As spoken to the Heritage Foundation by William J. Bennett, the cliché goes like this: "In America today, the longer you stay in school, the dumber you get, relative to peers in other industrialized nations" (Bennett, 2000).

This statement derives from the fact that American fourth graders were near the top in TIMSS, American eighth graders were average, and U.S. high school seniors were apparently near the bottom. I contend that the decline from Grade 4 to Grade 8 is real, but the decline between Grades 8 and 12 is not.

The fall off from Grades 4 to 8 stems from two sources. First, American textbooks are about three times as thick as those in other nations. TIMSS found that American teachers try to cover many more topics than those in other countries. The coverage is by necessity brief and shallow and doesn't "take." Secondly, American educators have traditionally considered the middle school years as the culmination of elementary school, a time for review and consolidation in preparation for high school. Even now, after years of pressure to accelerate mathematics, only about 15% of American eighth graders take algebra. About twice that proportion don't even have algebra or pre-algebra as an option.

Other countries have used the middle school years to introduce new material. Thus, Japanese students receive large amounts of algebra in seventh grade and plane geometry in eighth. The scope and sequence of mathematics needs to be rethought in the United States education system, but it is hardly a matter of students "getting dumber."

The acceptance of the TIMSS Final Year Study ("Final Year" because, as the TIMSS authors acknowledge, the final year in many countries is not equivalent to the American senior year of high school) requires the uncritical acceptance of a study so methodologically flawed I do not believe I could have gotten it past the undergraduate honors committee at the College of William and Mary, my alma mater. I have analyzed its many flaws elsewhere (Bracey, 2000). Suffice it to say here that when one compares subgroups of the American cohort who are most like their European peers, one finds American seniors rank average—the same rank as eighth graders.

Flawed or no, the TIMSS Final Year Study, as released by the U.S. Department of Education, was raw meat for the press. While the TIMSS Final Year Report emphasized the differences between many nations, the U.S. Department of Education's press conference made it seem that all other nations' final year students were peers with American seniors. That made for a banner day of bad headlines; in fact, American seniors were not taking the same math courses, for example, as their Japanese counterparts. The headlines included the following:

"U.S. 12th Graders Rank Poorly in Math and Science, Study Says" (Ethan Bronner, *New York Times*)

"U.S. High School Seniors Rank Near Bottom" (Rene Sanchez, *Washington Post)*

"U.S. Seniors Near Bottom in World Test" (Debra Viadero, *Education Week*)

"Hey! We're #19!" (John Leo, *U.S. News & World Report*)

"Why America Has the World's Dimmest Bright Kids" (Chester E. Finn, Jr., *Wall Street Journal*)

Can we expect better coverage in the future? Hard to say. As this is being written, it is only May 2002 and I've already had two op-eds in *The Washington Post* (Bracey 2002a, 2002b). On the other hand, a *Post* article on Edison schools looked like a plant to help its sinking stock price (Mathews, 2002). Mathews advised he was writing under extreme time constraints and it was not up to his usual level. One wonders where the impetus came from, to write under tight deadline without sufficient time for thorough investigation and reflection. It seems unlikely that the media, corporate types, and politicians can easily give up such the handy scapegoat that public schools provide.

CONCLUSION

Although today's education writers are providing increasingly fair, accurate, and objective reporting and analysis, the general public needs to remain highly critical of much that passes for education reporting. Political and corporate biases and private agendas often influence what media publish and broadcast about American public schools. The facts tell a very different story. The public needs to stay accurately informed.

ISLLC QUESTIONS

Standard 1

- How does Bracey's description of the media's negative portrayal of U.S. public school education impact educational leaders' ability to define and share a vision for learning with all members of the school community?
- How might educational leaders understand and address the media-influenced community view of education as a barrier to enacting the school vision?

Standard 4

- How might educational leaders who understand Bracey's argument use this awareness to respond to the diverse community interests and needs and mobilize community resources?

Standard 6

- How might educational leaders who understand Bracey's position use this information to effectively respond to the larger political, social, economic, legal, and cultural context while promoting the success of all students?

REFERENCES

Barrett, C. (2001). Interview with editors of *USA Today*. Printed in the November 8, 2001 edition.

Bell, T. H. (1988). *The thirteenth man: A Reagan Cabinet memoir*. New York: Free Press.

Bennett, W. J. (2000). *The state and future of American education*. Speech to the Heritage Foundation, March. Accessible at http://www.heritage.org.

Bracey, G. W. (1994, September). The media's myth of school failure. *Education Leadership*, pp. 80-84.

Bracey, G. W. (1997). *The TRUTH About America's Schools.* Bloomington, IN: Phi Delta Kappa International.

Bracey, G. W. (2000, May). The TIMSS "Final Year" Study and Report: A critique. *Educational Researcher,* pp. 4-10.

Bracey, G. W. (2002a, January 16). What they did on vacation: It's not schools that are failing poor kids. *The Washington Post,* p. A19.

Bracey, G. W. (2002b, May 5). Why do we scapegoat the schools? *The Washington Post,* p. B1.

Bracey, G. W. (2002c, June). Test scores, creativity, and global competitiveness. *Phi Delta Kappan, 83* (10).

Bronner, E. (1998, February 21). U.S. 12th graders rank poorly in math and science, study says. *New York Times,* p. A1.

Carson, C. C., Huelskamp, R. M., & Woodall, T. D. (1993, May/June). Perspectives on education in America: An annotated briefing. *Journal of Educational Research,* pp. 259-310.

Elley, W. P. (1992). *How in the world do students read?* Hamburg: Grindledruck. Available in the United States through the International Reading Association, Dover, Delaware.

Engibus, T. J., & Rust, E. B., (2000, September 7). The nation's "help wanted" crisis. *The Washington Post ,* p. A25.

Finn, C. E., Jr. (1998, February 25). Why the United States has the world's dimmest bright students. *Wall Street Journal.*

Gerstner, L. V., Jr. (2002, March 14). The test we know we need. *New York Times,* p. A31.

Gerstner, L. V., Jr., & Thompson, T. G. (2000, December 8). The problem isn't the kids. *New York Times,* p. A39.

Harwood, R. (1994, May 28). Reporting on, by and for an elite. *The Washington Post,* p. A29.

Henry, T. (2001, March 28). Scores go up for charters. *USA Today,* p. D9.

Kantrowitz, B., & Wingert, P. (1992, February 17). An 'F' in world competition. *Newsweek,* p. 57.

Lapointe, A. E., Askew, J. M., & Mead, N. A. (1992). *Learning mathematics.* Princeton: Educational Testing Service.

Lapointe, A. E., Mead, N. A., & Askew, J. M. (1992). *Learning science.* Princeton: Educational Testing Service.

Leo, J. (1998, March 9). Hey! We're #19! *U.S. News & World Report,* p. 14.

Manning, A. (1992, September 29). U.S. kids near top of class in reading. *USA Today,* p. A1.

Mathews, J. (2002, April 30). Putting for-profit company to the test. *The Washington Post,* p. A9.

Miller, J. (1991, October 9). Report questioning "crisis" in education triggers and uproar. *Education Week,* pp. 1, 32.

National Commission on Mathematics and Science Teaching for the 21st Century (2000). *Before it's too late.* Washington, DC: U.S. Department of Education.

Ogle, L., & Dabbs, P. (1996, March 13). Good news bad news: Does media coverage of schools promote scattershot remedies? *Education Week,* p. 46.

O'Neill, B. (1994, March 6). Anatomy of a hoax. *New York Times Sunday Magazine,* pp. 46-49.

Oplinger, D., & Willard, D. J. (1999a, December 13). In education, money talks. *Akron Beacon Journal*, p. A1.

Oplinger, D., & Willard, D. J. (1999b, December 14). Voucher system falls far short of goals. *Akron Beacon Journal*, p. A1.

Oplinger, D., & Willard, D. J. (1999c, December 15). Campaign organizer pushes hard for changes. *Akron Beacon Journal*, p. A1.

Oplinger, D., & Willard, D. J. (2002, April 10). Business breaks costing schools. *Akron Beacon Journal*, p. A1.

Reaves, J. (2002). Falling in line: An examination of education editorials appearing in four leading U.S. newspapers from the inauguration of George W. Bush to September 11, 2001. Available at www.asu.edu.edu/educ/epsl/epru.htm (Click on "Research Reports." After 2002, click on Archives Research Reports.)

Rothman, R. (1992, September 30). U.S. ranks high in international study of reading achievement. *Education Week*, p. 1.

Sanchez, R. (1998, February 25). U.S. high school seniors rank near bottom. *The Washington Post*, p. A1.

Schwartz, J. 1998. Pat journalism: When we prepackage the news, we miss the story. *Washington Post*, p. C1.

Viadero, D. (1998, March 11). U.S. seniors near bottom on world test. *Education Week*, p. 1.

Willard, D. J., & Oplinger, D. (1999a, December 12). Charter experiment goes awry: Schools fail to deliver. *Akron Beacon Journal*, p. A1.

Willard, D. J., & Oplinger, D. (1999b, December 14). Voucher plan leaves long list of broken vows. *Akron Beacon Journal*, p. A1.

Willard, D. J., & Oplinger, D. (1999c, December 15). School battle eludes voters, takes its cues from coalitions. *Akron Beacon Journal*, p. A1.

Lessons Learned

Educational leaders today face greater challenges than ever before. Population shifts have brought serious urban problems to suburban settings. Principals must now educate increasingly diverse students to higher achievement levels. This itself is a daunting task. What makes this more complicated, however, is that they must do this within a political and business environment that openly distrusts public schools and falsely brands them as "failing." Just when school leaders need more community support, many find themselves with less.

As Hodgkinson writes, few people live well, and school leadership today faces unprecedented challenges of teaching 21st-century values and skills to an increasingly diverse and changing student population. The 2000 U.S. census shows dramatic shifts in the student populace. One in every 5 children is growing up in poverty. Suburban as well as urban schools are educating a wider range of economically and racially diverse students from our own and other countries. Schools are also experiencing increased student transience as families frequently change home addresses and school attendance zones. Poverty and transience in white, black, Hispanic, and immigrant children make their learning more problematic. These realities create an achievement gap between states far greater than the differences between the United States and other countries. In addition, they impact school culture and student achievement in ways that make school leadership more complex and demanding.

Today's school leaders must design and initiate necessary interventions to address educating diverse students. Leaders must also work closely with parents, teachers, business, and government to sustain the programs over time if we are to meet both diversity and high-performance goals. This leadership requires an extensive range of professional and personal competencies.

Gaining the necessary public support for this demanding task becomes even harder when the media repeatedly and mistakenly portrays U.S. education as "failing." Bracey notes many examples of newspapers giving readers negative stories, omitting or suppressing facts that support public schools' successes, and highlighting ones that don't. Politicians and corporate America add to the distortions, Bracey says, to advance their own biases and agendas.

With increased diversity of students and community views on public education, today's educational leaders need enhanced professional and personal knowledge and skills to successfully address student learning.

Part II

Leading Change

3

Implementing Change at the Building Level

Michael Fullan

Overview

Starting and sustaining school reforms is difficult. No matter how promising a new idea, it cannot impact student learning if it is superficially implemented. Leadership for change requires using new materials, engaging in new behaviors and practices, and incorporating new beliefs. To do this, schools need to have or develop the principals' and teachers' capacity to work together over time while simultaneously attempting, monitoring, and refining improvements. They need program coherence to focus selectively and integratively on critical areas. In addition, schools need resources of time, materials, ideas, and expertise. Finally, principal leadership is key to causing the other factors to improve. Moreover, support from agencies outside the school including the district, regional, and state agencies and the community also impact school change.

IMPLEMENTING CHANGE
AT THE BUILDING LEVEL

The question of implementation is simply whether or not a given idea, practice, or program gets "put in place." In focusing on teaching and learning, for example, I have suggested that implementation consists of (1) using new materials, (2) engaging in new behaviors and practices, and (3) incorporating new beliefs (Fullan, 2001a). The logic is straightforward—no matter how promising a new idea may be, it cannot impact student learning if it is superficially implemented.

Concerns about implementation surfaced in the late 1960s after a flurry of innovative reforms failed to make a difference. The first-order problem that Sarason, Goodlad, and others (1984) identified at the time was that most innovations were at best "adopted" on the surface, but did not alter behaviors and beliefs. For the past thirty years, research and practice have focused on identifying key factors associated with failed or successful implementation. In this brief introduction, I will examine first, what we know about the dynamics of implementation at the building level, and second, what external-to-the-school issues should be considered.

Implementation at the Building Level

There has been a growing sense of urgency in society that schools must do a better job of teaching the young. Moreover, policymakers and citizens have demanded large-scale reform involving all or most schools, not just an innovative few. Models of Whole-School Reform have been generated to help the spread and depth of reform.

Still, there are perplexing problems. Datnow and Stringfield (2000) talk about the problem of initial and continuing implementation. In one study of eight schools that had implemented given reform models, only three had continued use of them after a few years. In another district, Datnow and Stringfield (2000) make the following report:

> By the third year of our four-year study, only one of thirteen schools was still continuing to implement their chosen reform designs. Reforms expired in six schools. A significant challenge to the sustainability of reforms . . . was the instability of district leadership and the politics that accompanied it. In 1995-1996 [the] then-superintendent actively, publicly promoted the use of externally developed reforms. During his tenure, the district created an Office of Instructional Leadership to support the designs' implementation. The following year, however, a new district administration eliminated this office, and district support for many of the restructuring schools decreased dramatically. (p. 198)

Figure 3.1

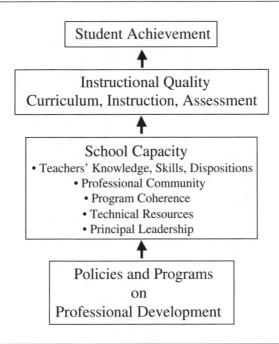

SOURCE: From *Professional Development That Addresses School Capacity* (Newmann, King, and Youngs, 2000).

If we look closely at the building level, we can identify the key factors and processes. The best up-to-date analysis is provided by Newmann, King, and Youngs (2000) in their recent case studies (see Figure 3.1).

First, the logic. Schools must focus on a constellation of quality curriculum, instruction, and assessment of student learning. If they do this, they can have a powerful impact on student learning. In order to do this, they must have or develop the *capacity* to work together over periods of time, all the while attempting, monitoring, and refining improvements. Newmann, King, and Youngs's identification of the five factors which comprise school capacity is very instructive.

1. Knowledge, skills, and dispositions of individuals

2. Professional community

3. Program coherence

4. Technical resources

5. Principal leadership

Knowledge, skills, and dispositions refer to the individual capability of teachers. One can enhance this by hiring teachers with desired traits and/or by providing professional development. Note the limitation, however. This is an "individualistic" strategy that won't work in isolation. Put another way, never send a changed individual into an unchanged environment. For this reason, effective schools have also built up their "professional learning community" in which principals and teachers work together over time. These interactive communities examine and reexamine their practices and results.

Most schools suffer from innovation overload—what Tom Hatch (2000) described as "multiple innovations colliding." Thus schools, to be effective, must work on "program coherence" by becoming more selective, integrative, and focused on those areas critical to the mission. Schools need "resources" to do all this. Technical resources refer to access to time, materials, ideas, and expertise. Schools need time for teacher collaboration to process ideas, enhance classroom expertise, and develop resources to increase student achievement.

Finally, Newmann et al. (2001) found that "principal leadership" was critical. In a sense, the best definition of school leadership is that which "causes" the previous four factors to get better and better; that is, effective leadership enhances individual development, professional community, program coherence, and access to resources.

The relationship of school capacity to implementation should be obvious. School capacity, as defined by Newmann et al. (2001), consists of the very strengths that produce better implementation. Stated differently, schools with higher capacity that take on given innovations operate in a way that is likely to improve access to materials and alter behaviors, skills, and beliefs of teachers within the school.

External School Factors

While we have an increasingly clear idea of what school capacity looks like, the key question is how to get more of it when you don't have it. Only a small proportion of schools are as good as the one depicted by Newmann and colleagues (Fullan, 2001a, 2001b). In order to get school capacity on a wider scale, we must turn our attention to the infrastructure for school reform. The infrastructure includes all those agencies and levels outside the school such as the community, the district, and regional or state agencies, policies, and programs. For example, returning to Datnow and Stringfield's (2000) study of school reform,

> We found that clear, strong district support positively impacted reform implementation, and the lack thereof often negatively impacted implementation. . . . schools that sustained reforms had district and state allies that protected reform efforts during periods

of transition or crisis and secured resources (money, time, staff and space) essential to reforms. . . . schools that failed to sustain reforms were sometimes located in districts that were "infamous for experimenting with new kinds of programs" but did not provide ongoing support for any of them. (pp. 194-195)

Such findings have led many of us to conclude that the district and other levels of the system are crucial if we want large-scale, sustainable reform. There is some evidence, for example, that districts and states can make a larger difference in many schools by using a strategy that integrates "accountability" and "capacity building." This is illustrated in Fullan (2001b) in which District #2 in New York City, San Diego City School District, and school districts in England are used as case studies. For example, England has dramatically increased its literacy and numeracy achievement in over 19,000 primary schools over a four-year period, using a reform strategy that increased accountability by naming and monitoring targets and capacity through substantial investments in new roles, new materials, and new opportunities for professional development.

CONCLUSION

In summary, we have an increasingly clear idea of what is required at the building level to achieve greater implementation that positively affects student learning. We need to have more case studies of what this looks like at the building level. More than that, however, we need strategies that will increase the number of schools engaged in successful reform.

This brings us full circle but leaves us with a paradox. Implementation, by definition, only occurs at the school and classroom level. Yet if schools are left on their own, only a minority will evidence the kind of school capacity needed, and fewer still will be able to sustain it. This is why rethinking the roles of districts and reevaluating state policies will be required in order to stimulate and support school-based capacity building.

The good news is that there is a growing focus on developing leaders at many levels (school, district, state). In *Leading in a Culture of Change* (Fullan, 2001b), I identified five crucial mind and action sets that leaders in the 21st century must cultivate: a deep sense of moral purpose, knowledge of the change process, capacity to develop relationships across diverse individuals and groups, skill in fostering knowledge creation and sharing, and the ability to engage with others in coherence making amidst multiple innovations.

Implementation, whether or not things change in practice, will always be at the heart of these new developments, and the building level will always be where the implementation buck stops.

ISLLC QUESTIONS

Standard 1

- According to Fullan, how does the educational leader promote the success of all students through a vision of learning that builds school capacity?

Standard 2

- How does the educational leader promote the success of all students by working at the building and district levels to manage the organization, operations, and resources?

Standard 3

- According to Fullan, factors external to the school exist. How does the educational leader promote the success of all students by recognizing and working with these external factors? What are these?

REFERENCES

Datnow, A., & Stringfield, S. (2000). Working together for reliable school reform. *Journal of Education for Students Placed at Risk, 5*(1 & 2), 183-204.

Fullan, M. (2001a). *The new meaning of educational change* (3rd ed.). New York: Teachers College Press.

Fullan, M. (2001b). *Leading in a culture of change*. San Francisco: Jossey-Bass.

Goodlad, J. I. (1984). *A place called school: Prospects for the future*. New York: McGraw-Hill.

Goodlad, J. I. (1998). *Educational renewal: Better teachers, better schools*. San Francisco: Jossey-Bass.

Hatch, T. (2000). *What's happening when multiple improvement innovations collide*. Menlo Park, CA: Carnegie Foundation for the Advancement of Teaching.

Newmann, F., King, B., & Youngs, P. (2000, April). *Professional development that addresses school capacity*. Paper presented at the annual meeting of the American Educational Research Association, Seattle, WA.

Wilson, K. G., & Daviss, B. (1996). *Redesigning education*. New York: Henry Holt.

4

Challenges to Leading and Sustaining School Change

William Patterson

Overview

Having a great idea for school change is not enough. Educators need a foundation for change that is shared by those implementing it. Establishing a set of shared beliefs and their implications for classroom practice can ensure that the change becomes part of the school culture. Patterson relates that after seven years of implementing mastery learning as principal of his school, he left his position there; within the next few years, the school dropped the program completely. On reflection, Patterson notes that without a clearly articulated philosophy and vision for change, the program would have failed even had the building and central office leadership remained. In his next school, the University of Denver High School, Patterson began planning with teachers by collectively identifying the philosophical basis for making decisions about the school and creating a document to guide their efforts in the short and long term. They developed a consensus around belief statements and their implications for daily practice within their

37

classrooms. This document provided direction for the long term as well as for daily decisions made in the classroom. The important information contained in the document is continually revisited to remind veteran staff and assimilate new ones.

In the early 1980s, the *A Nation at Risk* report ushered in a new round of pressures to improve schools in the United States. Paradoxically, the report seemed to have the effect of challenging schools to change substantively while giving them permission to adopt changes only incrementally. Schools could strengthen graduation requirements or add a few days to the school calendar and announce that they had responded to the challenge. The concern that such limited adjustments would not significantly alter the course of K-12 education prompted discussion at a Colorado state conference of education and business leaders in the late 1980s. One CEO posited that if he were producing a product in which 25% of the product fell off the line before completion and another 25% percent were defective upon completion, he would not solve the problem by adding 15 minutes to the workday.

At the time, I was principal of a 400-student high school in a Colorado resort community. Like many other schools, we felt the urgency to review what we were doing and determine how we could improve. Mastery learning was an approach that some schools were implementing, so we sent a districtwide team of teachers and administrators to visit the Johnson City School District in southern New York, a district that had gained national attention for effectively using the mastery learning approach for several years. The high school in Johnson City was particularly impressive. As we talked with students at random, we discovered that some families had moved to Johnson City specifically because of the high school's excellent reputation; and students and teachers alike relayed enthusiastic feelings about the school. Not only was a mastery learning program in place, but the lowest grade a student could receive for credit was 75 percent—this in a blue-collar community, not one whose schools were educating children of professors at a local university, not one where wealth made it possible to provide outside tutors on a regular basis or the finest school facilities. Yet the vast majority of students were succeeding at a higher level than those in our own community, one of the most educated communities in the country. No more students in Johnson City were failing than in our high school, where students could earn credit if they had a 60% average.

We returned to our school, shared what we had found with other staff members, and, with some strong encouragement from the central office administration, decided to move ahead with a mastery learning program and to raise our lowest passing grade to 75%. Over a 3-year period, we ran a pilot program, and then implemented mastery learning initially into one-third of our classes. By the third year, we had completely transformed into a mastery learning school. Meanwhile, we saw our students respond well to the increased expectations, although some struggled to reach 75% in every class and in every unit of instruction. Teachers started appearing at my office door indicating that the 7-period day with 50-minute classes was not working anymore. They needed more time to work with students. Some students were willing to stay after school as long as teachers would stay with them, but teachers were wearing out.

We established a committee to address the issues raised and decided to adopt an 8-period block schedule, one that today is used frequently across the country but was rarely used in 1987. We did find some schools in Utah that had moved to such a schedule and, after visiting some schools in that state, proceeded to implement a block schedule in the fall of that year. Those who believe that a school must take time to implement change should have visited our high school that spring. Students who took a lengthy petition to the school board protesting the proposed change from 50- to 90-minute periods delayed our move toward implementation. Those students who thought that we did not know what we were doing when we raised the bar to 75% were now convinced we were crazy. By the time the board of education approved our plan, it was April; yet the staff felt the need to make the change for the next school year.

As a staff, we met in interdisciplinary groups several times before the end of the school year to discuss how instruction would need to be different in a 90-minute period compared to a 50-minute period. Teachers had the summer to envision what their classes would look like and in most cases made a successful implementation in the fall of 1987. Teachers demonstrated how quickly and successfully a strategic change could take place if they were truly committed to it. The faculty had voted 33 to 3 in a secret ballot to move to a block schedule—although with the understanding that we would return to a traditional schedule after one year if they did not feel that it was working.

The faculty and I worked for the next four years, massaging the mastery learning system, working with students to help them reach at least 75%, and smoothing out the block schedule's wrinkles. I left in 1991, and within the next several years, the school dropped the mastery learning program and returned the lowest passing grade to 60%. Only the block schedule remains today.

What happened? I had been the principal at that high school for 11 years, and we had been implementing the changes during the last 6 years before I left. Yet most of what we had accomplished was dismantled fairly quickly. As I looked back with considerable disappointment, I believe that several things occurred that caused the school to return to "the way it used to be." Even though the faculty and I had developed a strong and trusting relationship over the years, they felt that much of the pressure to move to mastery learning came from outside the high school. At the time that I left, the two principle central office administrators left as well, causing a leadership vacuum. Under those circumstances, the appeal of the traditional program proved to be a stronger pull than a mastery learning program that was more difficult to maintain. Even though no more students were failing when 75% was the standard than when 60% was, it was considerably harder work to get some students to 75 than to 60. However, I believe the primary problem was the lack of a strong philosophical foundation for the changes we made. Even if leadership had been consistent and mastery learning had been easier to implement and maintain, I believe that ultimately the changes that we made would have collapsed.

Two things were missing. We had not as a staff determined on what basis we believed change needed to be made, nor had we identified what a classroom or the school needed to look like to reflect our philosophy. Both are critical pieces.

In the fall of 1994, the University of Denver (DU) gave me the opportunity to develop a high school on the DU campus. Based loosely on the principles of the Coalition of Essential Schools, the school opened in 1995 with a small student population of 40 and a targeted future enrollment of 200. For several months prior to opening, the newly hired teaching staff and I worked to determine what the school should look like. Borrowing again from what I had learned from Johnson City High School, we began with a discussion of what we believed about teaching and learning. Our purpose was to identify the philosophical basis for making decisions about the school and to create a document that could guide our efforts in both the short and long term. We agreed as a staff that among the problems schools face are the personal and organizational boxes that help to preserve our safety and comfort while preventing us from seriously exploring other options that might be better for our students. We wanted to avoid those kinds of boxes. Another issue that arose revolved around the difficulty in staying with the program once a course of action had been decided. Even the most sincere staff can become discouraged when the blips on the screen occur, and the day-to-day challenges of school life present themselves. We decided that we needed to develop a blueprint of our beliefs, beliefs that we would use as a foundation for discussion whenever we encountered those challenges. We took that discussion one step further, however, and agreed to some implications of our beliefs. Although the belief statements themselves provided the foundation for our program, the implications became just as important, for they translated our beliefs into our daily program.

Not only does a belief system such as we developed provide direction for the program, it also provides opportunities to examine cognitive dissonance for some staff members, especially those who are new to our school. For example, if a teacher says that he or she believes that students learn at different rates, then a classroom policy that does not allow for such differences is inconsistent with that belief. Upon being confronted with that inconsistency, a staff member can discuss how to remedy the situation in a way that is consistent with his or her beliefs.

The staff at the University of Denver High School agreed upon 16 different belief statements, ranging from "Students learn at different rates and in different ways" to "Students who develop a positive relationship with at least one adult in a school are more likely to be successful, stay in school, and graduate." The key issue is not necessarily the number of beliefs but the staff consensus on those beliefs. Even agreeing to one significant belief can change the way a classroom or a school looks and operates.

A school philosophy is worth nothing unless it is a living document that is represented in the day-to-day operations of the school, its teachers, and its administrators. When a problem arises regarding how the program at the University of Denver High School is operating, our philosophy, as presented in our belief statements, becomes a critical component of our discussion. We seek a solution that is consistent with those statements. They cannot become the old school accreditation documents that too often were put in a drawer and left there for several years. They must be continually revisited in order for the belief statements to be a living document.

One of the biggest problems in using belief statements to guide a program is finding the time and the enthusiasm among more experienced teachers to continually revisit them. For teachers who have worked in our high school for several years, discussing the belief statements several times a year can seem like old business; yet new staff must be assimilated into the program. If an environment is going to be intentional and planned, then the entire staff must participate in determining what that environment will look like, how to make it happen, and how to maintain it. Students will not assist in creating a positive school environment unless they see that the staff is dedicated to move in one direction. Although I spend time separately with new teachers, spending time together as a whole is critical. Teachers who have worked with the belief statements for several years are much more credible to new teachers than I will ever be. They know how the belief statements can be implemented in the classroom and what problems new teachers may face.

The need for variety when working with the staff is no different than the same need in the classroom; variety in the ways we address belief statements is absolutely necessary. At the University of Denver High School, we have sometimes discussed one belief statement per faculty meeting. On other occasions, I have created scenarios for us to discuss as a staff, wherein we have to apply what we believe to solve a simulated problem. At other times, I have asked different faculty members to take responsibility for presenting several belief statements to the whole staff. Regardless of how the statements are kept alive, they must be a planned and ongoing part of the school culture.

Change is difficult. Maintaining change is more so. I have been involved in working with teachers and administrators for the last 20 years in changing schools, and I have seen a lot of hard work go by the wayside because the necessary pieces were not in place. Having a great idea is insufficient. There must be a foundation for change that is shared by those people implementing the change. Establishing a system of beliefs and their implications is one way to ensure as much as possible that change is grounded in something substantial—that something exists independent of the current problem or of the personalities involved that will allow substantive change to occur and become a part of a school culture.

CONCLUSION

Commonly developed and shared belief statements about what a school should value and look like in daily practice provide essential criteria for short- and long-term decision making. Planning for school change that neglects to develop a consensus around its members' philosophical foundations and then place them into a continually revisited living document cannot sustain its direction or efforts.

ISLLC QUESTIONS

Standard 1

- How does the educational leader facilitate the development, articulation, implementation, and stewardship of a vision that is shared and supported by the school community? Why did the vision fail once the educational leader left?
- How does the educational leader eventually identify and remove barriers to implementing the school vision?
- What lessons does the educational leader learn about sustaining a shared school vision?

Standard 2

- How does the educational leader promote the success of all students by advocating, nurturing, and sustaining a school culture and instructional program conducive to student learning and staff professional growth?
- How does the educational leader gather more data and information about the situation from varied stakeholders before making decisions?
- How does the educational leader show value for conflict resolution and consensus building?

- How does the educational leader maintain a culture of high expectations? What caused the high expectations to collapse in his former school?
- How does the educational leader show knowledge of assessment strategies and multiple opportunities to learn (for faculty as well as students)?
- How does the educational leader value team process and stakeholder involvement for making decisions?

Standard 4

- How does the educational leader respond to community interests and needs and mobilize community resources?

Standard 6

- How does the educational leader promote the success of all students by understanding, responding to, and influencing the larger political, social, economic, legal, and cultural context?

5

The New
Effective Schools

Gordon Cawelti

Overview

Public education has a high priority on political agendas and has undertaken standards-based reform because of unsatisfactory student
achievement. Since one school, alone, cannot impact more than its own
students, Cawelti recently studied six successful school districts serving significant numbers of students from low-income families and what
these schools were doing to attain high levels of student achievement.
Findings included the following: restructuring for greater account-abil-
ity (decentralizing authority for change to the building level and
holding principals and teachers accountable for improving student
achievement; making central office leaders into mentors rather than
controllers); focusing on clear and important standards (often those
standards imposed by the state are not comprehensive enough to prepare students for tomorrow's world); and making use of the knowledge base about teaching and learning (principals must bring reliable

AUTHOR'S NOTE: The study of high-achieving school districts was done under a contract
with the Laboratory for Student Success, a regional educational laboratory in Philadelphia.

information and experiences about teaching and learning to teachers and provide time to discuss, analyze, practice, and make use of new teaching strategies).

Public education's number one issue is unsatisfactory student achievement. As a result, education is a high priority on political agendas. New findings growing out of the effective schools movement pioneered in the 1970s are helping to restore the productivity of schools and restore public confidence in communities where achievement has declined. These findings include attention to *restructuring* the way the system called a school or district operates to improve *accountability,* giving greater focus to *high standards of achievement* and making better use of the *knowledge base to improve teaching and learning.*

The nation's public schools continue to find themselves in the midst of long-term reform policies that are changing the way many states provide public education. Business leaders and those in higher education have articulated the need for this reform, citing high school graduates' lack of basic skills. Politicians and critics of public education note low rankings of U.S. students on international test comparisons, and these challengers often have their own solutions to the problem.

As a result of these varied factors, teachers and school leaders in every state find themselves in the midst of the so-called "standards-based reform," which has compelled them to focus instruction on the state-established curriculum and to improve student scores on tests designed to measure how well students meet these standards. There are endless discussions about whether such standards and tests are too easy or too tough or whether they even measure the right things. Even valid and reliable standardized tests sample only a small fraction of the knowledge universe that we want our students to understand and use, and all tests contain measurement errors. Too many states measure only the basic skills of reading, writing, and mathematics, with a net result of a substantial decline in the instructional time spent on the arts, science (especially in elementary schools), social studies, and health. The present accountability for schools, however, is assuring that all students achieve at high levels.

NEW RESEARCH ON EFFECTIVE SCHOOLS AND DISTRICTS

Many scholars contend that the school must be the center of change efforts to improve student achievement, and this continues to be a widely held viewpoint. The early work of Larry Lezotte, Ron Edmonds (1979), and Wilbur Brookover produced the Five Factor Theory, or the Effective School

"Correlates" as they are also known, which many schools applied in recent decades. More recently, Cawelti (1999b) studied six schools serving significant numbers of students from low-income families and reported on what these schools were doing to attain high levels of student achievement. These studies continue to show the importance of the principal's leadership, the need for focus on instruction and frequent assessment, the need for everyone to hold high expectations for all students, and the need for teachers who are deeply committed to educating economically disadvantaged students. More and more teachers are working on teams that regularly examine information about how well their students are doing as they seek ways to improve.

Thus we come to a central lesson about leadership. Great leaders do just two things—they decide what to do, and then they seek support to get things done.

For example, you decide a bond issue is needed to build schools and then go out and seek voter support at Rotary meetings and dozens of other avenues. President Roosevelt's job was to decide to declare war and then get Congress and the people to support what needed to be done to win the war. Likewise, educators decide to concentrate on the Five Factor Theory, and then make sure each school has a strong principal and teachers who understand the need to work in teams planning ways to improve.

Unfortunately, if one's attention is only on the school—rather than the system in which the school is a part—as the base for improvement, it will take a very long time to get the nation's low-performing schools up to higher achievement levels. With this in mind, the author recently undertook a study (Cawelti & Protheroe, 2001) of school *district* improvement to ascertain if there were any districts serving large numbers of children from low-income families where all or most of the schools showed substantial gains in student achievement over the past five years. While not a great many such districts exist, six successful districts were found and visited to determine what changes the teachers and school leaders believed had led to higher test scores. The findings tend to fall into the categories of (1) restructuring for greater accountability, (2) focusing on clear and important standards, and (3) making use of the knowledge base about teaching and learning.

This finding begins to suggest a new conception of effective schools that leaders will need to employ as they *make decisions* on what to do about low student achievement in their school or district and *enlist support* for getting these decisions implemented. Incidentally, this does not imply that such decisions are "made at the top" or arbitrarily. Normally the process of getting support for a decision begins with involving many people in the decision-making process. But sooner or later a decision must be made, and the leader is ultimately responsible for the decision's quality. If student achievement is very low, the decision to do nothing is a bad one.

The districts chosen for the study included two in Texas, one in West Virginia, and one in Idaho. Although they did not fully meet our criteria for inclusion in this study, we also looked at changes made in two large urban districts that had achieved good progress toward meeting the "all or most schools" criterion. Tests used to gauge "substantial improvement" in student achievement included the Texas Assessment of Academic Success, the Stanford Achievement Test–9th edition, the Iowa Tests of Basic Skills, and the Tests of Academic Progress. It is not the purpose here to go into the selection of these districts or report on how much improvement had been made. Suffice it to say the districts had gone a long way toward narrowing the gap in achievement normally found between minority children or those from low-income families and white or high-income students. For example, in the Brazosport Independent School District in Texas, the use of quality tools and an intense focus on high expectations, good instruction, and frequent assessment have essentially eliminated this gap.

The focus here is on the ways these districts changed from low-performing to high-performing districts. It is important to note that the growing recognition and conviction that all students can learn undergirds all successful activities and changes. When this belief is shared by many people, chances for success greatly improve.

RESTRUCTURING FOR
GREATER ACCOUNTABILITY

Even after leaders have made decisions, others often respond sluggishly and incompletely. The lack of clear accountability and the failure to identify those responsible for results can cause resistance to change at the school level because there are insufficient incentives to improve. In the districts we visited, each had undertaken one or more of the following changes in order to correct this lack of incentive and clarify who was responsible for improvement:

1. Decentralized authority to the building level, making obvious that the principal and staff were to be held responsible for improving student achievement. This included site-based budgeting, in some cases, but in every district it increased principals' and teachers' responsibility for resource allocation.

2. Increased reliance on the team structure as the basis for making plans to improve student achievement, including the annual plan for improvement submitted to the central office

3. The outsourcing of food services and benefits management as a means of increasing the focus on instruction

4. Increased choices for parents, including providing tuition for private schools if parents were not satisfied with the school to which their child had been assigned

5. More team use of instructional information about performance to analyze student achievement of particular students on particular instructional objectives

6. A change in the role of central office leaders from controlling, monitoring, and supervising to acting more as change agents, mentors, consultants, and advisors

Some of the districts were beginning to move much further than this by monitoring improvements in each school and taking action when higher test scores were not forthcoming. Responses included limiting principals' tenure, removing teachers who were not performing effectively, and even reconstituting schools (closing down and starting over). On the whole, however, it is still not clear what to do with "takeovers" of unsuccessful schools at either the district or state level.

The net effect of these changes is that they refocus efforts on student performance, and make it clear that the principal and staff are the ones accountable for improved results. Of course, many issues remain unresolved, such as promotion policies and high-stakes testing. Too much time is being spent on testing in some schools. In the final analysis, it is important to note that moving schools into a high-performing category is a major transition, and leaders must constantly be alert for excesses, omissions, and misdeeds.

FOCUS ON HIGH STANDARDS

All the new effective schools have decided to concentrate on a limited number of standards or else have had that decision made for them by the state education agency. Leaders are expected to guide discussions about how well test results in reading, mathematics, and writing reflect what the goals or standards for schools ought to be. The attention to these areas observed in the districts we studied tends to be on knowledge and skills that the state education agency assessed through standardized testing.

School leaders need to be developing far more comprehensive indicators of success than those measured by the state. Schools need success indicators for qualities today's students need as they prepare for tomorrow's world. For example, most jobs today require some degree of skill with computers, yet none of the districts we visited had tests for these skills that had to be passed for promotion. Certainly, a balanced program of general education will include attention to the arts, science, social studies, and health, but assessments in these subject areas are not prominent at the high school level and virtually nonexistent at the elementary level, except for in a few states such as Maine and Kentucky.

Here again, leaders need to be at the forefront of discussions about what the comprehensive indicators of student achievement ought to be in their districts and then work to get support for these decisions.

USING THE KNOWLEDGE BASE FOR IMPROVING INSTRUCTION

The most important question to ask about any pending change is the extent to which it will improve the daily instructional life of most students. In and of themselves, working in teams, setting standards, decentralizing, doing more testing, or changing from a controller to a mentor role will have no effect on classroom instruction. One may hope these factors will lead to such changes, but it is by no means a certainty. For example, several studies of site-based managed districts have shown no significant positive effect on student achievement.

The leader's job is to see that this issue of effective classroom instruction for all students remains at the forefront of discussions about changes in the school or district, and there are several resources to help with this. The Educational Research Service, the Association for Supervision and Curriculum Development, and the National Staff Development Council are several good sources of help. The difficult job is to bring teachers reliable information and provide the time to discuss, analyze, practice, and ultimately make use of new teaching strategies.

An example of another good resource is the *Handbook of Research on Improving Student Achievement* (Cawelti, 1995), in which I enlisted the help of scholars in the major disciplines to identify the teaching strategies for which the most and the best research exists. Here you will find 8 to 10 classroom teaching strategies for each subject such as science, mathematics, the arts, health, and other major fields. Experts indicate that these teaching strategies demonstrate improved achievement over traditional classroom practice. In addition, one generic chapter discusses those practices shown to be effective in several other relevant areas such as graded homework, direct instruction, and tutoring.

Marzano's recent publication (Marzano, Pickering, & Pollock, 2001) for the Association for Supervision and Curriculum Development (ASCD) discusses these as well as other practices such as reciprocal teaching, grouping, advance organizers, and various approaches to writing. Some of his work is based on meta-analyses of a large number of studies that measure the positive effects of particular strategies.

Many other such syntheses of classroom strategies exist. In addition, as leaders initiate their improvement plans, they need to make information available to teachers and principals on the effects of class size, pupil retention, instructional time on task, and other relevant policy issues. Moreover, a recent PDK Fastback (Owings & Kaplan, 2001) examines retention and social promotion.

The contribution of any one change in classroom practice does not tend to produce a very large increase in student achievement. Without going into the details of an effect size score, if meta-analysis of several studies on the use of analogies, for example, shows that their regular use produces an overall average increase of about a third of a standard deviation (an effect size of .33), this will result in an increase of 13 percentile points. Thus if a class using the practice began at the 40th percentile on the ITBS, it would rise to the 53rd percentile as a result of the new practice.

Teachers must realize that to make very large gains in student achievement and help reduce the gap between various student subgroups, they need to make other changes at the same time. Combining use of analogies, more frequent practice, and extensive tutoring, for example, would be much more likely to result in larger gains in student achievement.

CONCLUSION

The new effective school incorporates multiple considerations, including restructuring for accountability, more focus on a limited number of standards, and better use of research-based teaching practices. The knowledge base is not as precise as some would like, but that is true in other professions such as medicine; and we cannot afford to wait for it to be more conclusive.

Leaders need to make decisions about what they are going to undertake in their school or district to improve achievement, and they must realize that the larger task today may be getting support for whatever is decided. The ultimate test in many districts will be the leader's ability to develop a set of shared beliefs about the potential all students have for high achievement on goals important to their parents, employers, and politicians.

ISLLC QUESTIONS

Standard 1

- According to Cawelti, great leaders do two things. What are these and how does the leader develop, articulate, and implement a vision of learning that is shared and supported by the school community?

Standard 2

- How does Cawelti suggest that an educational leader build a school culture and instructional program conducive to student learning and staff professional growth?
- What was the impact on Brazosport School District in Texas from following this practice?

Standard 4

- How does Cawelti suggest mobilizing the community to support the academic success of all students?

REFERENCES

Cawelti, G. (Ed.). (1995). *Handbook of research on improving student achievement.* Arlington, VA: Educational Research Service.

Cawelti, G. (Ed.). (1999a). *Handbook of research on improving student achievement* (2nd ed.). Arlington, VA: Educational Research Service.

Cawelti, G. (1999b). *Portrait of six benchmark schools.* Arlington, VA: Educational Research Service.

Cawelti, G., & Protheroe, N. (2001). *High student achievement: How six school districts changed into high-performance systems.* Arlington, VA: Educational Research Service.

Edmonds, R. (1979). Effective schools for the urban poor. *Educational Leadership, 37*(1), 15-18; 20-24.

Marzano, R. J., Pickering, D. J., & Pollock, J. E. (2001). *Classroom instruction that works.* Alexandria, VA: Association for Supervision and Curriculum Development.

Owings, W. A., & Kaplan, L. S. (2001). Alternatives to retention and social promotion. *PDK Fastback, 481.* Bloomington, IN: Phi Delta Kappan.

Wohlsstetter, P. (1995). Getting school-based management right: What works and what doesn't. *Phi Delta Kappan, 71,* 22-26.

6

Politics and Education: A Conundrum for School Leadership

Gerald N. Tirozzi

Overview

Public schools are public and must be held accountable. Reform and political intervention have been constants in American public education during the past century, especially since 1965. Reforms address many of the outdated school practices that benefit both students and teachers.

Specific current political events impacting public school reform include the following: Title I of the Elementary and Secondary Education Act (ESEA), 1965 (a cornerstone of President Johnson's War on Poverty, Title I sought to improve the academic achievement of low-income students, stating that all children could learn a challenging curriculum and expecting school leaders to assure that it happened; equity and excellence had become goals of public schools; the "achievement gap" is a persistent pressure point that needs to be addressed); Individuals with Disabilities Education Act (IDEA), 1975 (promising parents that every child with a disability would receive a free, appropriate, and equal education; the

government promised to pay 40% of the costs but only pays 12%); and
A Nation At Risk, 1983 (This report seriously questioned the quality of
our schools and made suggestions for increased rigor for graduation
requirements, a restructured day, improved teaching, and accountability.).

Reform and political intervention in American public education have
been constants during the past century, taking on many forms and
offering many promises. I often ask audiences of educators, "Do you feel
reformed yet—is it over?" A story attributed to Claude Pepper, the legendary congressman from Florida, makes the point of the "staying power"
of reform. Supposedly, when Pepper died he asked the Lord, "Will we ever
have universal health care?" God's response was, "Yes, but not in my lifetime!" Educators might consider reform the same way.

The reality, however, is that reform should be viewed as favorable—if
it truly addresses many of the stagnant practices and outdated methodologies that permeate the teaching and learning process. In effect, the status quo of education practice is under scrutiny. The charge to promote
change during the past 35 years has come mainly from the political
process, particularly at the federal and state levels. This "process" has
dramatically affected public education and has had a major impact on
school leadership.

Public education is rooted in the political arena. The word *public* makes
it so! Consider the fact that the largest percentage of most local municipal
budgets, and a major share of state funding, goes directly to public
schools. Funding of our nation's education system is often at the center of
the local and state budget process with the financial impact hitting the taxpayers. This issue has been exacerbated by changing demographics, which
portray senior citizens as the fastest growing block of U.S. voters. Senior
citizens who have no school-age children and who face fiscal constraints
in their retirement years, are not enamored with the idea of their taxes
being raised to support other people's children. Older Americans truly
represent a constituency that merits the attention of school leaders, challenging them to develop outreach and create advocacy. In addition, community organizations, parent groups, and the business community have
become significant political players, demanding greater accountability for
student achievement and better use of fiscal resources in public education.

It is important to understand the political forces that have shaped the
educational landscape over the past 35 years. It is fair to state that the
forces of change and the political will to transform our system of public
education reached its nadir during this period. At no other time have there
been so many financial resources, legislative mandates, federal intervention
initiatives, and business/corporate interventions to shape the direction of
U.S. public education.

The most significant political pressure points can be traced to six key events:

1. The 1965 enactment of Title I, which is now a major component of the Elementary and Secondary Education Act (ESEA)

2. The 1975 enactment of the Individuals with Disabilities Education Act (IDEA)

3. The 1983 publication of *A Nation At Risk*

4. The Goals 2000 initiative of the late 1980s

5. The standards movement of the mid 1990s

6. The accountability/high-stakes testing initiatives of the past few years

Taken individually, each has been a catalyst for reform. Taken collectively, they have become a coalescing force that has transformed the political landscape of public education—and has had a major impact on the leadership of our nation's schools. Chief state school officers, superintendents, principals, and school board members, who are not conversant with the new lexicon of reform and the political will driving the reform, are truly out of touch with reality and will have a difficult time surviving the tidal wave of school change. The key point is that school leadership must be practiced within the context of the political climate.

To gain a perspective on these catalytic events and their significance for leadership, we need to review each and gain a greater understanding for, and appreciation of, the role of school administrators in the critical times that lie ahead. This is one parade that school leaders cannot follow; they must be up front and leading it!

TITLE I OF ESEA

Originally created in 1965, Title I (which has also been known as Chapter 1) is the nation's largest federal elementary and secondary program, with a present appropriation of $8.6 billion. The focus of the program is to improve the academic achievement of low-income children, and was a cornerstone of President Johnson's "War on Poverty." Title I makes a bold and challenging statement that *all* children can master a challenging curriculum and meet high academic standards—with the expectation that school leaders can provide the vision and skills to see these goals through to fruition. In effect, the level of expectation has been raised, and equity and excellence have become the goals for all of our nation's schools. One of the major challenges for public education is to address the persistent achievement gap that exists in U.S. schools. As state testing and exit examinations become the norm, the greatest "pressure point" of accountability for school administrators is, and will continue to be, their ability to significantly close the gap.

INDIVIDUALS WITH DISABILITIES EDUCATION ACT (IDEA)

In 1975, Congress passed landmark legislation, promising parents that every child with a disability would receive a free, appropriate, and equal education. Now called the Individuals with Disabilities Education Act (IDEA), this legislation promoted the inclusion and equality of one of our most disenfranchised groups of citizens. The dilemma for school leaders, charged with implementing this federal mandate, is that Congress has not met its fiscal obligation to support the program. Initially, Congress committed to funding 40% of the cost of special education. The fact is that the federal government provides only 12% of the funding—and local and state budgets are providing 88% of special education costs! This reality places a major and onerous financial burden on school leaders to meet the escalating cost of educating children with special needs. In passing IDEA, Congress made a strong moral statement and political commitment to our nation's disabled citizens, but the statement rings hollow without the funding to back it up.

A NATION AT RISK

The report *A Nation at Risk*, released in 1983, shook the foundations of public education. It called into serious question the quality of our schools, demanding higher academic standards, more rigorous high school graduation requirements, a restructured school day and year, and improved teaching and accountability for educational leaders to bring the reform agenda to fruition.

The report warned that "the education foundations of our society are presently being eroded by a rising tide of mediocrity that threatens our very future as a nation" (p. 6). It also captured the attention of politicians, policymakers, and the public with a dramatic conclusion: "If an unfriendly foreign power had attempted to impose on America the mediocre educational performance that exists today, we might well have viewed it as an act of war" (p. 6).

The staying power of *A Nation at Risk* is evident to this day, as shown by a significant increase in high school graduation requirements, a rush to institute state academic standards, a national movement to improve teaching, and the promotion of assessment and accountability.

I can personally speak to the political influence of this report, in that my appointment as a chief state school officer in Connecticut was announced on the same day the report was released. The strong and dramatic message of the report made it possible for me to open policy and political doors and develop and implement a broad and sweeping reform agenda in my state. The advantage the report gave to educational leaders was not necessarily embodied in its recommendations, but rather in the opportunity it presented to capitalize on its message and tone to awaken both the public and political will to address and support timely and necessary changes in public education.

GOALS 2000

In October of 1989, President George H. W. Bush convened a national educational summit in Charlottesville, Virginia, attended by the nation's governors, selected policy gurus, and corporate leaders. The outcome of the summit was an agreement on educational goals for our nation's schools. The goals gained even greater credibility when Congress enacted them in 1994 as the Goals 2000 legislation.

This far-reaching legislation became the framework for President Clinton's educational reform agenda, and was a driving force in the administration of Secretary of Education Richard Riley.

The Goals 2000 legislation became a catalyst, especially for states to implement the established goals and assess their attainment. This unique partnership among the White House, Congress, governors, and corporate leaders placed education once again in the public spotlight, and provided new and demanding challenges to school leaders and policymakers across the United States. In effect, Goals 2000 made a political statement and set forth national expectations for our schools—expectations that have driven the focus and efforts of school administrators for the past decade.

STANDARDS

The standards movement is rooted in the garden of politics, as legislators and policymakers have been largely responsible for driving the agenda to develop rigorous academic standards. To this end, all states—to varying degrees—have implemented legislation for standards-based reform. The statewide focus on "what students should know and be able to do" in core academic subjects has become a mantra for school leaders. This movement has served to shift the educational policy structure from the local level to greater state control. Inherent in this paradigm shift has been a greater emphasis on holding school superintendents and principals responsible for state-mandated programs and initiatives. This emerging political direction has also impacted school districts' curricula, instructional methodologies, professional development, assessment models, and leadership training. In addition, the state-driven standards movement has caused districts and schools to direct and redirect their financial resources as they align their programs with the new standards.

HIGH-STAKES TESTING

Against the backdrop of standards-based education, there has been an aligned political will to assess the extent to which the standards are being achieved. Of particular note has been the emphasis on high-stakes testing—which means that a single test determines whether a student graduates from high school, or is promoted to the next grade. This emphasis on accountability for demonstrable improvement in student achievement, often embodied in a *single test*, has placed enormous pressure on school leaders. The reality is that the school districts, and the individual schools within the district, are the focal points of accountability—placing the superintendent and the principals in the "spotlight" of accountability. The key observation is that the leadership roles within a school district are more easily identified as the positions to which responsibility and accountability can be affixed, as opposed to more closely scrutinizing the performance of classroom teachers.

The political nature of testing and accountability has a firm foundation in the business community where performance analysis, profit margins, and a "bottom line" mentality are commonplace. Corporate America has become a significant player in the political process of holding schools accountable. The reliance of the business world on data-driven decision making is reflected in a corporate adage, "In God we trust; all others bring data"!

CONCLUSION

There are other initiatives that could be cited to make the point that national public policy and politics have dramatically driven the educational agenda for the past 35 years. In addition, there are numerous state-driven policies and legislation that have sought to reform public education—in many cases, having an even greater impact on schools and classrooms within a state.

It should also be noted that the "political campfire" has been fueled by the escalating debate regarding the need for competition with other public schools. The rising tide of privatization initiatives (e.g., vouchers, school choice, magnet schools, Edison Project) has heated up the discourse among policy gurus and legislative leaders to hold public schools accountable, and to allow educational options for students who are in failing schools. The privatization of American public education looms as the centerpiece of political resolve over the next 10 to 20 years.

The legendary congressman from Massachusetts, Tip O'Neill, once said, "All politics are local." While local control still borders on being sacrosanct in the United States, the political power—especially that of local school boards—has eroded. The new focus of power has shifted to the nation's statehouses, and witnessed a greater involvement at the federal level. This shift must be clearly understood by school leaders as they chart a course for their schools and districts. It is imperative that school administrators analyze and comprehend the significance of the educational "megatrends" of the past 35 years, all of which have been largely directed by the political process.

It is safe to say that the presence of politics in public education will not diminish in the future. In fact, it may very well intensify, as we become more of a global village, driving international competitiveness and placing even greater pressure on schools to educate all children to high academic levels.

When individuals state that public education should be divorced from politics, they are simply not in touch with the real world. Our nation's economic growth, democratic way of life, military strength, international standing, and social fiber are inextricably linked with the quality of its public schools. Thomas Jefferson captured the imperative of education centuries ago in his insightful statement, "A nation that is ignorant and free is one that never was and never will be."

Mr. Jefferson's cogent warning merits reflection as a political statement regarding the essential nature of public education for a free and democratic people. Contemporary political leaders—using different words, and offering them in a different context—are driving an agenda, which speaks not only to a free and public education, but also to one that brings into clear focus the need for equity and excellence for *all* students. In effect, the bar has been raised. Are school administrators paying attention?

Educational leaders are faced with a conundrum. They can either allow the political process to continue to set the school reform agenda and the related terms and conditions thereof, or they can be active and vocal participants in the discourse, informing and instructing the debate with their expertise and experience. The latter is the role of a leader; the former is that of a casual observer. Administering a school district or school in an environment that is politically motivated is *not* a spectator sport—it needs active participants. Let's take the field!

ISLLC QUESTIONS

Standard 6

- Why does Tirozzi believe that politics will take an even more important role in education?

- How does Tirozzi recommend that educational leaders respond to and influence the larger political, social, economic, legal, and cultural context of educational reform?

REFERENCE

National Commission on Excellence in Education (1983, April). *A nation at risk: The imperative for educational reform.* Available online: http://www.ed.gov/pubs/natatrisk/

Lessons Learned

Leading change is a relatively new role for principals. The heightened public emphasis on school accountability hands principals the final responsibility for student achievement. To do this, today's principals are expected to understand how to restructure their organizations and how to make better use of the knowledge base to improve teaching and learning. These responsibilities for organizational change mark a significant transition in the principal's role from the traditional school operations manager to that of activist instructional leader. It is a position that requires additional preparation, professional and personal resources, and time.

As Gordon Cawelti observes, "Great leaders do just two things—they decide what to do, and then they seek support to get things done." Likewise, Michael Fullan notes, no matter how promising a new idea, it cannot impact student learning if it is superficially implemented. Gerald Tirozzi adds that public schools are public and must be accountable. All three writers address how successful principals can impact change.

As leaders in an era of high accountability, principals must effectively address people and task factors in the change process. Principals cannot *mandate* change. Change requires many to act in concert over time. Influencing others' beliefs and actions requires a broad complement of leadership skills. Principals must assist teachers and communities to identify and act on clear and important goals about teaching and learning. As fulcrums for change, principals bring together the vision, people, resources, and actions into a cohesive force that makes a positive difference for students and teachers.

Today's principals must deeply understand the change process and deftly integrate ideas about the nature and direction of the desired changes, the people who must genuinely comprehend and commit their efforts to put them into practice, and the actions that will make improvements happen. As they do, principals bring coherence to the many aspects of school improvement. They understand and clearly express where they are leading the school. They recognize the complexity of change and how to effectively facilitate the ideas, people, and actions over the long term to best advantage.

As instructional leaders, principals must help teachers focus on student achievement. Effective principals bring clear and important goals beyond those demanded by the state, and access reliable information, experiences, and the knowledge base about teaching and learning to increase student achievement. Principals become the "teachers of teachers," helping faculty use instructional practices that reflect a reliable knowledge base. Their common goal is to help all learners reach high standards required for high-stakes achievement as well as for fuller personal, civic, and career effectiveness in tomorrow's world.

In addition, principals as leaders of change recognize that they must accomplish more than just getting teachers to try out instructional innovations. Indeed, school leaders must transform their school culture if practices to enhance teaching and learning are to become ingrained parts of daily school life. The school culture reflects its members' values, beliefs, and behaviors. Without creating a school climate that supports the desired changes, no improvements will last. Building school culture takes frequent nurturing. New teachers need thoughtful induction into the belief and behavior network. Mature teachers need reinforcement and renewal of important beliefs and practices to keep them growing. Faculties need celebrations to commemorate their progress and achievements.

Without a supportive environment where they truly believe and feel commitment to the changes, teachers may comply with administrative expectations; but they will rarely make the innovations part of their own professional repertoire. Instead, new approaches remain "fads," readily exchanged for the next one rather than becoming a lasting style that works. School leaders of change must structure and direct the ongoing process of teachers' vision sharing, "buy-in," skill building, and acting on behaviors if real classroom changes that benefit students' learning are to occur.

Clearly, leading change requires principals to have certain essential personal qualities. They need ample emotional, physical, and intellectual energy for continuously thinking about where they are going. They must maintain a strong daily focus on the beliefs and practices that will turn the desired changes into realities for teachers and students. As leaders, they need keen people skills to help key stakeholders understand, embrace, and act on personal commitments to the shared goals. Moreover, change leaders require a long-term view to repeatedly create and renew followers who will act in good faith on their common goals when classroom doors close.

Finally, it is important for principals as leaders of change to accept their responsibilities as "public educators," accountable not only to the taxpayers and parents for effectively educating students to meet high standards. Principals also have the obligation to educate their communities about teaching and learning and to be proactive participants, influencing their local, state, and national education agendas. With their expertise and experience, principals can thoughtfully inform and influence the educational reform discussion. As research studies continue to show, principal leadership is an essential component for effective schools.

Part III

Teaching and Learning

7

Curriculum and Instruction: Critical and Emerging Issues for Educational Leadership

Robert J. Marzano

Overview

Curriculum and instruction have always been critical to the success of public education. *A Nation at Risk* (1983) brought strong focus to our students' low achievement in international comparisons. Varied reform efforts ensued, and the efforts to raise student achievement through an increasingly rigorous curriculum and clear standards for what all students should be able to know and do in certain subjects became the common goals. Unfortunately, this has produced too much content targeted as "essential" for the K-12 system to accommodate. Likewise, research on instruction shows that effective teaching accounts for two-thirds of the total effect of schooling on student learning. The impact of going to an effective school as opposed to an ineffective school is an increase in achievement of about 34 percentile points. Having an effective teacher accounts for about 26 percentile points.

What specific teachers bring to the schooling process is the major influence on achievement for students *at all achievement levels.*

While curriculum and instruction have always been critical to the success of public education, their importance was made more prominent with the publication of *A Nation at Risk* in 1983 (National Commission on Excellence in Education). The primary assertion of the report was that U.S. students were not performing well in traditional academic areas and, in fact, had demonstrated a marked decline in their performance. As evidence, the report offered research findings such as the following:

- Average achievement of high school students on most standardized tests is now lower than 26 years ago when Sputnik was launched.
- International comparisons of student achievement, completed a decade ago, reveal that on 19 academic tests, American students were never first or second and, in comparison with other industrialized nations, were last seven times.
- The College Board's SATs demonstrate a virtually unbroken decline from 1963 to 1980. Average verbal scores fell over 50 points and average mathematics scores dropped nearly 40 points. (p. 7)

Ramsey Seldon, Director of the State Assessment Center at the Council of Chief State School Officers, notes that after the publication of *A Nation at Risk*, educators set out to change what they could through new policies, such as those that increased the rigor of graduation requirements. Yet the results generated by these new policies were less than satisfactory. "We found that this first wave of reform didn't have dramatic effects. So there was a feeling of urgency that the education system needed to be stronger, and that in addition to what states and districts were doing, we needed a stronger presence at the national level . . . " (in O'Neil, 1995, p. 12). For the most part, the "presence at the national level" translated into a mandate for increased rigor in the content of the curriculum U.S. students were expected to master.

This expectation was made explicit in September of 1989 when President George H. W. Bush called the nation's governors together for an education summit in Charlottesville, Virginia. Shepard (1993) explains that at this summit, President Bush and the nation's governors, including then-governor Bill Clinton, agreed on six broad educational goals to be reached by the year 2000. These goals and their rationale were published under the title *The National Goals Report: Building a Nation of Learners* (National Education Goals Panel [NEGP], 1991). Two of those goals related specifically to achievement:

Goal 3: By the year 2000, American students will leave grades four, eight, and twelve having demonstrated competency in challenging subject matter, including English, mathematics, science, history, and geography; and every school in America will ensure that all students learn to use their minds well, so they may be prepared for responsible citizenship, further learning, and productive employment in our modern economy.

Goal 4: By the year 2000, U.S. students will be first in the world in science and mathematics achievement. (p. 4)

Soon after the summit, two groups were established, the National Education Goals Panel (NEGP) and the National Council on Education Standards and Testing (NCEST). Collectively, these two groups were charged with addressing (among others) the unprecedented question, "What subject matter knowledge should U.S. students be expected to master?" The work and influence of these two groups created a flurry of activity by subject matter specialists to identify the knowledge and skills essential to their subject areas. By the mid-1990s, specialists in no fewer than a dozen subject areas had generated documents articulating what students should know and be able to do regarding their subject matter content—the standards all students should meet.

The standards movement has been one of the most influential curriculum movements of the twentieth century, if not the most influential. At no time in U.S. history has there been such a comprehensive and focused effort to identify the knowledge and skills essential for students to master. However, the standards movement has unwittingly created more problems than it has solved. This is due to the lack of parsimony in the content identified as essential for students to know. For example, commenting on the quality of the standards documents, Chester Finn noted that "the professional associations, without exception, lacked discipline. They all demonstrated gluttonous and imperialistic tendencies" (Diegmueller, 1995, p. 6).

At the time of Finn's statement in 1995, the standards documents, taken together, weighed about 14 pounds, stood 6 inches tall, and contained over 2,000 pages. Since, then, more documents, more pounds, and more inches have been added to the total mass of standards. By contrast, the Japanese national curriculum fits into "three slender volumes, one for elementary schools, one for lower secondary schools, and one for upper secondary schools" (Ravitch, 1995, p. 15).

The impact of *A Nation at Risk* on U.S. curriculum was profound. For the first time, an attempt was made to specify the knowledge and skills that should be addressed in specific subject areas. Unfortunately, the effort had the unintended consequence of producing too much targeted content for the K–12 system to accommodate.

In addition, *A Nation at Risk* targeted instruction as a domain in need of reform. However, the link between the quality of student performance and the quality of teaching was less directly stated than was the link between the quality of performance and the curriculum. For example, the report made indirect allusions to a need for more qualified personnel in the teaching profession: "Persons preparing to teach should be required to meet high educational standards, [and] to demonstrate an aptitude for teaching. . . " (p. 21).

Since the publication of *A Nation at Risk*, the importance of instruction as a critical factor in effective school reform has been validated in a number of ways from a number of perspectives. For example, one review of the research over the last three decades found that of the total effect schooling has on student learning, the teacher accounts for two-thirds of that effect (Marzano, 2000). More specifically, in a given year, the impact of going to an effective school, as opposed to an ineffective school, is an increase in achievement of about 34 percentile points. Of this increase, having an effective teacher accounts for about 26 percentile points. Stated differently, if a student who is at the 50th percentile in academic achievement transfers from an ineffective school to a highly effective school, she can expect an increase in academic achievement of about 34 percentile points which would place her at the 84th percentile. However, 27 points of this 34-point expected gain are dependent on whether she has an effective teacher. If she is assigned to an ineffective teacher in that same school, she can expect an increase in achievement of only about 7 percentile points.

Clearly, what specific teachers bring to the schooling process, as opposed to what the school in general brings to bear, is the major influence on student achievement. This fact is most forcefully made by researcher William Sanders and his colleagues (see Sanders & Horn, 1994; Wright, Horn, & Sanders, 1997). Reporting on 30 separate studies across 3 grade levels (3-5) and 5 subject areas (math, reading, language arts, social studies, and science) with some 60,000 students, the researchers came to the following conclusion:

> The results of this study will document that the most important factor affecting student learning is the teacher. In addition, the results show wide variation in effectiveness among teachers. The immediate and clear implication of this finding is that seemingly more can be done to improve education by improving the effectiveness of teachers than by any other single factor. *Effective teachers appear to be effective with students of all achievement levels regardless of the levels of heterogeneity in their classes.* If the teacher is ineffective, students under that teacher's tutelage will achieve inadequate progress academically regardless of how similar or different they are regarding their academic achievement. (Wright et al., 1997, p. 63)

While this finding provides great hope, it also includes a rather somber warning. If teachers are not using effective instructional practices, their students fall further and further behind in their learning. Unfortunately, the results of another study, the *Third International Mathematics and Science Study* or TIMSS, as it is popularly referred to, provided evidence that teaching practices in the United States, at least in some classrooms, leave much to be desired. TIMSS was a large-scale, comparative study of the education systems in 41 countries. TIMSS researchers examined mathematics and science curricula, instructional practices, and school and social factors in all participating countries. One of the more publicized findings was that, in general, U.S. fourth-grade students did relatively well when compared to students of similar ages in other countries; eighth-grade students less so; and twelfth-grade students performed quite poorly. In a provocative *Wall Street Journal* article entitled, "Why America Has the World's Dimmest Bright Kids," Chester Finn (1998) described the findings in the following way:

> Today the U.S. Department of Education officially releases the damning data which come from the Third International Mathematics and Science Study, a set of tests administered to half a million youngsters in 41 countries in 1995. But the results have trickled out. We learned that our fourth-graders do pretty well compared with the rest of the world, and our eighth-graders' performance is middling to poor. Today we learn that our 12th-graders occupy the international cellar. And that's not even counting the Asian lands like Singapore, Korea and Japan that trounced our kids in the younger grades. They chose not to participate in this study. (Sec. A, p. 22)

One finding that was not well publicized was the difference in instructional practices employed by U.S. teachers as opposed to teachers in those countries that performed better. Specifically, the study found that teachers in other countries employed instructional strategies that engaged students more deeply and in higher cognitive ways than did U.S. teachers (see Forgione, 1998).

The challenges for educational leaders regarding curriculum and instruction are fairly clear. On the curriculum side is the need to decrease the amount of content teachers are expected to cover and students are supposed to learn. To date there have been some efforts to this end. For example, in 1998, researchers at McREL (Marzano, Kendall, & Cicchinelli, 1998) surveyed U.S. adults as to the standards they considered most essential for students to learn. Out of 255 standards, the top 25 are reported in Table 7.1.

The results of this effort imply that one positive step educational leaders can take toward decreasing the amount of content addressed in

Table 7.1   Top 25 Standards Identified by U.S. Adults

Subject Area	Standard
1. Health	Understands aspects of substance use and abuse
2. Language Arts	Uses grammatical and mechanical conventions in written compositions
3. Health	Understands the relationship of family health to individual health
4. Health	Knows essential concepts about the prevention and control of disease
5. Technology	Knows the characteristics and uses of computer software programs
6. Health	Knows how to maintain mental and emotional health
7. Geography	Understands the characteristics and uses of maps, globes, and other geographic tools and technologies
8. World History	Understands the causes and global consequences of World War II
9. Life Work	Displays reliability and a basic work ethic
10. Life Work	Operates effectively within organizations
11. Health	Knows the availability and effective use of health services, products, and information
12. Health	Understands essential concepts about nutrition and diet
13. U.S. History	Understands the causes of the American Revolution, the ideas and interests involved in shaping the revolutionary movement, and reasons for the American victory
14. Life Work	Manages money effectively
15. U.S. History	Understands the causes of the Civil War
16. Health	Knows essential concepts and practices concerning injury prevention and safety
17. Life Work	Makes general preparation for entering the work force
18. Technology	Knows the characteristics and uses of computer hardware and operating systems

Subject Area	Standard
19. Health	Understands the fundamental concepts of growth and development
20. Mathematics	Understands the general nature and uses of mathematics
21. Mathematics	Understands and applies basic and advanced properties of the concepts of measurement
22. Life Work	Pursues specific jobs
23. Science	Understands basic features of the earth
24. Health	Knows how to maintain and promote personal health
25. Civics	Understands the meaning of citizenship in the United States, and knows the requirements for citizenship and naturalization

national and state standards is to conduct a survey such as this with their local teachers, parents, and community members.

Relative to instruction, the clear challenge for educational leaders is to increase the use of effective instructional strategies. Again, some progress has been made in this direction. In a series of studies, researchers at McREL (see Marzano, 1998; Marzano, Gaddy, & Dean, 2000; Marzano, Pickering, & Pollock, 2001) identified nine categories of instructional strategies that have impressive track records in terms of enhancing student achievement. These are reported in Table 7.2.

While it is not necessarily true that all teachers should use all of these strategies all of the time, it can be said that classroom teachers should be expected to exhibit skill in all of these areas, and then have a rationale for picking and choosing those strategies to use in a given lesson for a given subject area.

The challenges of the next decade for educational leaders regarding curriculum and instruction are not small. However, there is enough cumulative research and theory to provide educational leaders with the content with which substantive changes can be made. We need to reduce the amount of curriculum for K-12 teachers to cover and students to master. Teachers need to increase their use of effective instructional strategies. We know which strategies increase student achievement and the percentile gain associated with each. Classroom teachers should be able to demonstrate skills in all areas of effective instruction and should have a rationale for using them in different learning situations.

Table 7.2   Categories of Instructional Strategies That Affect Student
Achievement

Category	Percentile Gain Associated With Category
Identifying similarities and differences	45
Summarizing and note taking	34
Reinforcing effort and providing recognition	29
Homework and practice	28
Nonlinguistic representations	27
Cooperative learning	27
Setting objectives and providing feedback	23
Generating and testing hypotheses	23
Questions, cues, and advance organizers	22

ISLLC QUESTIONS

Standard 2

- How does Marzano suggest educational leaders promote the success of all students by advocating, nurturing, and sustaining a school culture and an instructional program conducive to student learning and staff professional growth? Specifically, what educational practices should be clearly evident throughout a school?

REFERENCES

Diegmueller, K. (1995, April 12). Running out of steam. *Struggling for standards: An Education Week special report.* Washington, DC: Education Week.

Finn, C. (1998, March 25). Why America has the world's dimmest bright kids. *Wall Street Journal.*

Forgione, P. D., Jr. (1998). Commissioner's statement in *Pursuing excellence: A study of U.S. twelfth-grade mathematics and science achievement in international context* by S. Takahira, P. Gonzales, M. Frase, & L. H. Salgonik, pp. 5-6. Washington, DC: National Center for Educational Statistics.

Marzano, R. J. (1998). *A theory-based meta-analysis of research on instruction.* Aurora, CO: Mid-Continent Research for Education and Learning. (ERIC Document Reproduction No. ED 427 087).

Marzano, R. J. (2000). *A new era of school reform: Going where the research takes us.* Aurora, CO: Mid-Continent Research for Education and Learning.

Marzano, R. J., Gaddy, B. B., & Dean, C. (2000). *What works in classroom instruction?* Aurora, CO: Mid-Continent Research for Education and Learning.

Marzano, R. J., Kendall, J. S., & Cicchinelli, L. F. (1998). *What Americans believe students should know: A survey of U. S. adults.* Aurora, CO: Mid-Continent Research for Education and Learning.

Marzano, R. J., Pickering, D. J., & Pollock, J. E. (2001). *Classroom instruction that works: Research-based strategies for increasing student achievement.* Alexandria, VA: Association for Supervision and Curriculum Development.

National Commission on Excellence in Education. (1983). *A nation at risk: The imperative for educational reform.* Washington, DC: Government Printing Office.

National Education Goals Panel (1991). *The national education goals report: Building a nation of learners.* Washington, DC: Author.

O'Neil, J. (1995). On using standards: A conversation with Ramsey Seldon. *Educational Leadership, 52* (6), 12-14.

Ravitch, D. (1995). *National standards in American education: A citizen's guide.* Washington, DC: Brookings Institute.

Sanders, W. L., & Horn, S. P. (1994). The Tennessee value-added assessment system (TVAAS): Mixed-model methodology in educational assessment. *Journal of Personnel Evaluation in Education, 8,* 299-311.

Shepard, L. (1993). Setting performance standards for student achievement: A report of the National Academy of Education Panel on the evaluation of the NAEP trial state assessment: An evaluation of the 1992 achievement levels. Stanford, CA: Stanford University, The National Academy of Education.

Wright, S. P., Horn, S. P., & Sanders, W. L. (1997). Teacher and classroom context effects on student achievement: Implications for teacher evaluation. *Journal of Personnel Evaluation in Education, 11,* 57-67.

8

Enhancing Teaching

Linda Darling–Hammond

Overview

Teaching that ensures diverse students' learning requires a transformation in the ways that our education system attracts, prepares, supports and develops expert teachers. Teacher expertise is one of the most important school factors influencing student achievement. Instead of trying to address teacher shortages with ill-conceived "emergency" licenses for unprepared and underprepared individuals, states and schools can enact policies and practices to ensure more high-quality teachers for students. These approaches include providing subsidies for high-quality teacher preparation, competitive salaries, streamlining selection and proactive recruitment, mentoring and induction for beginning teachers, high-quality professional development, and redesigning schools to support teaching and learning.

For many decades, the United States education system has tried to improve student achievement by tinkering with various levers in the great machinery of schooling: New course requirements, curriculum packages, testing policies, management schemes, centralization initiatives, decentralization initiatives, and a wide array of regulations and special programs have been tried, all with the same effect. Reforms, we have learned over and over again, are rendered effective or ineffective by the knowledge, skills, and commitments of teachers and other professionals in schools. Without know-how and buy-in, innovations do not succeed. At a time when the success of individuals and societies depends more than ever before on their ability to learn, our ability to remain a strong and prosperous democracy depends, more than anything else, on our ability to teach. Teaching that ensures the learning of diverse students will require, in turn, a transformation in the ways in which our education system attracts, prepares, supports, and develops expert teachers who can teach in more powerful ways.

WHY IS QUALITY TEACHING A PRESSING ISSUE?

Since 1983, when *A Nation at Risk* warned of a "rising tide of mediocrity" in American schools, a massive education reform movement has been underway. Educators in the K–12 system have been urged to raise standards, redesign schools, and rethink curriculum to enable students to compete in an increasingly technological economy that demands high levels of knowledge and skill. Much of the press for reform is economic. 1950 saw 50% of the nation's labor force working at routine jobs on factory assembly lines or farms, whereas only 10% of today's jobs require such low levels of skill. Twenty years ago, a high school dropout had a 2-out-of-3 chance of getting a decent job; today the chances of such a person getting any job at all are less than one in two, and the job will pay half what it would have paid two decades ago. Meanwhile, nearly 70% of the new jobs being created are the kind of "thinking work" for which schools have typically prepared only a small minority of their students.

Over the last decade, reforms have sought to increase the amount of academic coursework and the number of tests students take, in hopes of improving achievement. These initiatives have made a great difference in what courses students choose to take: In 1983, only 14% of high school students took the number of academic courses recommended in *A Nation at Risk*. By the mid-1990s, more than 50% had taken this set of recommended courses. Despite these changes, achievement scores improved little and actually declined slightly for high school students in reading and writing. Meanwhile, international tests published in 1996 and 2000 continue to show U.S. high school students ranking below the median in mathematics and physical science and well behind peers in Asia and Europe. While course mandates have been enacted, the overall quality of learning seems not to have improved. Clearly, the quality of teaching students receive must become as much a focus of attention as the number of courses they take.

Those who have worked to improve schools over the last decade have found that every aspect of school reform—the creation of more challenging curriculum, the use of performance-based assessments, the implementation of decentralized management, the invention of new model schools and programs—depends on highly skilled teachers. Successful programs or curricula cannot be transported from one school to another where teachers do not know how to use them well. Raising graduation requirements has proved to be of little use where there are not enough qualified teachers prepared to teach more advanced subjects well. Mandates for more math and science courses have been badly implemented because of chronic shortages of teachers prepared to teach these subjects. Course content is diluted, and more students fail when teachers are not adequately prepared for the new courses and students they must teach. In the final analysis, there are no policies that can improve schools if the people in them are not armed with the knowledge and skills they need.

HOW DOES THE NEED FOR INVESTMENTS IN TEACHING IMPACT TODAY'S SCHOOLS?

The kind of complex learning needed for problem solving, invention, and application of knowledge rather than rote memorization depends on skillful teaching that does far more than "cover the curriculum." It requires teachers who understand how to represent critical ideas in powerful ways, can systematically organize a useful learning process, and can adapt instruction to the different approaches students use for learning. Expert teachers are diagnosticians who can take all of these variables into account and teach in reciprocal relationship to their students' learning. The task is not one that can readily be "teacher-proofed" through curriculum packages, textbooks, or testing systems, as schools have tried to do for most of this century. Teaching so that all students actually learn to achieve at high levels requires that teachers learn about learning—the structures of their disciplines and how these translate into critical curriculum concepts, strategies for diagnostic assessment as well as evaluation, and a repertoire of effective teaching methods.

A growing body of research finds that teacher expertise is one of the most important school factors influencing student achievement, far outweighing the lesser but generally positive influences of small schools and small class sizes. Teachers' knowledge of subject matter, student learning, and teaching methods are all important elements of teaching effectiveness and contribute greatly to a teacher's impact on student achievement.

Despite the critical importance of teacher knowledge and expertise, 40 states continue to issue emergency licenses for teachers, which allow people to teach with little or no preparation. Although no state will permit a person to write wills, practice medicine, fix plumbing, or style hair without completing training and passing an examination, these states fill nearly 100,000 vacancies a year with teachers who do not meet basic requirements. The vast majority of these underprepared recruits work in schools serving low-income and minority children, exacerbating the inequalities in education they already face. The 1996 report of the National Commission on Teaching and America's Future noted that, "Most states pay more attention to the qualifications of the veterinarians treating America's cats and dogs than to those of the people educating the nation's children and youth."

Until recently, teaching was not a focus of efforts to improve education. Through most of this century, teaching in U.S. schools has been treated as a form of semi-skilled labor that requires little more than the ability to "get through the book" with the aid of a few simple routines and tricks of the trade. The preparation of teachers has been a low status, under-resourced activity on most college campuses, and the old adage—"those who can, do; those who can't, teach"—described the patterns of recruitment in many colleges and school districts. Professional development has been characterized by occasional one-shot workshops on "flavor-of-the-month" topics, rather than a process of sustained learning and development of sophisticated practice. The result has been an uneven teaching force and few well-developed mechanisms for transmitting what is known about effective teaching to those charged with doing it. Efforts to invest in teaching have begun to change this situation in many states and school districts across the country, although there is still much variability. Especially now, as teachers must enable higher order learning on the part of students with a wide range of needs, it is critical that we invest in skilled and knowledgeable teaching in all communities.

WHAT ARE THE ALTERNATIVES?

While there are many challenges, policy can make a difference in the availability of qualified teachers to all schools. Such policy includes at least the following:

Subsidies for High-Quality Training

One important consideration in solving problems related to the supply of qualified teachers is the fact that better-prepared teachers enter and stay in teaching at much higher rates. For example, studies suggest that 5-year programs have entry and retention rates significantly higher than those of 4-year undergraduate programs, which in turn have retention rates significantly higher than those of short-term alternative certification programs or emergency routes. These differences are so substantial that it is actually less expensive, once the costs of preparation, recruitment, induction, and replacement due to turnover are taken into account, to prepare a teacher in a high-quality program than to train a teacher through a quick route that leads to high turnover.

One successful model is the North Carolina Teaching Fellows program, which provides $20,000 inservice scholarships to 400 high-ability high school seniors a year who enroll in intensive teacher education programs throughout the state. The Fellows do not have to pay back their scholarship if they teach for at least 4 years in North Carolina schools. The program has recruited more than 4,000 Fellows to teaching—a large number of them in high-need fields like math and science and in urban school districts. When the program was studied, 75% of all Fellows had completed their 4-year obligation, were still teaching in the public schools, and were rated as exceptional by their principals.

Competitive Salaries. One major cause of teacher shortages in cities and poor rural districts is that few states have equalized school funding or teachers' salaries so that districts can compete equally in the market for well-prepared teachers. In 1986, Connecticut sought to rectify this situation, having experienced severe shortages of qualified teachers in its cities for more than two decades. With a major investment through its Educational Enhancement Act, Connecticut spent over $300 million in 1986 to boost minimum beginning teacher salaries in an equalizing fashion that made it possible for low-wealth districts to compete in the market for qualified teachers. This initiative eliminated teacher shortages in the state, even in the cities, and created a surplus of applicants. At the same time, the state raised licensing standards, instituted performance-based examinations for licensing and a beginning teacher mentoring program, required teachers to earn a master's degree in education for a continuing license, invested in training for mentors, and supported new professional development strategies in universities and school districts. Since then, Connecticut has posted significant gains in achievement, becoming one of the top-scoring states in the nation in mathematics and reading, despite an increase in the proportion of students with special needs during that time. Equalization of salaries and improvements in teacher education and induction have led to similar improvements in states like Kentucky and North Carolina as well.

Streamlined Selection and Proactive Recruitment

Some districts have hiring procedures that are so cumbersome and dysfunctional that they chase the best-prepared candidates away instead of aggressively recruiting them. Others have focused intently on attracting well-qualified teachers and have changed their hiring practices. A glimpse of the possible can be seen in the New Haven Unified School District, located midway between Oakland and San Jose, California, which serves approximately 14,000 students, three-quarters of whom are students of color, most of them low-income and working class. Twenty years ago, the district was the poorest district in a low-wealth county, and it had a reputation to match. Families who could manage it financially sent their children elsewhere to school. Today, New Haven Unified School District, while still a low-wealth district, has a well-deserved reputation for excellent schools. Every one of its 10 schools has been designated a California Distinguished School. All have student achievement levels well above California norms for similar schools.

How did they do it? While school districts across California scrambled to hire qualified teachers, often failing to do so, New Haven had in place an aggressive recruitment system and a high-quality training program with local universities that allowed it to continue its long-term habit of hiring universally well-prepared, committed, and diverse teachers to staff its schools. One factor in its success is that, despite having lower per-pupil expenditures than many surrounding districts, New Haven spends the lion's share of its budget on teachers' salaries. For example, while a nearby district spends substantially more money per pupil, New Haven's beginning teacher salaries are nearly one-third higher. New Haven's personnel office uses technology and a wide range of teacher supports to recruit from a national pool of exceptional teachers. All vacancies are posted on its Web site, which draws inquiries from all over the country. Each inquiry receives an immediate e-mail response. With the use of electronic information transfer (for example, the personnel office can electronically send vacancy information directly to candidates and send applicant files to the desktop of any administrator), the district can provide information to candidates that urban districts might never think would be available to them. Viable applicants are interviewed immediately in person or via video conference (through a local Kinko's), and if they are well qualified with strong references, they may be offered a job that same day. Despite the horror stories one often hears about the difficulty of out-of-state teachers earning a California teaching credential, New Haven's credential analyst in the personnel office has yet to lose a teacher recruited from out of state in the state's credentialing maze.

Among the many factors contributing to the district's success in recruiting teachers and serving students, one significant strategy is the district's investment in teacher education. The district was one of the first in the state to implement a Beginning Teacher Support and Assessment Program that provides support for teachers in their first two years in the classroom. All beginning teachers receive such support from a trained mentor who has release time for this purpose. Many beginning teachers report that they chose to teach in New Haven because of the availability of this strong support for their initial years in the profession. In addition, with the support of California State University, Hayward, the district designed an innovative teacher education program that combines college coursework and an intensive internship conducted under the close supervision of school-based educators. Because interns function as student teachers who work in the classrooms of master teachers, rather than as independent teachers of record, the program simultaneously educates teachers while protecting students and providing quality education. The fruits of these efforts show in New Haven's steadily increasing student achievement as well as its success in finding and keeping good teachers.

Mentoring and Induction for Beginning Teachers

New Haven's investment in beginning teacher mentoring is increasingly being replicated elsewhere, with similar results. The number of teachers who participated in formal induction programs almost doubled during the decade 1981 to 1991. By 1991, 48% of all teachers with fewer than three years of experience and 54% of public school teachers had experienced some kind of induction program during their first year. Depending on the nature of the programs—such as whether they focus on support as well as evaluation and whether they help teachers address real problems of practice—these induction initiatives may make a substantial difference in teacher recruitment and retention. In addition to providing vital guidance and learning for new teachers, research suggests that teacher mentoring reduces the early attrition from the profession, especially when programs are designed to support new teachers in the development of guided, collegial practice and inquiry.

Several districts have created models of beginning teacher induction and career-long learning that have been replicated with significant success in other settings. Peer review and assistance programs initiated by AFT and NEA locals in Toledo, Cincinnati, and Columbus, Ohio; Rochester, New York; and Seattle, Washington, have been successful in helping beginners learn to teach and in helping veterans who are having difficulty to improve their teaching or leave the classroom without union grievances or delays. Each program was established through collective bargaining and is governed by a panel of 7 to 10 teachers and administrators. The governing panel selects consulting teachers through a rigorous evaluation process that examines teaching skills and mentoring abilities. The panel also approves assignments of tenured teachers to intervention status (through self-referral or referral made by principals) and oversees appraisals of intern (beginning) and intervention teachers.

The intensive assistance is provided by consulting teachers who are freed up to focus on this job. This ensures that adequate help and documentation will occur over the course of the year. The consulting teacher is selected for teaching excellence and generally is matched by subject area and grade level with the teacher being helped. This increases the value of the advice offered and the credibility of the judgment rendered. In these districts, overall attrition of beginning teachers has decreased and beginners become competent sooner. In Rochester, for example, retention of beginning interns is 90%, as compared with only 60% before the program was put into place. In Cincinnati, attrition of beginning teachers has been close to 5% annually since the program was put into effect.

High-Quality Professional Development

Developing the type of knowledge and skill needed by today's teaching force requires that most teachers move far beyond what they themselves experienced as students, and that they learn in ways that are more powerful than simply reading and talking about new ideas. Learning to practice in substantially different ways than one has personally experienced cannot occur through theoretical imaginings or unguided experience alone. It requires a much tighter coupling of experience and theory. Good professional development bears little resemblance to the "drive-by" workshops that treat teachers to daylong lectures and handouts—just as good education for students bears little resemblance to rote memorization of information without opportunities to apply it. Teachers learn well just as students do—by studying, doing, and reflecting; by collaborating with other teachers; by looking closely at students and their work; and by sharing what they see.

Good settings for teacher learning provide plentiful opportunities for research and inquiry, for trying and testing, and for talking about the results of learning and teaching. Professional development strategies that improve teaching share the following features:

- Experiential: engaging teachers in concrete tasks of teaching, assessment, and observation that illuminate the processes of learning and development
- Grounded in participants' questions, inquiry, and experimentation as well as profession-wide research
- Collaborative: involving a sharing of knowledge among educators
- Connected to teachers' work with their students as well as to exploration of subject matter and teaching methods
- Sustained and intensive: supported by modeling, coaching, and problem solving around specific problems of practice
- Connected to other aspects of school change

Inquiry models of professional development may include such activities as teacher study groups, teacher research, school-based coaching, or teacher networks. In New York City's Community School District #2, teachers can utilize a professional development laboratory (PDL) where one teacher can spend 3 weeks working in the same classroom as an expert resident teacher who uses specific practices. While she is visiting this resident teacher, a skilled substitute works with the teacher's students, using the same kinds of practices. When the 3-week PDL experience is over, the teacher can return to the resident teacher and to other school-based consultants for expert coaching as she applies the new practices in her classroom. The district also uses teams of instructional consultants to work with groups of teachers within schools to develop particular strategies. Teachers and principals visit and observe one another, develop study groups on topics of current interest, and work together to solve problems of practice. The focus is on sharing, analyzing, and improving practices in the context of how they affect learning.

Content-based professional development is particularly effective when it is grounded in concrete problems of practice. For example, one study found that California's intensive "student curriculum workshops" in elementary mathematics caused teachers to change their practices and improved their students' learning. Teachers studied and used specially designed "replacement units" to teach mathematics, discussing them with colleagues and learning from each other's experiences. The curriculum workshops offered teachers the opportunity to collaborate on learning new content and new strategies for teaching it, grounded in their own day-to-day work. Other examples of content-based professional development include the subject-matter collaboratives that California formed around the state's curriculum framework and the National Writing Project. Both use summer institutes to bring teachers together around specific curriculum topics to share successful strategies, discuss current research, and sharpen practice through reflection, analysis, and study.

One positive trend is the engagement of prospective and veteran teachers in studying research and conducting their own inquiries through cases, action research, and the development of structured portfolios about practice. Teachers report that they learn a great deal from analyzing their own and others' practice and measuring it against standards that reflect accomplished teaching. This process is substantially assisted when teachers develop a portfolio based on teaching artifacts (videotapes, lesson plans, student work) and reflections on their work. When teachers examine portfolios and talk with one another about this evidence, they discover matters about which they disagree, have different interpretations, or use the same terms to mean different things. They begin to develop shared standards and common language with which to examine and discuss teaching and learning. The portfolio approach is the cornerstone of National Board certification, as well as teacher induction models supported by the Interstate New Teacher Assessment and Support Consortium (INTASC). Teachers say they learn much from developing a portfolio based on teaching artifacts—videotapes, lesson plans, student work, and so on—and then reflecting on their work in light of professional standards of practice.

All of the approaches described above shift from old, "fill-the-vessel" models of teacher training to a model in which teachers are regularly engaged in evaluating their practice and use their colleagues for mutual assistance. Theory is brought into the school setting; teachers see how what they are learning relates to the classrooms they are in; professionals who work at the same site share and leverage information to form a common base of experience and understanding. The result is a greater appreciation for what matters and what works, as well as what needs to change to promote student success. But at least one barrier to this internally driven and sustained model of professional development is today's typical school environment.

Redesigning Schools
to Support Teaching and Learning

A final critical area for recruiting and retaining excellent teachers is the restructuring of school organizations and of teaching work, including a reallocation of personnel and resources so that teachers have time to work intensively with students and collaboratively with each other. Teaching in large, bureaucratic settings that do not enable teachers to come to know their students well or to work and plan with other teachers is exhausting, non-rewarding work. It is especially counterproductive in urban areas where students face many challenges and need a great deal of personal attention. Factory-model high schools in which teachers see 150 or more students daily, cycling anonymously though the classroom in fragmented 45-minute periods, create alienation and anomie because they support neither learning nor teaching well.

Studies of school organization consistently find that small schools (with enrollments of roughly 300 to 600) promote higher student achievement, higher attendance, lower dropout rates, greater participation in school activities, more positive feelings toward self and school, more positive behavior, less violence and vandalism, and greater postschool success. These outcomes are also found in settings where students have close, sustained relationships with a smaller number of teachers throughout their school careers. This can be achieved when teachers can work for longer periods of time with smaller total numbers of students, either by teaching a core curriculum to one or two groups of students rather than a single subject to several groups, or by teaching the same students for more than one year. Schools in which students remain with a cohort of their peers also foster a sense of community and a set of continuing relationships that are important to learning and to the affiliations needed to sustain trust and effort. Not incidentally, schools with these communal features have lower turnover of teachers and are easier to staff, regardless of the neighborhood or students they serve, since they provide teachers the opportunity to be successful.

Developing such schools requires rethinking organizational forms and norms that have developed over many decades. Successful schools have changed curriculum, assessments, and schedules to provide longer periods of time for in-depth learning and teaching; they have also developed new patterns of staffing and resource use, including greater investments in teaching rather than non-teaching functions. In order to afford both smaller pupil loads for teachers and greater time for collegial work, more of the staff who are now working in pullout programs, administrative roles, and support offices are working in the classroom, as they do in most other industrialized countries. For example, in contrast to European and Asian countries that allocate 60 to 80% of their education personnel to classroom teaching, the bureaucratic organization of U.S. schools means that only about 43% of education staff are regularly assigned as classroom teachers. This allocation of staff and resources to the periphery of the classroom maintains large class sizes and pupil loads for teachers and reduces their opportunity to plan and work together.

Structuring school time so that teachers have adequate preparation, consultation, and collaboration time does not have to be an add-on expense or an either-or sacrifice that supports professional development at the expense of teachers' time with students. But it does require creative thinking and fresh approaches to the fragmented specialization that drives school staffing today. Schools that have restructured their staffing have been able to create shared planning time for teachers without added costs. For instance, instead of having pullouts and large numbers of aides for Title I and special education, these positions can be turned into classroom teacher slots so as to lower teacher-to-student ratios, spread workloads more evenly, and provide more individualized attention to each student. In Boston, these pullout positions constituted 40% of the teaching staff. Merely redeploying staff reduced class sizes and expanded planning time substantially in schools that chose to rethink their organizational assumptions. The expertise of specialists reassigned to teaching teams can be shared with teachers through teaming, in-class consultation, and staff development they conduct. Teachers can work in teams that share responsibility for a number of students. Classes in aligned subjects, such as English, history, and writing, can be taught in block schedules by interdisciplinary teams. Longer class periods (90 to 120 minutes) and fewer classes reduce teaching loads and expand planning time for teachers in middle and high schools. All of these strategies have been used in new, smaller restructured schools that have had extraordinary success with students and have enabled a higher degree of teacher learning, co-planning, and collaboration.

In short, school leaders need to set the expectation and provide the opportunity for teaching to become a learning profession. School norms and structures need to be redefined to support the collaborative exploration and enactment of new content and practices. Movement is beginning to occur toward collaborative, inquiry models of professional development and toward revamping school organization to create new opportunities that enable study, reflection, problem solving, and collegial learning. Making this movement widespread is the challenge facing school leaders today.

CONCLUSION

All students need quality teachers if they are to achieve at high levels. The data clearly show the difference that teacher effectiveness makes. Policy changes can increase the number of effective teachers working with students.

ISLLC QUESTIONS

Standard 1

- What issues does Darling-Hammond suggest are barriers to educational leaders' and communities' vision of learning?
- What suggestions does Darling-Hammond offer to remove these barriers to their vision of learning?
- What practices to secure quality teachers can school principals use, and which are the responsibility of the school division's Human Resources Department? In which areas can school and central office work collaboratively?

Standard 2

- How do the teacher quality issues that Darling-Hammond raises impact the school culture and affect the instructional program and staff professional growth?

Standard 3

- How do the suggestions for increasing the pool of quality teachers impact the efficient and effective management of the school organization from the school and Human Resources perspectives?
- How do these issues impact procedures to maximize student learning, support sound fiscal management, and use effective problem-framing and problem-solving skills?

Standard 4

- How do Darling-Hammond's suggestions impact educational leaders' collaboration with communities to secure community resources to address school issues?

Standard 5

- What aspects of the teacher quality issues affect educational leaders' ability to act with integrity, fairness, and ethics?

Standard 6

- How do educational leaders' response to the teacher quality issue reflect the larger political, social, economic, legal, and cultural context?

REFERENCES

Darling-Hammond, L. (1997). *The right to learn.* San Francisco: Jossey-Bass.

Darling-Hammond, L., & Sykes, G. (2001). *Teaching as the learning profession: A handbook of policy and practice.* San Francisco: Jossey-Bass.

National Commission on Teaching and America's Future. (1996). *What matters most: Teaching for America's future.* New York: Author.

9

Enhancing Teacher Quality

Thomas S. Mawhinney
Laura L. Sagan

Overview

Preparing future teachers to become effective classroom teachers is an important means to renew our profession. The cooperative teacher relationship in developing quality teachers and building a school's learning organization and culture is critically important. In addition, becoming a mentor for another teacher enhances the quality of the mentor's practice as well. In a time of increased accountability for student achievement, however, encouraging seasoned teachers to give up teaching their curriculum to work with preservice teachers becomes a challenge. To address this, the principal and teachers at Rhineback High School, New York, built a partnership with the state teachers college to immerse the faculty, students interns, and apprentice teachers in the teacher-training process.

The twelfth-grade English teacher approached the principal in the hall in an obviously agitated state. "I've had it with student teachers," he stated emphatically. Apparently, his student teacher, who had been struggling for the previous 2 weeks, had called in and left a message that she would not be returning to complete her student-teaching requirement.

This bit of news dismayed the administrator, because he was trying to encourage more of the high school faculty to work with student teachers. Many seasoned teachers were reluctant to give up teaching their curriculum for an 8-week period, especially in classes facing a culminating New York State Regents examination, the results of which would be published in the local newspaper. This latest breakdown in the mentoring of a preservice teacher only reinforced with the veteran faculty the futility of accepting a student teacher. Knowing the importance of the cooperating teacher relationship in developing quality teachers and in building the school's learning organization and culture, school administrators were uncertain as to how to change this veteran staff's attitude.

Rhinebeck High School is a small, rural high school, located in the Hudson Valley about 100 miles north of New York City. The student population is largely middle- to upper-middle-class with about 5% qualifying for a free or reduced lunch. Approximately 80% of the graduating seniors attend a 2- or 4-year college. Annual New York State Regents examination scores are typically well above the state average. Out of a total student population of 425, minorities comprise 2%. There are 35 faculty, 8 support staff, and 5 clerical staff. Bulkeley Middle School became part of our building 4 years ago, and we have several faculty members in common. Bulkeley contains 335 students, 18 faculty, and 7 support staff.

Every spring and fall, the local teacher training colleges send Rhinebeck High School and Bulkeley Middle School correspondence asking for the names of faculty members willing to accept student teachers. Semiannually, we disseminate the colleges' request form to all Rhinebeck teaching staff. Typically, the response is minimal.

This had to change for several reasons. We knew from the literature that becoming a mentor for another teacher enhances the quality of not only the preservice teacher's practice, but the mentor's as well (Rowley, 1999). We also had a vision of creating a school culture where teaching and learning were the most important aspects of what went on in the building. We wanted to nurture an environment where everyone's first priority is improving academic achievement by enhancing pedagogy. We initiated teacher-learning groups (Mawhinney, 2000) to foster this culture, but we wanted to build on this by forming a partnership with the state teachers college to immerse our faculty in the teacher-training process.

The major obstacle facing any kind of change in our school has been the administrator-faculty relationship that existed in the building. Because of the animosity generated by the decade-long tenure of a previous principal, the veteran teachers immediately dismissed any administrator-generated idea. Shared decision making usually meant that the principal made a decision and shared it with the faculty. Despite efforts to involve the staff, they usually banded together to endorse the status quo. Therefore, to ask them to take on more student teachers when they were unhappy taking on any would be difficult at best.

Ironically, both the plan and the solution to this dilemma were teacher-driven. One of our middle school teachers was an adjunct faculty member at the nearby state university where he taught a secondary methods course. Knowing the high school principal's interest in teaching and learning, he approached the administrator about doing a workshop with the methods students when they made their mandatory visit to the middle/high school. The high school principal subsequently taught a 2-hour workshop on the vastness of the teaching knowledge base titled, "Everything I Know About Teaching, I Learned in High School." Our school's university involvement further increased when this teacher turned over his methods course to another middle school faculty member who was involved with the high school principal in an instructional leadership doctoral program at St. John's University.

A requirement of the second instructor who took over the methods course was that the preservice teachers had to teach a social studies lesson to an eighth-grade class. Knowing I had been trained in observing and analyzing teaching (Saphier, 1993) based on *The Skillful Teacher* (Saphier & Gower, 1997), she asked me to conduct teacher observations with her. This partnership received such positive feedback from the university students that the dean of the secondary education department called and asked if we would be willing to take a cohort of preservice interns every semester. Again, we eagerly accepted, knowing that having apprentice teachers in the building would be a stimulating experience for our faculty.

The eighth-grade teacher and the principal began to develop a program for the interns that included exposure to learning styles (Dunn & Dunn, 1993), Socratic Seminars (Letts, 1994), research-based strategies (Marzano, Pickering, & Pollock, 2001), and the parameters of teaching (Saphier & Gower, 1997). Because teachers are more inclined to respond to a colleague than to an administrator, the teacher petitioned other faculty to conduct workshops with the interns on areas of their individual expertise. Subsequently, high school and middle school teachers conducted mini-workshops on school law, creating teacher portfolios, integrating the curriculum, and mind mapping. The interns and methods students were ecstatic that they were receiving a higher level of training and exposure to teaching methodologies than their fellow students who were interning at other schools.

This collaboration and increased interest by the university led us to examine the possibility of Rhinebeck High School and Bulkeley Middle School becoming professional development schools. (Abdal-Haqq, 1998; Darling-Hammond, 1997; Goodlad, 1990). We arranged a meeting with several of the university's School of Education faculty. While impressed with our efforts, no one volunteered to make our partnership a more formal one. Also discouraging was the fact that the college hired retired public school faculty to supervise student teachers. These retired teachers may have been good practitioners, but were not necessarily trained in observing teachers and providing helpful feedback.

Having the interns in our building has encouraged our veteran faculty to accept student teachers. Mature teachers had the opportunities to meet and know prospective preservice teachers before their student teaching experience and made more knowledgeable decisions on becoming a cooperating teacher the following year. Several faculty even granted the interns an occasion to teach a model lesson with the principal observing. The longer the interns were in the building, the more our faculty were willing to have them come in and observe their practice. Discussion about teaching took place between the observing interns and the practicing teachers. If the interns wanted to see a particular aspect of teaching—classroom management, organization, technology in the classroom, team teaching—we had teachers they could observe. The change was obvious—during the spring semester we had over 13 student teachers in the building. For two small schools, that was a significant increase. Most of the preservice teachers had negotiated their placement directly with the cooperating teachers during their internship. Following the practicums, every cooperating teacher reported a positive mentoring experience.

Bringing change to veteran teachers was difficult. Involving them in knowledge gathering, give-and-take discussions, and shared decision making had not worked. The negative faculty had too much power and convinced the majority that change is equivalent to giving in to the latest fad. Therefore, introducing change gradually, inviting teachers to buy in, and slowly increasing teacher involvement was a much more compatible way to introduce change in our school. No one was mandated to run a mini-workshop or take a student teacher, and yet it happened.

The intern and methods programs, however, have not worked for all university students. Some entered the program with preconceived notions and beliefs that teaching was just "chalk and talk." Some college faculty and supervising teachers supported these beliefs. But most were excited and grateful for the opportunity to observe quality pedagogy. We would have done some things differently in instituting this partnership with a teacher training college. Plans are in place to improve the system.

We have volunteered to train retired public school teachers hired to supervise student teachers. We are also continuing our efforts to invite university professors into our school to work with faculty and to teach courses. We also plan to increase the number of teachers involved in teaching workshops and working with interns. Eventually, we would like to train all our teachers in observing and analyzing teaching.

Becoming a professional development school is our long-term goal. We feel we are on the right course.

CONCLUSION

Finding the means to make mentoring happen within a high-stakes context offers challenges to educators, but the payoff is high. Mentoring preservice and "apprentice" teachers builds skills for both mentor and mentored and helps create a genuine learning environment.

ISLLC QUESTIONS

Standard 1

- How does this educational leader facilitate the implementation of a vision of learning that is shared and supported by the school community?
- How does this educational leader identify and remove barriers to this vision?

Standard 2

- How does this educational leader advocate and nurture a school culture and instructional program conducive to student learning and staff professional growth?
- How does this educational leader maintain a culture of high expectations?
- How does this educational leader support conflict resolution and consensus building?
- How does this educational leader gather more data and information before making decisions?
- How does this educational leader treat all individuals with dignity and respect?

Standard 4

- How does this educational leader collaborate with community members and mobilize community resources?
- How does this educational leader give credence to individuals and groups with conflicting opinions?
- How does this educational leader secure community resources to solve school problems?

Standard 6

- How does this educational leader understand, respond to, and influence the larger political, social, economic, legal, and cultural context?

REFERENCES

Abdal-Haqq, I. (1998). *Professional development schools: Weighing the evidence.* Thousand Oaks, CA: Corwin.

Darling-Hammond, L. (1997). *The right to learn: A blueprint for creating schools that work.* San Francisco: Jossey-Bass.

Dunn, R., & Dunn, K. (1993). *Teaching secondary students through their individual learning styles: Practical approaches for grades 7-12.* Boston: Allyn & Bacon.

Goodlad, J. I. (1990). *Teachers for our nations schools.* San Francisco: Jossey-Bass.

Letts, N. (1994, April). Socrates in your classroom. *Teaching K-8, 24*(7), 48-49.

Marzano, R. J., Pickering, D. J., & Pollock, J. E (2001). *Classroom instruction that works: Research-based strategies for increasing student achievement.* Alexandria, VA: Association for Supervision and Curriculum Development.

Mawhinney, T. S. (2000). Who's teaching whom? Building a culture of learning in your school. *NASSP Bulletin, 84* (617), 73-76.

Rowley, J. B. (1999). The good mentor. *Educational Leadership, 56*(8), 20-22.

Saphier, J. (1993). *Making supervision and evaluation really work.* Carlisle, MA: Research for Better Teaching.

Saphier, J., & Gower, R. (1997). *The skillful teacher.* Acton, MA: Research for Better Teaching.

10

Using Technology to Change School Learning Culture

Alan November

Overview

Technology reorganizes the culture of learning. Its real impact on learning lies in the opportunity to develop new relationships between teaching and learning and to rethink the relationship of the learner to the world. Technology creates an environment to teach students real-world problem solving as it empowers learners to direct and manage their own learning beyond schools' confines. The teacher's role in this context becomes one of engaging students in identifying their own real-world problems and then deciding which technologies are needed to research, compile, and communicate findings. Amid this potential, educators must address educational equity that would help all families have the capacity to be Web-connected learning centers, so no child falls behind.

In 1983, one of my high school students profoundly changed my vision of education and helped me to understand why so many students are underserved by traditional schools.

On a late Friday afternoon, hours after the last student left for the day, Yves was discovered in the computer lab. He had broken in. The natural response of the teacher who discovered this was to punish him. The possibility that this student had broken into the classroom to learn was certainly not the teacher's first thought. Why else would a student break into a classroom unless he or she were up to mischief?

As Director of the Alternative School, and Yves' advisor, I got the call to "deal with" him. Imagine a student who does not like school, someone who does not worry about completing work on time or at all, who has no academic aspirations but who is a good kid. At that time the concept that this student had broken into school to learn was a disconnect for me, too. But there Yves sat, busily striking the Chiclet-like keys on the Commodore Pet computer. An audiotape drive was plugged into the back of the computer. I did not understand any of it, but clearly, Yves was fascinated by what he was doing.

Today, nearly 20 years later, I am not puzzled when I find students wanting to work on technology all night. I understand the empowered feeling of building models, writing code, communicating with people around the world, or creating music with a tool that gives boundless access to information and feedback to the learner. It can be an exhilarating feeling. As Csikszentmihalyi has described (1991), you are deep in the flow of learning and creating.

In my own home, I have a hard time convincing my 14-year-old daughter that she needs to sleep and that it is time to stop working on her Web site. Jessie gives the Golden Cauldron Award to students who write in the style of J. K. Rowling, author of the Harry Potter books, and gets submissions from around the world. As Yves did before she was born, Jessie initiated and developed the work on her own, using a computer.

What really amazed me 20 years ago was Yves' confidence in his ability to manage his own learning. When I had sorted out that he really wanted to learn programming, I suggested that he take a summer school course. He looked at me as if I were suggesting that he go to jail.

His response was, "I could do the whole course in a weekend!" He wasn't bragging (well, maybe a little); he was stating fact. Here was this kid who, in all likelihood, was not going to graduate because he didn't have enough credits—classes bored him. At the same time, he was claiming that he could complete a computer programming course in a weekend. How could he? His assertion was a direct challenge to our concept of time and space and learning.

In 1983, I was happily teaching social studies and had never even touched a computer. It was all a foreign land to me. The math department owned every computer and ran the computer labs, and all they taught was programming—BASIC, Pascal, and LOGO.

At that time, my roommate was a Harvard Business School professor in the area of computer systems. I was so excited by Yves' desire to learn that I went home and asked Roger what computer programming language I should learn so I could think about teaching a computer course during the following year. Working with more students in this new environment had enormous appeal to me.

In his professorial way, Roger told me I was asking the wrong question. "You do not need to teach programming anymore. Software tools are coming. What you really need to teach is problem solving. Very few people will need to program their own tools. Technical skills are essential but critical thinking is more important."

"But what does the curriculum for critical thinking look like?" I asked him. "What do we do on the first day of class?"

Roger explained that I should engage students in identifying their own real-world problems and then figure out what technologies are needed to solve them. At that time, the concept of using technology as an environment to teach real-world problem solving was new. My colleagues at school were somewhat befuddled by my request to develop a new computer course that did not follow a syllabus of a programming language. But I figured Roger, with his doctorate from MIT and his full-time work at the Harvard Business School, knew what he was talking about. This was not the first time that the direction that schools were taking with technology turned out to be a dead end.

By virtue of his breaking and entering, Yves graduated. And I began a journey that still motivates me today. At first, my goal was simply to understand the special relationship many students have with technology (save them one at a time). But now, I find myself exploring ways to reorganize the culture of learning.

In 1983, the critical question about technology for many schools was, "What programming course should we teach?" Technology was not a central theme for building a new learning culture or asking fundamental questions about the empowerment of learning. In my view, many schools remain stuck in a technocentric view of technology's impact. While questions like "When should we teach PowerPoint?" are necessary, technology's real impact on learning lies in the opportunity to rethink the relationships of time, space, and the connectivity of the learner to the world. Ultimately, the role of the teacher, student, family, and community will all be redefined. Technology will impact our architecture (both the buildings and the rooms in which we teach), our understanding of the definition of a course, the concept of assessment, our value of educational equity, and the loneliness of one teacher in a classroom. It is likely to be a 10- to 20-year process.

I believe the fundamental questions to ask today revolve around learner empowerment. "What is the balance of the locus of control between the school and the learner?" "How many students can we teach to be self-directed?" "What are the new relationships between teaching and learning?" "Can we prepare fearless learners?" "Can we make the boundaries of schooling (grades, disciplines, family) permeable to the flow of information and knowledge?"

The empowered or fearless learner is not something that our traditional school culture was designed to produce. Indeed, we have inherited an institutional design that purposely creates a relationship in which the student is dependent on the organization called school to manage learning. In many ways, our traditional concept of schooling aligned with the industrial world of work these students would eventually enter, in which having a job meant you have a boss who tells you what to do, where to do it, when to do it, and how well you are doing it. The organization provided the basic work design. Having too many educated or empowered people who manage, design, and evaluate their own work could even be counterproductive.

In the emerging "knowledge society" based on access to enormous amounts of information and global communications, the empowered worker who has the self-discipline to manage and create work is an asset instead of a potential liability. People with the discipline to manage their own work within an interdependent communications system are in high demand. In the knowledge economy, simply knowing a subject is not enough. The ability to take action on what you know produces economic viability.

SKILLS FOR A KNOWLEDGE SOCIETY

For the most part, schools are still preparing individuals for a manufacturing society that no longer exists. The skills that served students well before are no longer effective in the new knowledge society. To prepare students for employment in today's and tomorrow's economy, effective schools must help individuals learn to do the following:

- Organize poorly structured problems while recognizing problems that no one else can see
- Access information and people around the world
- Use all necessary tools, including information, for their work
- Understand how to be independent and interdependent, working with others (no matter where they are located) to solve problems
- Be responsible for the quality of their own work
- Communicate their findings to audiences that will give them feedback that they can use to constantly improve their work

- Know what they don't know and how to find resources that can inform decisions
- Be self-organized and self-motivated so they can figure out what they need to know
- Structure their own work organization and environment

BEST PRACTICES FOR SCHOOLS INTEGRATING TECHNOLOGY INTO TEACHING AND LEARNING

To prepare students for the emerging information economies and societies, educational leaders must change the schools' learning culture and use technology to create an environment in which to teach critical thinking and problem solving. The following Best Practices can guide school leaders, teachers, and students in making this a reality.

- Vision: Focus on building a community of learners that supports fearless learning and global citizenship.
- It will be essential for every teacher to have a Web site that is a robust environment for supporting the empowered learner. Curriculum maps, assessment links to resources, examples of outstanding student work (from any school in the world), and support tools for the family can all be organized on the Web.
- Online learning will have the biggest impact on the current design of schooling. We need to set a goal that every student will take at least one online course in order to graduate. Just as we assume every teacher can read and write, every teacher will build online activities into their courses. There is no need to learn Web programming; new software will make it very easy for teachers to add resources to their Web sites.
- All students and teachers must become information literate. Like language in print, the Internet has a grammar. There are tools to cross-reference sites. Patterns of links can be analyzed for bias.
- Staff development processes need to involve children. Teaching teachers to use technology in labs after school only addresses their technical ability. What we really need is to teach teachers to understand the impact of technology on how children learn and behave. More and more teachers should bring one or two students with them to staff development to understand how children learn and how they can be part of the team that returns to class to help the other students.
- Collegiality: School leaders have the opportunity to publish the best practices of every single teacher. Every teacher now has the capacity to share his or her knowledge and wisdom. We are also learning that many at-risk students are more willing to accept criticism from an

anonymous reviewer over the Web than from the teacher in the room. We need to build networks of teachers working together.

- Standards: The Web can be used to provide teachers with much more information than they currently have access to. We have tools that can provide pretests across the standards. Essentially, every course will be on the Web 24/7.
- Educational equity is currently in jeopardy. We must set a goal that every family has the capacity to be a center of learning. We will move from buying desktops to handheld devices during the next five years. Every student will need one. Every family will need access to the Web, but access is not enough. We must set a goal to build skills within every home to access enormous amounts of information and people. My worst fear is that, if the public schools do recognize the enormity of technology's impact and do rethink the fundamental relationships between information and knowledge control, we will have unwittingly doomed our concept of educational equity. People who can afford the access at home and have the skills to build an empowered learning environment will buy it.
- Time and space: Our concept of time and space needs to shift. School hours are no longer just 8 to 3—students can log onto to a computer any time. Take a look at the Web site for the Education Program for Gifted Youth at Stanford, www.epgy.org, to see an example of how K–16 math curriculum is already accessible to students on the Web.

CONCLUSION

The emerging knowledge society requires empowered workers with the self-discipline to manage and create their own work within an interdependent communications network. Knowledge is more than knowing; it is using that knowing to solve real-world problems. Educational leaders, teachers, and students must rethink how they use technology for teaching and learning if students are to be fully prepared to enter tomorrow's world.

ISLLC QUESTIONS

Standard 1

- How did working with Yves prompt November to identify and remove barriers to the school's vision?
- How does November recommend that technology influence the vision for all schools?

Standard 2

- How did November's new awareness of technology and learning change his thinking about the principles of effective instruction?
- How do these beliefs affect curricular programs' design, implementation, evaluation, and refinement?
- How does this vision impact measurement, evaluation, and assessment strategies?

Standard 3

- How does November recommend flexibility in dealing with students' learning needs?

Standard 4

- How does November's vision for technology, teaching, and learning respond to diverse students' needs?
- What alternative plans of action does November imply by using technology to influence curriculum, instruction, staff development and collegiality, and standards?

Standard 6

- How does November's understanding of technology respond to and influence the larger social, economic, and cultural context?
- Explain November's concerns about educational equity.

REFERENCE

Csikszentmihalyi, M. (1991). *Flow: The psychology of optimal experience.* New York: HarperCollins.

11

Integrating Technology Into Instructional Design

Frank M. Betts

Overview

The personal computer's popularity in our economy and personal lives makes its use for teaching and learning a critical issue. Little agreement exists, however, about how to integrate technology with instructional design most effectively to increase the effectiveness of teaching and learning. This lack of consensus lowers educators' morale and increases resistance to further use of technology in instruction. The author identifies two barriers to reaching technology's educational potential: the digital divide that separates students who have computer and Internet access from those who don't; and the lack of an effective process to integrate computers and telecommunications with current instructional practice. Betts offers examples of practical solutions to both obstacles, including school-based and foundation grants for hardware and the nine-step "BEST FIT" approach for curriculum and technology integration.

The issue in this chapter is not whether to use technology to support teaching and learning or what technologies to use. The widespread use and importance of the personal computer in virtually every aspect of the economy and our personal lives has made the "whether" and the "what" questions irrelevant. Now the critical issue facing educational leaders is how to best use technology to achieve instructional goals.

Although both research and popular opinion support the premise that using technology in schools will increase the effectiveness of teaching and learning, little agreement exists about how to integrate technology with instructional design most effectively. The absence of a successful process for integrating technology into teaching and learning produces a mishmash of frequently conflicting, counterproductive approaches and wasted effort. This results in lowered morale and increased resistance to further use of technology in instruction. Without an effective instructional design practice, introducing technology into the teaching and learning process will generate a defective product.

Computer use in schools has paralleled their applications in business; initially, in the 1950s, computers in schools were used to "batch-process" administrative functions. In the 60s and 70s, the terms "teaching machines" and "programmed instruction" had come into vogue. The predominant instructional model was still the one-to-many lecture mode, so it should be no surprise that teachers used computer technology for the passive delivery of content to the student and for scoring short-answer, standardized tests. With the steep learning curve and lack of interactivity, available applications proved to be relatively ineffective for delivering content. Computer scoring of tests, however, was fast and cost-effective, thereby contributing to the proliferation of standardized tests.

As Peter Senge (1990) pointed out, it frequently requires contemporaneous breakthroughs in seemingly disparate disciplines in order to realize a new technology's potential. In his example of commercial aviation, breakthroughs in the 1920s and 30s in aluminum metallurgy and fabrication, one-piece fuselage design, the retractable landing gear, and the radial engine were all necessary to achieve a power-to-weight ratio sufficient to make air transport economically viable. Similarly, in education, the Carnegie Corporation's (1983) increased focus on education contributed to revived interest in individualization, brain-based and self-directed learning, and problem-based and hands-on approaches to teaching and learning (National Commission on Excellence in Education, 1983). The creation of the personal computer, the ubiquity of the telephone, the creation of the Internet (ARPANET [Advanced Research Projects Agency Network], 1969) and subsequently the World Wide Web (CERN/SLAC [European Laboratory for Particle Physics/Stanford Linear Accelerator Center], 1991), in combination with the renewed interest in constructivist approaches to teaching and learning, have made possible fundamental changes in the delivery of instruction.

When every child and every family has entrée to a computer with Internet access and e-mail 24/7, instruction need no longer be constrained to 14.5% of a student's waking hours, as is now the case under the traditional 180-day, 7-hour-per-day schedule.[1] Ample evidence exists, both quantitative and qualitative, that using technology to extend instruction into the home and community—engaging parents, students, and the public in a continuous learning process by delivering relevant information in an interactive mode—increases student achievement in school.

Two barriers prevent us from realizing the educational potential of such a model: (1) The so-called *digital divide*, which separates individuals who lack computers and Internet access from those who do; and (2) the lack of an effective process by which to integrate the use of computing and telecommunications technologies with current instructional practice.

In mid-2002, the digital divide is a reality that represents a major obstacle to realizing the educational potential of the technologies now within reach. According to data reported in *Falling Through the Net, Toward Digital Inclusion* (2000) and *A Nation Online* (2002), 94.1% of households have telephones, 56.5% of them have computers at home, while 50.5% have Internet access. The most needy families economically and academically are the least likely to have access to computers and telecommunications resources outside of school. Eliminating the digital divide is not, strictly speaking, an issue for schools; it is a national concern. In a time of increased state-mandated, high-stakes testing, schools should consider whether or not they have the desire and resources to make computers and Internet access available to all students outside of normal school hours.

There are two approaches to doing so: (1) a school-based approach; and (2) a community-based approach. The Washington Heights, New York, Mott Hall School program is an example of a school-based approach in which the school district bought $1,500 laptops for all students and then leased them to families at $30 per month (www.motthall.org). The families also assume the cost of Internet access. Cost, maintenance, and the logistics of moving the laptop between school and home are major issues.

The Computers for Kids Foundation on Colorado's Western Slope is a community-based approach in which a nonprofit organization was created for the purpose of eliminating the digital divide (www.c4kfoundation.org). The foundation collects and refurbishes donated computers, installs them in the homes of students, trains parents, creates a "virtual school" to deliver instructional content on the Web, and trains teachers in its use. This program also provides free Internet access and e-mail services, as well as after-installation support using high school students trained during the refurbishing phase of the process. Information is exchanged between home and school via the Web or inexpensive USB flash hard drives, which eliminates the problems of moving computers between school and home. Cost is still an issue—about $500 per family for the complete program, all of which comes from gifts and grants raised by the community-based foundation.

Elimination of the second barrier to the successful use of technology, the lack of an effective process by which to integrate the use of computing and telecommunications technologies with current instructional practice, is solely the purview of each school. Success depends primarily upon a professional development program that adequately prepares teachers to integrate the use of technology with best practices in instruction.

An effective professional development program will accomplish three goals:

1. Achieve agreement on a set of instructional strategies that are most likely to improve student achievement across all content areas and all grade levels

2. Achieve proficiency and consistency in the use of these strategies to deliver content of the curriculum

3. Achieve agreement on a consistent, complementary approach to integrating the use of technology with the most effective instructional strategies and content of the curriculum

Sufficient evidence exists to indicate which strategies are most effective for improving student achievement; for example, those cited by Marzano, Pickering, and Pollock in *Classroom Instruction That Works* (2001). As the musician said, when asked by a New York City tourist, "How do you get to Carnegie Hall?" proficiency in application comes from "Practice, practice, practice!"

Integrating technology into instruction requires a systematic process that begins with the teacher asking the question, "How do I achieve the best fit for using technology to support my instructional goals?"

The BEST FIT approach (Betts, 1994) is based on the premise that computing and telecommunications are enabling technologies that can be used in three ways:

1. Facilitating technologies used to increase productivity of an existing instructional process—e.g., the use of a word processor to support the writing process

2. Integrating technologies that allow students to analyze the relationships between events or disciplines—e.g., the use of the computer for dynamic modeling or simulations

3. Transforming technologies used to change the nature of the instructional process from whole group, teacher-directed instruction toward collaborative, self-directed learning—e.g., problem-based learning supported by 24/7 Internet access to instructional resources, including the teacher, parents, and outside experts

The choice and specific use of computers and telecommunications is derived from a nine-step instructional design process presented and discussed in Table 11.1.

Table 11.1 Nine Steps to a Best Fit

Nine Steps to a BEST FIT	Example
Step 1: Inventory the curriculum to choose the subject area and topic and essential learning.	**Subject:** Science, Ecology **Topic:** Students will study predator-prey relationships in order to gain a better understanding of how the inter-relationships between ecological factors (weather, human population, food supplies, etc.) affect animal populations. **Learning:** Methodological—casual loop modeling Content-Understanding ecological systems.
Step 2: Select the most effective instructional strategy for the chosen topic.	Nonlinguistic Representation; Cooperative Learning; and Generating and Testing Hypotheses.[a]
Step 3: Determine how to use at least one of the three FIT applications of technology to best support the desired learning and instructional strategy.	**Facilitative:** Internet access to the Forest Service database for the target area and a graphing calculator or computer spreadsheet will speed up data collection and graphic analysis; word processing or presentation software for the final report. Email and online discussion for sharing data and discussing hypotheses. **Integrative:** Use of a computer with STELLA, Powersim, or VenSim modeling software to create dynamic models of the hypothesized relationships between ecological factors. **Transformative:** Students work in teams, supported by Forest Service and Natural History Museum staff, communicating by email and online discussion groups at the RMMS virtual school site.[b]
Step 4: Determine the availability of technologies to support the selected FIT application(s).	Dialup 26K Internet access available to all students from home; broadband access available in school or at the local community Cyber Center. All teachers have 24/7 Internet access; teachers need dynamic modeling software for use at home.

(Continued)

Table 11.1 Continued

Nine Steps to a BEST FIT	Example
Step 5: Select and/or acquire the needed technologies and prepare or revise the instructional design for the unit or lesson.	Select and acquire a dynamic modeling package. Distribute software and conduct a 2-day workshop. Update Internet browsers; verify email addresses; select discussion moderators and set up discussion groups.
Step 6: Assess the teacher's skill in using the proposed instructional design and applications of technology; train or retrain as necessary.	Teachers require additional training and practice in the use of causal loop archetypes and dynamic modeling software. The PD study group should review D. H. Kim, *Systems Archetypes I*, Waltham, MA: Pegausus and/or F. M. Betts, *Systems Thinking*, ASCD Online PD Course, http://www.ascd.org.
Step 7: Practice, practice, practice.	PD Study Group members prepare and critique sample units.
Step 8: Deploy in the classroom.	This five-week unit will be presented in the Spring quarter in Ecology 301 by the Math-Science team.
Step 9: Evaluate and adjust practice as needed.	Participation in the online discussion during Weeks 1 & 2 was too meager—need better preparation in class and cues, questions & advance organizers online. Students had difficulty downloading data from the Forest Service database—download the data and provide .pdf and .xls versions of the files to students on the school server.

a. Adapted from *Classroom Instruction That Works*, by R. J. Marzano, D. J. Pickering, & J. E. Pollock (2001), Alexandria, VA: ASCD.

b. The Rocky Mountain Middle School (RMMS) is a hypothetical example of the best practice, Internet technology-enhanced school described in V. E. Hancock & F. M. Betts, "Back to the Future," *Learning and Leading with Technology*, April 2002, Eugene, OR: ISTE. Visit the RMMS at http://rmms.c4kfoundation.org.

The BEST FIT model provides a simple, systematic, consistent approach to the otherwise complex process of integrating curriculum, instruction, and technology. It is most effective in a multi- or cross-disciplinary environment. It cannot compensate for an inadequate curriculum or lack of knowledge and skill in identifying and implementing effective instructional practices in the classroom.

Without such a model, we have little choice but to continue to develop and deliver curriculum in essentially the same ways we have done for over 200 years, dis-connected and dis-integrated from a vision of the future in which "The new basic skills for the twenty-first century will require students to . . . access, analyze and communicate information successfully . . . through the use of technology to create their own knowledge" (Phillipo, 1992).

CONCLUSION

Community resources and effective professional development provide means to overcome barriers to using personal computers to enhance teaching and learning. The equity issues inherent in the digital divide are a national concern that schools should address. A simple, systematic, consistent approach to integrating curriculum, instruction, and technology—plus practice, practice, practice—guides teachers to use PCs to increase student learning.

ISLLC QUESTIONS

Standard 1

- How does the author suggest that school leaders identify and remove barriers to the school's vision?
- How does the author envision technology as a means to develop a shared vision with the school community?

Standard 2

- How does the author see technology as a means to maintain a school culture of high expectations?
- How does the author's BEST FIT model demonstrate knowledge of principles of effective instruction?

Standard 3

- How does the author envision principals using technology to maximize student learning?
- How does the author use principles of effective learning when he suggests ways for teachers to fully learn how to integrate technology into teaching and learning?

Standard 4

- What approaches does the author propose for schools to develop family partnerships to overcome the "digital divide" and promote learning?
- What examples does the author give of securing community resources to solve school problems?

Standard 5

- How does the author promote equity and fairness in use of resources?

Standard 6

- How does the author suggest that educational leaders respond to and influence the larger political, social, economic, legal, and cultural context?

NOTE

1. Assumes a total of 365×14 = 5110 waking hours versus [180 days × 7 hours/day = 1260 total school hours] − [(6×10/60 transition hours/day × 180 days) + (.83 lunch hours/day x 180) + (28 hours in-service) + (14 hours parent conferences) + (.83 hours free/study periods × 180)] = 739.2 hours available for directed study in school (five 50-minute periods/day).

ANNOTATED REFERENCES

Betts, F. M. (1994). Technology and the coherent curriculum. [ASCD videotape]. In P. Neal (Ed.), *Facilitator's guide to teaching and learning with technology.* Alexandria, VA: Association for Supervision and Curriculum Development. This is the original version of the BEST FIT model.

Brooks, J. G., & Brooks, M. B. (1993). *In search of understanding: The Case for the constructivist classroom.* Alexandria, VA: Association for Supervision and Curriculum Development Presents five overarching principles of pedagogy and examples of instructional designs in which teachers encourage student autonomy and use draw data and primary sources to investigate real-world problems, and where curiosity and inquiry are valued.

Caine, R. N., & Caine, G. (1991). *Making connections: Teaching and the human brain.* Alexandria, VA: Association for Supervision and Curriculum Development. This is one of the first and best explications of the impact of cognitive research on the design of instruction.

Falling Through the Net: Toward Digital Inclusion. (2000, October. Washington, DC: U.S. Department of Commerce. (http://www.ntia.doc.gov/ntiahome/digitaldivide)

Hancock, V. E., & Betts, F. M. (2002, April). Back to the future: Preparing learners for academic success in 2004. *Learning & Leading with Technology*. Eugene, OR: International Society for Technology in Education. This essay is a research-based scenario about teaching and learning in a "wired" community.

Harris, J. (1998). *Design tools for the Internet-supported classroom*. Alexandria, VA: Association for Supervision and Curriculum Development. Harris offers examples of ways to use the Internet to support work in the classroom.

Marzano, R. J., Pickering, D. J., & Pollock, J. E. (2001). *Classroom instruction that works*. Alexandria, VA: Association for Supervision and Curriculum Development. This is a more complete discussion of nine research-based strategies for increasing student achievement, four of which were cited in the BEST FIT example.

A Nation Online (2002, February). http://www.esa.doc.gov/508/esa/nationonline.htm

National Commission on Excellence in Education. (1983, April). *A nation at risk: The imperative for educational reform*. Washington, DC: Government Printing Office.

Phillipo, J. (1992). *The twenty-first century school: Linking educational reform with the effective use of technology*. Marlborough, MA: Center for Educational Leadership and Technology.

Senge, P. (1990). *The fifth discipline*. New York: Doubleday. The fifth discipline—*systems thinking*—is a way of looking at the world in terms of patterns and relationships that is congruent with brain-based and constructivist learning and lends itself especially well to the use of technology, as suggested by the BEST FIT example in this chapter.

12

Professional Development in Instructional Technology

Richard W. Shelly

Overview

Educators are accountable for what is being taught and how it is being taught. Increasingly, as national, state, and professional organizations' standards drive curriculum, the importance of curriculum design, development, implementation and accountability grows. Curriculum benchmarking is a quality control process involving multiple stake-holders who make formative adjustments to curriculum that keep it effective and relevant. Curriculum benchmarks express one's institutional vision, mission, beliefs, and strategic policies: the school's "big picture" superimposed on each course.

AUTHOR'S NOTE: This work is based on an article originally published by R. W. Shelly, 2000, "From Literacy to Fluency in Instructional Technology: Taking Your Staff to the Next Level." *NASSP Bulletin, 84*(614): 61-70.

Some problems are good to have. For example, our faculty was computer literate. We had no anti-technology Luddites who raised moral, ethical, or professional arguments against the excesses of modern technology. They used computers routinely in classrooms and labs. Quantity of hardware and software was neither a barrier nor a hurdle. Times were changing, and what educators previously referred to as "technology" (i.e., computers) had now burgeoned to include many technologies. New information technologies, options, and communications devices were being touted. Digital devices were impacting the business marketplace. Powerful new software applications were becoming available almost daily. How could we capitalize on these opportunities and challenges? Moreover, how can a principal take a computer-literate faculty and transform them into a technology-fluent faculty? How might we take our staff to the next level, that is, from good to very good? Our answer was called "IPD", Individual Professional Development in Instructional Technology.

The following were our underlying principles and assumptions:

- Professional development is a dynamic process and not a series of dog-and-pony shows.
- Relevance to the teacher and actual transfer to the classroom are pivotal and primary criteria for all that is done.
- Student use and facility in the application of new technologies to construct their own knowledge and to build capacity is a manifestation of teacher effectiveness with these technologies.

Our school is a regional, specialized secondary school for science, mathematics, technology, and student research. Students come for one half-day and return to their home high schools for subjects such as English, social studies, and foreign languages.

Several challenges needed to be overcome in planning and implementing our model. Experienced teachers, in particular, are perhaps more wary of "new ideas." Having seen programs, models, and innovations come and go, they could have been a hard sell. Their legitimate questions included whether a plan was needed, whether the benefits would outweigh their investment of time and energy, and questions about the model's probable efficacy for improving instructional strategies. Others expressed past experiences of dissatisfaction with the lack of flexibility and choice in the professional development process. Still others voiced concern about the need for more collaboration and peer support. Teachers described dissatisfaction with divisionwide inservice offerings that did not apply, were not specific to a particular discipline, or were often entry-level applications that did not meet their needs.

Several factors led us to believe that we could make something significant happen. As a group, our faculty had experience in entry-level technology. We were, relatively speaking, "technology-rich"—not in terms of "stuff," but in how we employed computer and digital technologies with our students. We had the infrastructure to provide technical support on short turnaround on a continuing basis. We had faculty who provided network and routine technology support as part of their contract. Our connectivity was state of the art with both fiberoptic and wireless networks already in place. We were poised to budget for and to purchase the tools to use newer technology-based strategies in our classrooms and labs. As a group, we believed that the plan would be sustainable because it fit with other ongoing organizational initiatives, including required divisionwide inservice credits, recertification requirements, and objectives for faculty supervision and evaluation.

We saw an opportunity to dovetail this initiative with others already established within our school. This was, in the eyes of our staff, not just another hoop to jump through. Organizationally, we had a clear goal and a mandate in our mission to utilize and to disseminate fruitful innovations and strategies in mathematics, science, and technology. Our priority and our strength were the faculty's professionalism and competence using technology in the classroom. We had in place an established protocol for peer observation and cognitive coaching. We wanted to improve our collaboration, sharing, and feedback. We wanted to advance our level of competence in applications of technologies beyond the fundamentals.

The basic professional development design is twofold. During the first year of implementation, and subsequently for teachers new to the school regardless of years of experience, all faculty have a technology-related objective as their formal evaluation objective. Following the first year, approximately 50% of faculty had a similar technology objective for evaluation. Our design valued flexibility as well as accountability because of the focus and the options available. In providing options for faculty, we agreed to value alternatives rated according to relevance and the degree of correlation with actual subsequent classroom implementation.

We looked at the research in professional development, specifically in the use of instructional technologies. What became evident were common characteristics of successful programs in instructional technologies. First, "success" seemed to be defined as relevance and utilization of the technologies in the classroom as well as documented student achievement. It was clear that research-based correlations between specific technologies and student achievement appeared tentative and enormously complex at best. More straightforward, however, were correlations between types of professional development and the voluntary, observable uses of the technologies in the classroom.

Three categories of activities representing varying degrees of correlation with subsequent voluntary classroom use structured our model. Each category includes a cluster of options for teacher choice. Within each category, options bear a similar number of points. Each teacher was required to accumulate a total of 9 points by choosing 2 items from the 3-point group, 1 from the 2-point group, and 1 from the 1-point group.

In the 3-point category, which stressed research-based classroom applications, we included the following items:

- Presenting a targeted technology application in a discipline at a focused regional or national professional conference of one's choice
- Demonstrating a "new" application or "new" technology during a planned teacher observation
- Presenting a new technology application in an internal team or departmental training session
- Acting as the "on-call" in-house faculty consultant or expert in a new software application or type of hardware in one's discipline
- Presenting course- or discipline-specific models to colleagues regarding Internet and online features and applications that support teaching and learning

At the 1-point level, items remained relevant to the Instructional Technology (IT) effort, but showed either considerably less research-based correlation or were items that our faculty wished to try. Examples included the following:

- College credit in a technology application
- Publishing in a technology-focused periodical
- Participation in an ongoing external technology interest group
- Working with a professional external to our school on an area of technology expertise with particular relevance to a course or discipline

The characteristics for 2-point items are intermediate in that they occupy intermediate levels of group size (small), slightly larger locus of learning objectives (department-level), slightly wider origin of perceived need (schoolwide), and greater levels of teacher connections or networking. Examples of 2-point items include department- or team-level professional development, incorporation of a technology or application observed by peer observation, or a relevant inservice technology that connects directly to the teacher's personal technology objective.

We assigned learning options to the model's 3-point categories based on how closely each matched our core values. For example, important factors included group size, the locus of learner objectives, specificity and level of focus in the course or discipline, type and sophistication of the technology, probable organizational support and/or reward, the origin of the perceived need for the technology, the level of professional collegiality, and the level of the initiative's ongoing management. A 3-point item was highly individualized (in the teacher's area of interest) as opposed to a districtwide generic topic ("the importance of instructional technology in the classroom"). Other 3-point items valued applications in a focused course or discipline (e.g., the use of a specific kind of spreadsheet in the creation of matrices in a calculus class) as opposed to a generalized application (e.g., "using spreadsheets"). A new technology with advanced content received higher value than a basic technology with introductory content. An item with a high organizational support base of money, resources, and time had more value than one with low support or no perceived benefit. Teachers' real needs earned higher value than entire school district's institutionalized needs. A highly interactive pursuit among our own teachers or a similar virtual learning community held greater value than an isolated individual activity with no sharing or collegiality. The 3-2-1 categories were not entirely exclusive and were used as a means of classifying or categorizing teacher options according to research-based efficacy.

What we don't yet have is clear research documenting the efficacy of this model in impacting student achievement. Such a study should be performance-based, and not merely a reflection of indirect indicators or retrospective opinion.

Nevertheless, we learned that an approach that brings professional development in instructional technology closer to home, to the real needs of teachers and their students, tends to elevate quantity and quality of technology-based classroom strategies. Use of a wider range of technologies became more seamless, more integral in the classrooms and labs. Our teachers uniformly saw a quantum step in their ability and confidence. Motivation to keep up the momentum was high in the pilot's second year. Comments from teachers reflect that they liked the flexibility, the freedom and control, and their increased capacity to engage students using the technologies. As a principal, I saw a level of support, collegiality, engagement, and satisfaction with a process, namely "professional development," that I had not seen before. Something went right.

CONCLUSION

Principals can use the curriculum benchmarking process to provide evidence that leads to curriculum effectiveness, and communicate with a wider audience of teachers, students, and community experts. The results are a closer connection between what is intended, taught, learned, assessed, and practiced and a means to systematically adjust what and how students learn to best meet a school's goals for student achievement.

ISLLC QUESTIONS

Standard 1

- How does the educational leader facilitate the development, articulation, implementation, and stewardship of a vision of learning that is shared and supported by the school community?

- How does the educational leader recognize and celebrate the contributions of the school community?
- How does the educational leader identify and remove barriers to the school vision?

Standard 2

- How does the educational leader advocate, nurture, and sustain a school culture and instructional program conducive to student learning and staff professional growth?
- How does the educational leader gather more data and information about the situation from all stakeholders before making decisions? What data still need to be obtained to draw conclusions about this professional development model and student achievement?
- How does the educational leader value team process and stakeholder involvement before making decisions?
- How does the educational leader maintain a culture of high expectations?
- How does the educational leader use understanding of human growth and development?

Standard 3

- How does the educational leader effectively frame the problem and use problem-solving skills?
- How does the educational leader use the support system effectively and efficiently?

Standard 5

- How does the educational leader act with integrity to ensure fairness in the use of resources?

Standard 6

- How does the educational leader show understanding, respond to, and influence the larger political, social, economic, legal, and cultural context?

Lessons Learned

In *Powerful Learning* (ASCD, 1998), Ronald Brandt describes conditions that increase student learning. People learn well when what they learn is personally meaningful; when what they learn is challenging and they accept the challenge; and when what they learn is appropriate for their developmental level. People learn well when they can learn in their own way and have some degree of choice and control; when they use what they already know as they construct new understandings; when they have opportunities for social interaction; and when they get helpful feedback. In addition, people learn well when they acquire and use learning strategies; when they experience a positive emotional climate; and when the learning environment supports the intended learning. Effective teaching, appropriate curriculum, and available technology infused into the process to increase curricular relevance and student engagement help learners meet all these criteria.

What every student needs most is an effective teacher. Robert Marzano writes that what specific teachers bring to the schooling process is the major influence on student achievement for learners at all achievement levels. The data on effective teaching's impact on student achievement are staggering. Effective teaching accounts for two-thirds of the total effect of schooling on student learning. Principals need to use successful practices to hire, keep, and develop teachers and assure that all students have opportunities to work with the best.

Similarly, Linda Darling-Hammond reminds us that all school reform efforts depend on highly skilled teachers. The evidence connecting teacher effectiveness and student achievement is so compelling that teaching itself is becoming a focus of school improvement efforts. Given these data, the practice of states issuing "emergency" teaching licenses that permit individuals to fill the nearly 100,000 vacancies yearly with little or no preparation is troubling. Darling-Hammond suggests policy and practice changes to reduce the teacher shortage and make qualified teachers available to all schools. Alternatives include providing subsidies for high-quality teacher preparation, offering competitive salaries, streamlining the teacher selection process, extending proactive recruitment, providing intensive induction and mentoring for beginning teachers, investing in high-quality professional development, and redesigning schools to better support teaching and learning.

High-quality teaching and an appropriate curriculum can help students (and their principals) successfully meet many accountability measures. Effective curriculum reflects an organization's values as they are implemented into each classroom. Curriculum is a set of meaningful information and skills, not desiccated facts by which to better sort multiple-choice answers. Unfortunately, as Marzano clearly suggests, today's high-stakes testing often places contradictory demands on principals. On the one hand, principals are responsible for assuring that all students meet the state-defined standards of what students are supposed to know and do at each grade level, as embodied in standardized tests. Regrettably, these tests are often based on a politically driven curriculum that is too large for students to learn in the allotted time.

On the other hand, educators have enough cumulative theory and research to support effective curricular and instructional practices. Teachers often ignore these practices in their rush to "cover the content" in time for these make-or-break assessments. This creates a serious leadership and teaching quandary with important consequences for all players.

Both teaching and curriculum undergo important changes when teachers learn how to effectively use technology as an engine to drive student learning. As Alan November writes, technology in the schoolhouse should bring profound changes in the way we understand and structure teaching and learning. Correctly used, technology reorganizes the learning culture. Its real impact on learning lies in the opportunity to rethink the relationships of time and space, and the relationship of learning to the world. Powerful learning results.

Technology increases student learning because it puts students in the center of their own education. This wired—and increasingly wireless—environment, empowers students to become active learners. When students define the problems to explore because they are genuinely interested in knowing the answers, they give learning tasks a personal meaning; and they actively pursue knowledge because it matters to them. Interacting with technology also provides occasions for prompt feedback to clarify their thinking; and it offers novelty with access to new information sources and an endless range of topics to study. Interacting with information, technology, and critical thinking, students develop the habits of mind to ask thoughtful questions that will guide their studies inside and outside school.

Likewise, technology used correctly also changes the relationship between teaching and learning. Teachers are no longer "information deliverers" or "content coverers," when, with a few clicks, students can instantly access more information than their teachers will ever know. Instead, teachers must learn how to listen to students' interests and help them connect their present understanding to larger questions that extend knowledge in directions of students' interest yet within developmentally appropriate levels.

Finally, educators must address issues of educational equity. All students need access to the technology and the learning processes that develop their thinking, problem-solving, and communication skills, and give them substantial content knowledge in fields essential to future success, including preparation for higher education and well-paid employment. Many students rely on school to provide these learning experiences. The "digital divide"—between students who have access to robust technology and those who do not—must not limit the academic, social, or economic advancement of individuals without the resources at home to continue learning not just what they want to know but also how to learn.

Principal leadership is needed to ensure that all students have access to the highest quality teaching, meaningful curricula, and the tools to learn it, while they simultaneously meet community and state expectations for measured achievement. Leadership in classroom changes to successfully incorporate these seemingly conflicting dimensions lives at the heart of the principal's emerging role.

REFERENCE

Brandt, R. S. (1998). *Powerful Learning*. Alexandria, VA: Association for Supervision and Curriculum Development.

Part IV

Meeting Individual Learners' Needs

13

What Instructional Leaders Need to Know About Special Education

Chriss Walther-Thomas
Michael F. DiPaola

Overview

Today, special education seeks to provide students with disabilities with access to the general education curriculum and appropriate support to facilitate academic progress. Principal leadership is critical to assuring that disabled students have effective learning programs. Administrative leadership is the most powerful predictor of positive teacher attitudes about special needs students' success in the regular curriculum. To help special needs students learn, principals can do the following: create a positive school culture that supports their academic success, use knowledge of special education laws that protect students' rights, understand how teachers and specialists can better assist disabled students, and work continuously and collaboratively with their key stakeholders to address all students' learning needs. Principals must also provide high-quality professional development for all personnel to enhance disabled students' outcomes.

Since the passage of the *Education of All Handicapped Children Act* (now known as the *Individuals with Disabilities Education Act* [IDEA]) in 1975, schools have been challenged to meet both the intent and the spirit of federal laws regarding the education of students with disabilities. Over this period, special education services have changed significantly. Students with disabilities are no longer segregated from their general education peers. Today, a primary function of special education is to provide students with disabilities access to the general education curriculum and appropriate support to facilitate academic progress.

As public thinking about special education has evolved, so have the academic expectations in general education. Over the past two decades, the nation has embraced a far-reaching set of academic reforms designed to ensure higher student performance and greater professional accountability. Consequently, public scrutiny of student test scores and demands for professional accountability have never been higher (National Association State Boards of Education [NASBE], 1992; National Commission on Teaching and America's Future [NCTAF], 1996). Today schools are expected to provide rigorous academic programs to an expanding array of students, many of whom have unique learning needs (e.g., special education, English as a second language, Title I, homeless).

It is not surprising that principals' roles have changed dramatically because of these new realities. During the 1970s, principals' roles began evolving, in large measure because of early research on effective schools that directly linked principal functions to student achievement. Over time, the linkage between instructional leadership and the development of academically challenging programs has been well documented in the literature (Council of Chief State School Officers [CCSSO], 1996; National Association of Elementary School Principals [NAESP], 2001). Effective principals create effective learning environments.

In 1997, Congress reauthorized the *Individuals with Disabilities Education Act* (IDEA). Because of mounting concerns among advocates that students with disabilities were being excluded from many school reform initiatives, several key provisions were added to the law. Today, school leaders must ensure that students with disabilities have access to the general education curriculum, appropriate support, and that their progress is monitored in a number of ways, including through their participation in local and state assessments.

As special education has become more complex, it has become increasingly evident that principals need to have a clear understanding of their roles and responsibilities in this process. Because effective special education is student- and site-specific, well-informed and principled leadership is critical. Recently, the Council for Exceptional Children (CEC) published a guide for principals on implementing IDEA (CEC, 2001). This document, developed in collaboration with the National Association of Elementary School Principals (NAESP), asserts that the principal's role is pivotal in the academic success of students with disabilities: "The principal's values, beliefs, and personal characteristics inspire people to accomplish the school's mission" (p. 19). Effective building-based leaders create a culture and climate for change by engaging others in leadership roles that result in a shared vision and a mission that faculty, staff, and students support. In addition, they communicate the school's core values and vision to family and community stakeholders, address tough issues that arise, and ensure that accomplishments are recognized (DiPaola, in press). They lead the way in ensuring the rights of students with disabilities and their families, modeling acceptance and support, and guaranteeing that faculty and staff have the skills and encouragement needed to provide effective learning programs. Their knowledge, skills, and attitudes influence the development of appropriate and meaningful individualized education plans (IEPs) (Walther-Thomas, Korinek, McLaughlin, & Williams, 2000).

During the past decade, the Council of Chief State School Officers (CCSSO) has led a national initiative to create a common vision to ensure effective school leadership. Through the CCSSO-sponsored Interstate School Leaders Licensure Consortium (ISLLC), a set of unified standards has been developed and a corresponding professional development process has been recommended to ensure use of research-based practices in preparing principals for their roles (CCSSO, 1996, 1998, 2000). It is important to note that these documents infrequently refer to "students with disabilities" specifically. However, they emphasize the importance of quality education for *all* students. This broad-based support for inclusive schools and responsive school leadership, coupled with changes in federal rules and regulations (see, for example, United States Department of Education [USDOE], 1997, 2001), now ensure better access to the general education curriculum, more comprehensive program improvement and progress monitoring, and, in the end, stronger student outcomes.

BEST PRACTICES FOR BUILDING LEADERS

Emerging research suggests that students with disabilities can be included successfully in reform-focused schools (Klingner, Arguelles, Hughes, & Vaughn, 2001; NASBE, 1992; National Council on Disability [NCD], 1995).

In these inclusive learning environments, stakeholders believe that *all* students, including those with disabilities and other risk factors, can learn. Recently, the CEC and the NAESP suggested that effective principals can ensure greater academic success for students with disabilities and others at risk by addressing five key dimensions of school: organization, curriculum and instruction, professional development, climate, and student assessment (CEC, 2001). These recommendations are in line with the ISLLC's central mission of helping create leaders for student learning by grounding criteria and standards for school leaders' professional practice in a deep knowledge and understanding of teaching and learning. Together, these documents offer a comprehensive leadership framework for the development and delivery of effective special education services that are grounded in six key principles.

Principle 1: Effective Principals Create a Positive School Culture That Embraces Shared Leadership

Effective principals create a context that fosters academic and social success for students with disabilities (CEC, 2001). Their behaviors clearly convey the message that their schools are learning communities in which students and adults continually expand their capacity to create desired outcomes. Principals cannot effectively advocate for students with disabilities unless they have a clear understanding of disabilities and the laws that protect the educational rights of students with disabilities (Bateman & Bateman, 2001).

Clearly, most principals face more daily leadership and management responsibilities than they can realistically hope to accomplish. Data from a recent statewide study indicate that principals need more resources to provide effective school leadership (DiPaola & Tschannen-Moran, 2001). Principals simply cannot personally perform all the tasks that are expected of them. They need to know how to nurture professional growth within their schools and how to develop shared leadership (Fenwick, 2000). Consequently, they must have distributive leadership skills that enable them to organize their schools in ways that capitalize on the collective skills, knowledge, and experiences of stakeholders (Hughes, 1999). By doing so, school leaders create better learning environments for all students, more productive and satisfying work environments for staff members, and more realistic jobs for themselves that enable them to focus on critical instructional issues.

While research has shown that the principal is not always *the* critical player in providing support of lasting change in instructional practices, it is clear that someone assumes that role (Gersten & Brengelman, 1996). Effective principals know their own professional strengths and interests, and can realistically assess the time constraints they face. They know their staff members' talents, skills, and professional growth interests and needs. Most importantly, effective principals know how to foster shared leadership to provide lasting support of new instructional initiatives. Skillful principals know how to nurture the professional development of local facilitators who have a strong understanding of the instructional model, effective teaching skills, and commitment to sustained implementation of various innovations. By providing these instructional leaders with support and encouragement, principals can build support networks that facilitate lasting implementation.

Principle 2: Principals Understand Special Education Laws and the Related Roles and Responsibilities of Educators

While principals do not need to be disability experts, they need a working knowledge of disabilities, a clear conception of the unique challenges various conditions present, and a thorough understanding of laws that protect the educational rights of these students (CEC, 2001; Turnbull & Cilley, 1999). Effective principals need a working knowledge of IDEA, especially some of the key amendments that have changed special education planning requirements (CEC, 1997, 2001). For example, states must establish performance goals and indicators for students with disabilities that are more closely aligned with goals for typical students. New IEP provisions must describe how the student's disability will affect his or her involvement in the general education curriculum, and IEP goals should be more closely related to that curriculum. In addition, states and local districts must include students with disabilities in their assessment programs and provide appropriate testing accommodations as needed.

While specific duties associated with the special education process vary from district to district, principals hold the key to school-level compliance. Yet research has shown that most principals are inadequately prepared to lead local efforts to create learning environments that emphasize academic success for students with disabilities (Katsiyannis, Conderman, & Franks, 1995). In a recent state study of principals, those surveyed identified "help and information about implementing successful special education programs" as their greatest need (DiPaola & Tschannen-Moran, 2001, p. 7).

In developing and designing job expectations for teachers, specialists, and paraprofessionals, principals must consider and plan for the needs of students with disabilities. Without adequate understanding of effective special education service delivery, principals may unintentionally thwart efforts to provide quality support services for students with disabilities because of competition from other pressing demands (Bateman & Bateman, 2001; CEC, 2001).

By understanding teacher and specialist demands more fully, administrators can provide more appropriate and focused support (e.g., specific resources, relevant information, and delegation of decision-making power) to facilitate their efforts, reduce stress, and increase job satisfaction. Few novice teachers are well prepared to address the broad range of instructional needs they encounter on the first day of school. While initial preparation programs provide preservice teachers with critical entry-level skills, all effective teachers need ongoing support and professional development to ensure that they use research-based strategies in their classrooms.

Attrition in the ranks of special education teachers and specialists is significant; almost half of all special educators leave the field within 5 years. Gersten and colleagues (2001) found that principals are critical to the success or failure of special educators. The research showed that principal support, or lack thereof, had strong effects on "virtually all critical aspects of (special education) teachers' working conditions" (2001, p. 557). The researchers suggest that administrators who understand the challenges that special educators face are better prepared to provide their teachers with more appropriate support that can help reduce both stress and role dissonance. This study adds support to a growing body of research that has demonstrated the importance of building-level support on special educator satisfaction, performance, and retention (e.g., Billingsley & Cross, 1991; Boe, Barkanic, & Leow, 1999; Boe, Bobbitt, & Cook, 1997). Building support helps alleviate teacher stress, increases participants' sense of professional development opportunities, and affects overall job satisfaction.

Principle 3: Effective Principals Are Problem Solvers

While principals may be personally committed to new initiatives, unless they can win the support and commitment of their school community, their best efforts will yield few results (Fullan, 2001). Therefore, effective administrators possess a deep commitment to continuous improvement that is coupled with a thorough understanding of the change process and the ability to work creatively with others to address issues that emerge over time (Kouzes & Posner, 1995). They know how to mobilize their schools to tackle challenging issues and confront problems that have not yet been addressed successfully (Heifetz, 1994). In brief, they see themselves as change agents who work collaboratively with others to increase their school's capacity to involve stakeholders, envision a better future for all students, guide meaningful curriculum development, and monitor student progress. For example, calls for more inclusive education coupled with demands for higher academic standards and greater accountability are forcing many changes in longstanding instructional practices and professional mindsets. Because these changes in "how things are done" are unsettling, effective principals, in collaboration with other school leaders, must address a two-pronged problem—"the social-psychological fear of change and the lack of technical know-how or skills to make the change work" (Fullan, 2001, p. 41). To overcome these issues, school teams need to work together to create mechanisms that can provide support, skill building, coaching, and risk taking.

Fullan (2001) notes that relationships are essential in all successful change initiatives. "If relationships improve, things get better. If they remain the same or get worse, ground is lost. Thus school leaders must be consummate relationship builders with diverse people and groups" (p. 5). Principals need skills that enable them to work collaboratively with students, families, school professionals, and community leaders to ensure that effective educational programs are provided.

Walther-Thomas and colleagues (2000) noted that schools become more inclusive as they become more collaborative. Effective leaders know how to build positive relationships that increase the "social capital" of their schools (Coleman, 1990). By creating and supporting relational networks that facilitate ongoing dialogue, support, and sharing among teachers, administrators, students, and families, the social capital grows as stakeholders work together for the benefit of all learners including those with disabilities and others at risk. These relational networks are particularly critical to the lasting success of special education efforts (Bateman & Bateman, 2001; Gersten et al., 2001; Miller et al., 1999). By building trust, improving and increasing communication, and sharing knowledge and skill about effective ways to serve all students, the synergy of teamwork takes hold and all participants benefit (Wasley, Hampel, & Clark, 1997).

Principals who recognize the importance of ongoing collaboration ensure that all students are included in academic programs and extracurricular activities (NAESP, 2001a). By creating mechanisms that facilitate ongoing communication, problem solving, and progress monitoring, emerging concerns can be resolved promptly—ensuring better student success and less professional stress and aggravation. Research suggests that it is the values and actions of principals and general educators, as mediated by overall school culture, that influence special educators' sense of collegial support (see, for example, Billingsley, 1993; Billingsley & Cross, 1991; Miller, Brownell, & Smith, 1999).

Principals need to work closely with their teams to ensure that effective evaluation systems are in place to monitor student progress and ensure data-based decision making. They also need to ensure that teachers and specialists have the knowledge and skills necessary to make appropriate instructional modifications to ensure academic progress. Principals also must create appropriate alternatives to retention and social promotion of students with disabilities (CEC, 2001; NASBE, 1992; Owings & Kaplan, 2001).

Principle 4: Effective Principals Are Good Role Models

Principals have ethical as well as legal responsibilities to ensure that students with disabilities are educated appropriately. Effective principals communicate, through their own actions and behaviors, personal commitments to the spirit of the laws that safeguard the educational rights of these students. Specifically, they model inclusive practices such as valuing individual and team efforts, recognizing the dignity of all people, believing people are doing their best, sharing leadership responsibilities, envisioning a better future for all school community members, and demonstrating the school's commitment to the academic success of all learners (Kearns, Kleinert, & Clayton, 1998; Klingner, Arguelles, Hughes, & Vaughn, 2001).

When principals assume primary responsibility for the education of all students and serve as the instructional leader for all staff members, educational opportunities for all students improve. As effective change agents, principals must see themselves as role models for others in their schools. Their actions provide reassurance and guidance for others about the value of the team's goals. For example, Villa, Thousand, Meyers, and Nevin (1993) reported that in a study of 32 schools implementing inclusive education programs for students with disabilities, administrative leadership was the most powerful predictor of positive teacher attitudes about the process. As Fullan notes, schools that embrace significant and lasting changes engage in ongoing "reculturing" in which new expectations, structures, and patterns emerge to support new initiatives (2001, p. 44). Principals play critical roles as facilitators in this process. Effective principals model shared leadership and a collaborative work culture. In such schools, reculturing efforts are recognized as the sine qua non of progress.

Effective principals need well-honed interpersonal communication skills. They must model effective leadership as two-way communication by seeking information from staff members, families, students, and others as well as disseminating information to these constituencies. Novice principals must be familiar with existing organizational procedures and processes related to communication (e.g., chain of command, communication flowcharts) and recognize the expectations for effective communication. Emphasizing effective communication within the context of principals' accountability helps ensure that administrators understand the value placed on these skills and processes by district leadership (Bateman & Bateman, 2001; NAESP, 2001b).

Principle 5: Effective Principals Facilitate Ongoing Professional Development

Principals must be instructional leaders who are familiar with effective, research-based practices. Given the many competing demands for their time, classroom teachers may need assistance to stay current with the literature on best practices. Research shows that teachers are more likely to follow through with academic and behavioral interventions suggested by specialists if they know that they will be held accountable for implementation (Noell & Witt, 1999). Therefore, principals need to work with teachers to ensure that effective practices are implemented and that teachers have the support, tools, and decision-making power required to make appropriate instructional decisions and modifications.

Schools that focus on instructional issues and provide high quality professional development for all personnel produce enhanced outcomes for students with disabilities and for others at risk for school failure (Kearns et al., 1998). Many teachers and specialists being asked to "collaborate" with one another are poorly prepared for this task. For many, preservice education did not prepare them to work with other adults in roles such as collaborative problem solvers, co-teachers, consultants, and paraprofessional supervisors. Consequently, many need additional skill development to perform these roles effectively.

Numerous studies have demonstrated that administrative leadership facilitates lasting implementation of research-based instructional practices (Fullan & Stiegelbauer, 1991; Gersten et al., 2001; Klingner et al., 2001). Thus administrative support, or lack thereof, has been shown to affect the extent to which classroom teachers implement interventions designed to improve the performance of low-achieving students (Fuchs, Fuchs, Harris, & Roberts, 1996). Effective principals work with teacher leaders to determine individual and group learning needs within their buildings. Together, they develop ways for knowledge building and sharing to take place—recognizing a broad range of learners' skills and experience. One size does not fit all in effective professional development. For example, by identifying teachers who have exemplary knowledge and skills related to effective instruction and developing ways that they can share their skills in context (e.g., mentoring, coaching, workshop presentations for interested colleagues, book groups, hosting classroom observations), principals can provide shared leadership opportunities, recognize talent and effort, and establish structures for collaborative and professional growth.

Principals should be aware of available resources and know how to access these sources of support to ensure appropriate services for students with disabilities. They need to encourage the efforts of others to share useful resources with one another, such as electronic and print materials developed by state and federal offices, professional organizations, community agencies, district-level specialists, and family advocacy groups.

Finally, effective principals understand that what is monitored, measured, and rewarded is what gets done. To that end, they ensure classroom implementation of academic and behavioral interventions for students with disabilities by monitoring instruction and using annual performance evaluations to identify areas for improvement and to recognize individuals who do exemplary work daily. Effective and ongoing management, supervision, and encouragement help ensure that teachers and specialists work together to implement effective instructional programs, manage classroom behavior, and monitor student performance continuously.

CONCLUSION

Clearly, the performance expectations for administrators, teachers, and students have changed dramatically over the past 25 years. In today's rigorous academic learning environments, effective principals provide instructional leadership that facilitates collaboration, program development, and ongoing performance monitoring. In 2001, President George W. Bush proclaimed that no child will be left behind in America's public schools. Ensuring appropriate educational opportunities for students with disabilities and others at risk is one of the most crucial challenges facing administrators today. For the president's ambitious promise to become a reality, principals must create communities of support that can address the unique learning needs of all students, including those with disabilities.

ISLLC QUESTIONS

Standard 1

- How do the authors see the principals' role in defining and enacting a shared vision for the education of all students?
- How can principals use IDEA to identify and remove barriers to disabled students' education?

Standard 2

- How do the authors view shared leadership and team process as a means to assure appropriate education for students with disabilities?
- Why do the authors consider shared leadership essential when dealing with the education of disabled students?

Standard 3

- In what ways do the authors believe principals can maintain a culture of high expectations and flexibility in dealing with students' learning needs by supporting all teachers and specialists who work with special needs students?

Standard 4

- How do principals and other educational professionals use IDEA and other special education regulations to respond to diverse students' learning needs within the regular education program?

Standard 6

- How do the authors see principals' involvement with special education laws and school-related practices as an example of responsiveness to the larger political, social, legal, and cultural context? How can a school work with stakeholders to change its instructional practices and include special needs students?

REFERENCES

Bateman, D., & Bateman, C. F. (2001). *A principal's guide to special education.* Arlington, VA: Council for Exceptional Children.

Billingsley, B. S. (1993). Teacher retention and attrition in special education: A critical review of the literature. *Journal of Special Education, 27*, 137-174.

Billingsley, B. S., & Cross, L. H. (1991). Teachers' decisions to transfer from special to general education. *Journal of Special Education, 24*, 496-511.

Boe, E. E., Barkanic, G., Leow, C. S. (1999). *Retention and attrition of teachers at the school level: National trends and predictors.* (Data Analysis Report No. 1999-DAR1). Philadelphia: University of Pennsylvania, Center for Research and Evaluation in Social Policy.

Boe, E. E., Bobbitt, S. A., & Cook, L. H. (1997). Whither didst thou go? Retention, reassignment, migration, and attrition of special and general education teachers from a national perspective. *The Journal of Special Education, 30*, 371-389.

Coleman, J. S. (1990). *Foundations of social theory.* Cambridge, MA: Belknap.

Council for Exceptional Children. (1997). *IDEA 1997: Let's make it work.* Arlington, VA: Author.

Council for Exceptional Children. (2001). *Implementing IDEA: A guide for principals.* Arlington, VA: Author.

Council of Chief State School Officers. (1996). *Standards for school leaders.* Washington, DC: Author.

Council of Chief State School Officers. (1998). *Propositions for quality professional development for school administrators.* Washington, DC: Author.

Council of Chief State School Officers. (2000). *Collaborative development process for school leaders.* Washington, DC: Author.

DiPaola, M. F. (in press). Daily challenges for school leaders. In N. Bennett, MP. Crawford, & M. Cartwright (Eds.), *Leadership and effective education.* London: Sage.

DiPaola, M. F., & Tschannen-Moran, M. (2001). *The 2001 study of Virginia principals.* Richmond: Virginia Department of Education.

Fenwick, L. T. (2000). *The principal shortage: Who will lead?* Cambridge, MA: Harvard Graduate School of Education, The Principals' Center.

Fuchs, D., Fuchs, L. S., Harris, A. H., & Roberts, P. H. (1996). Bridging the research-to-practice gap with mainstream assistance teams: A cautionary tale. *School Psychology Quarterly, 11*, 244-266.

Fullan, M., with Stiegelbauer, S. (1991). *The new meaning of educational change.* New York: Teachers College Press.

Fullan, M. (2001). *Leading in a culture of change.* San Francisco: Jossey-Bass.

Gersten, R., & Brengelman, S. U. (1996). The quest to translate research into classroom practice: The emerging knowledge base. *Remedial and Special Education, 17*, 67-74.

Gersten, R., Keating, T., Yovanoff, P., & Harniss, M. K. (2001). Working in special education: Factors that enhance special educators' intent to stay. *Exceptional Children, 67*, 549-453.

Heifetz, R. (1994). *Leadership without easy answers.* Cambridge, MA: Harvard University Press.

Hughes, L. W. (1999). The leader: Artist? Architect? Commissar? In L. W. Hughes (Ed.), *The principal as leader* (2nd ed., pp. 3-24). Upper Saddle River, NJ: Merrill/Prentice Hall.

Katsiyannis, A., Conderman, G., & Franks, D. J. (1995). State practices on inclusion: A national review. *Remedial and Special Education, 16,* 279-287.

Kearns, J. F., Kleinert, H. L., & Clayton, J. (1998). Principal supports for inclusive assessment: A Kentucky story. *Teaching Exceptional Children, 31* (2), 16-23.

Klingner, J. K., Arguelles, M. E., Hughes, M. T., & Vaughn, S. (2001). Examining the school-wide "spread" of research-based practices. *Learning Disabilities Quarterly, 24,* 221-234.

Kouzes, J. M., & Posner, B. Z. (1995). *The leadership challenge.* San Francisco: Jossey-Bass.

Miller, M. D., Brownell, M. T., & Smith, S. W. (1999). Factors that predict teachers staying in, leaving, or transferring from the special education classroom. *Exceptional Children, 65,* 201-218.

National Association of Elementary School Principals. (2001). *Leading learning communities: NAESP standards for what principals should know and be able to do.* Alexandria, VA: Author.

National Association State Boards of Education. (1992). *Winning ways: Creating inclusive schools, classrooms, and communities.* Alexandria, VA: Author.

National Commission on Teaching and America's Future. (1996). *What matters most: Teaching for America's future.* New York: Author.

National Council on Disability. (1995). *Improving the implementation of the Individuals with Disabilities Act: Making schools work for all of America's children.* Washington, DC: Author.

Noell, G. H., & Witt, J. C. (1999). When does consultation lead to intervention implementation? *Journal of Special Education, 33,* 29-41.

Owings, W. A., & Kaplan, L. S. (2001). *Retention and social promotion: A history and alternatives to two public failures.* Bloomington, IL: Phi Delta Kappa Fastback.

Turnbull, H. R., & Cilley, M. (1999). *Explanations and implications of the 1997 amendments to IDEA.* Upper Saddle River, NJ: Merrill/Prentice Hall.

United States Department of Education. (1997). *Individuals with Disabilities Act.* Washington, DC: Author.

United States Department of Education. (2001). *Elementary and Secondary Education Act.* Washington, DC: Author.

Villa, R., Thousand, J., Meyers, H., & Nevin, A. (1993). *Regular and special education teachers and administrators' perceptions of heterogeneous education.* Unpublished manuscript.

Walther-Thomas, C. S., Korinek, L., McLaughlin, V. L., & Williams, B. (2000). *Collaboration for effective inclusive education: Developing successful programs.* Boston: Allyn & Bacon.

Wasley, P., Hampel, R., & Clark, R. (1997, May). The puzzle of whole-school change. *Phi Delta Kappan, 78* (9) 690-697.

14

Making Inclusion Work

Patricia Jordan Rea

Overview

School data showed special needs students with markedly lower achievement and social outcomes, low involvement in school activities, and poor school attendance compared with their non-disabled peers. The principal brought a consultant to help coordinate and facilitate the strategic planning process to design improved ways of educating special needs students. Training teachers to make the inclusive practices work, selecting an evaluation model, and making midcourse corrections occurred. After one year's implementation, students performed better on all measures.

Serving students with disabilities is a challenge for 21st-century schools. Not only does litigation's threat ratchet up the stakes, but burgeoning numbers of identified students and shortages of properly credentialed special education teachers have made staffing, scheduling, and the mechanics of meeting federal and state mandates considerably more

---

AUTHOR'S NOTE: The school name is fictitious in order to maintain the confidentiality of the consultation relationship.

difficult. These factors, along with increased accountability, serve as the backdrop for Meadow Rock Middle School's change initiative.

Meadow Rock Middle School, situated in the center of a sprawling suburban community in the southeast United States, could be called a typical American middle school. It has approximately 1,300 students in the sixth, seventh, and eighth grades. Twenty-two percent are from minority groups and 10% receive free or reduced-price meals. Approximately 13% (169 students) are identified with disabilities under federal regulations. Eighty-three percent (140) of those identified have learning disabilities, emotional/behavioral disorders, or other health impairments. Ninety-seven percent (37) of those with the health impairment label are diagnosed with attention deficit disorder (ADD). Seventy-two staff members work at the school, including 64 classroom teachers, 2 guidance counselors, an itinerant school psychologist, a school nurse, an itinerant school social worker, two assistant principals, and a principal. Ten of the classroom teachers currently serve as special educators. Twelve percent of the staff represent minority groups. Meadow Rock has enjoyed a largely positive relationship with parents and community members. It has an active parent-teacher association and several active parent support groups for various activities. It enjoys a reputation supported by statistics for high academic achievement, competent teachers, and a positive atmosphere. Over time, it has experienced changes common to many schools: growing diversity in its student population, increasing emphasis on accountability, and an escalating presence of social concerns reflected in both its students and staff.

As part of its reflective response to these issues, Meadow Rock staff undertook a self-assessment and subsequently identified delivery of special education services as an area of concern. When compared to their non-disabled peers, these students demonstrated markedly depressed academic and social outcomes, low involvement in school activities, and poor school attendance (see Tables 14.1, 14.2, 14.3, and 14.4.). Staff suspected these data were related to students' receiving special education services in self-contained rather than general education classes, a factor increasingly documented by research. The inclusion of students with disabilities in general education classrooms, with the support of special educators teaching collaboratively with general educators, is often the remedy of choice. Even within the district, other schools had begun inclusion initiatives.

Meadow Rock leaders believed that successfully meeting challenges required a strategic planning process. Without targeted, comprehensive planning, efforts to alter service delivery for disabled students are less likely to be effective. Poorly planned initiatives often fall into the "been-there, done-that" discard pile. Consequently, Meadow Rock began its comprehensive planning to include more students with disabilities in general education classrooms a year before the intended implementation.

In an era of limited resources and multiple competing agendas, clear communication between school administrators and central office decision makers is

Table 14.1 Academic Achievement

	Student Data BEFORE Improved Special Education Service Delivery				Student Data AFTER Improved Special Education Service Delivery			
	% of participation		% scoring at or above grade level		% participation		% scoring at or above grade level	
	Students WITH Disabilities	Students WITHOUT Disabilities	Students WITH Disabilities	Students WITHOUT Disabilities	Students WITH Disabilities	Students WITHOUT Disabilities	Students WITH Disabilities	Students WITHOUT Disabilities
Standardized Tests	62	97	36	82	83	98	42	81
	% of participation		% meeting minimum standard or above		% participation		% meeting minimum standard or above	
State Competency	68	98	32	84	80	98	45	89

Table 14.2 Behavioral Outcomes

	Student Data **BEFORE** Improved Special Education Service Delivery		Student Data **AFTER** Improved Special Education Service Delivery	
	Students WITH Disabilities	Students WITHOUT Disabilities	Students WITH Disabilities	Students WITHOUT Disabilities
% Suspended 1–10 Days	14	6	10	3
% Suspended 11 or More Days	2	<1	1	<1

Table 14.3 Social Outcomes

	Student Data **BEFORE** Improved Special Education Service Delivery		Student Data **AFTER** Improved Special Education Service Delivery	
	Students WITH Disabilities	Students WITHOUT Disabilities	Students WITH Disabilities	Students WITHOUT Disabilities
% in Extracurricular Activities	12	82	22	82
% in Cocurricular Activities	9	74	13	76

Table 14.4 Attendance Outcomes

	Student Data **BEFORE** Improved Special Education Service Delivery		Student Data **AFTER** Improved Special Education Service Delivery	
	Students WITH Disabilities	Students WITHOUT Disabilities	Students WITH Disabilities	Students WITHOUT Disabilities
% Absent Fewer Than 10 Days	71	93	79	92

critical. Meadow Rock's initial request for support was strengthened by data. Facts speak louder than anecdotes—Meadow Rock included data-driven statements such as, "Currently we have 15 students with disabilities participating in the ninth-grade history coaching classes after school, 8 more than last year. We calculate that 21 students would be more appropriately served and demonstrate high pass rates if we were staffed differently."

Armed with hard data on discrepant outcomes, Meadow Rock's leaders engaged central office administrators in their pursuit of improved outcomes for students. One offer of support came in the form of grant funds to hire an outside consultant to coordinate and facilitate the strategic planning process. The following sequence of events was set into motion:

IDENTIFICATION OF KEY PLAYERS

Leadership team members identified individuals with a stake in the initiative's outcome: general and special education teachers, parents, students, school administrators, district administrators, support staff, and community members. Care was taken to include a core group able to articulate the effort's purpose, to identify its advantages and pitfalls, and to recognize the difficult, long-term nature of systemic organizational change. Another important group was teachers with either formal leadership roles, such as grade-level chairpersons or team leaders, and informal roles with influence in the school, willing to join administrators in the initiative.

ESTABLISHMENT OF REGULARLY SCHEDULED MEETINGS

Regular meetings with tight, purposeful agendas were scheduled. The principal communicated the importance of consistent attendance and participation and completion of assigned committee work.

IDENTIFICATION OF A VISION, MISSION, GOALS, AND OBJECTIVES

The consultant stressed the importance of a common purpose for the work, creating target goals, and defining strategies to reach those goals. Over several sessions, the committee created its vision for a blended service delivery system characterized by general and special educators working together as instructional teams. In addition, decision making based on student need and strength rather than on arbitrary factors related to disability classification, administrative convenience, or student deficits would guide actions.

Goals focused on training teacher teams and reorganizing students so appropriate instructional groupings occurred throughout the day. Issues were to be addressed within the context of the entire school program rather than treating special education as a separate, add-on program.

CREATION OF AN IMPLEMENTATION PLAN

The team agreed that the initial steps should center around training and planning, both of which are well documented in theory and in practice. The committee assessed staff readiness to provide collaborative special education services and the current service delivery. Then Meadow Rock vigorously planned a training program involving graduate class enrollment, conference attendance, on-site workshops, professional reading and study groups, mentorships, and networking. A database of opportunities, participation, and feedback aided the group in tailoring this training program to meet the staff needs.

Concurrently with the training, staff members planned collaborative service delivery for the upcoming school year. Steps included reviewing students' individual education plans (IEPs); devising tentative blended class rolls based on IEPs; recommending staff assignments derived from licensure, experiences, and skills of teachers; and developing a plan to inform and educate the school and the community of anticipated changes, their necessity, and potential benefits. The team sought diligently to address all issues. Knowing there are no guarantees and the unexpected does occur, the team tried to foresee difficulties and strategize to minimize their impact.

DEVELOPMENT OF AN EVALUATION PLAN

Meadow Rock's team members knew that their initiative's success would depend on a systematic review of outcome data. Therefore, they built evaluation systems for each facet. They evaluated the training's usefulness and the strategic planning process itself. They also crafted a program evaluation to assess and correct for missteps as quickly as possible. Data consisted of student integration into general curricula, course grades, standardized test scores, school attendance, involvement in extracurricular and cocurricular activities, and anecdotal feedback from students, staff, and parents. (See Tables 14.1, 14.2, 14.3, and 14.4.) Data were aggregated and disaggregated in ways to facilitate prompt and positive changes. Consistent review led to routine mid-course corrections that kept any risk taking on the part of staff, parents, and students from being interpreted as failures of either themselves or the initiative. Illustration of such changes included the following:

- Two students, one with learning disabilities and another with emotional disturbance, were determined to require a more restrictive environment than the general education setting. Even with extensive support, accommodation, and modification, they did not derive the benefits necessary for success. Their IEPs were revised to reflect service delivery within the special education setting.

- Four students, one with emotional disturbance and three with attention deficit disorder, required revisions in their IEPs to include a Behavior Management Plan. Their IEP committees decided that the students' success in general education was negatively impacted by behaviors that warranted more specific behavior management strategies and supports.

- Nine students, three with learning disabilities, one with emotional disturbance, and five with attention deficit disorder were determined to no longer need a resource special education class to support their academic performance. Therefore, time in a segregated placement could be replaced with more time in general education classrooms.

- Two general education and three special education teachers received more training in strategy development and implementation because of the special challenges involved in teaching content classes, such as science and social studies, to students with very low reading levels.

- An additional paraeducator was assigned to assist with in-class service delivery to support students requiring monitoring and encouragement. The increase in personnel allowed teachers more flexibility in grouping and regrouping students for instruction and freed the teachers to deliver more direct instruction rather than to monitor independent drill and practice.

Meadow Rock's critical features that helped to blend general and special education programs included the following:

A representative advisory group to provide a forum for ongoing problem solving. Constituents of the initiative can take unresolved concerns to this advisory group for reflection and assistance. Workable suggestions may be generated at that level or referred to the building administrators for solutions. The advisory group must always keep the principal, as the individual responsible for the school, fully informed of its workings. By reciprocal agreement, it is also critical that the principal keep the advisory group apprised of information that may impact its perspective, decisions, and advice.

Targeted, high-quality, needs-based professional staff development; consistent, organized gathering of data, including evidence of what occurs in classrooms day to day. For instance, classroom observations included a systematic collection of data on seating arrangements, group assignments, pupil-teacher interactions, curricular modifications, and co-teaching situations. Such evidence aids teachers and administrators in continuous modification of classroom practice to meet student need. Logical, objective modification of the instructional program was based on data, such as alteration made in staff assignments. An instructional group needing more intensive instructional intervention might require the service of a special educator rather than a paraprofessional originally assigned to the group. A switch would be in order, and the justification would be systematic, objective data. For instance, when a general education teacher became concerned that a student with disabilities in his science class was failing because of poor test performance and questioned the appropriateness of the placement, staff reviewed the situation and decided to revise the testing format to include two sessions rather than giving the test all at once. The student's performance improved dramatically to the B-C range. The central office was continually involved in planning, problem solving, and celebration of success.

Availability of resources and supports.

Acceptance of periods of confusion and discouragement when the initial excitement wears off and the true difficulty of the work is glaringly apparent. It is human nature to approach new adventure with enthusiasm. However, undertaking systemic change is a challenging, long-term endeavor. Progress is often not readily apparent nor is it neatly sequential. Consequently, it is important that implementers be prepared for plateaus.

Realistic estimations of time and energy necessary to make systemic change a reality.

After a year of commitment and hard work, Meadow Rock Middle School implemented its well-planned and publicized initiative to improve special education services through collaboration. Leadership team members and staff adhered as closely as possible to their strategic plan. There were, however, unexpected and unavoidable complications. Three potential collaborating teachers left the school. A key administrator was reassigned to another school. Students with complex profiles enrolled, increasing demands on teacher resources. Some students included in general education classes for the first time experienced a decline in grades, triggering anxiety for students and parents. Maintaining the integrity of planning time became more difficult as daily events captured people's attention and distracted them from the goal. Staff meetings, parent conferences, grading papers, committee assignments, and so on, are all immediate time-snatchers and can easily divert energies away from more long-term, global projects.

However, both planners and participants agreed that successes far outweighed problems. Students did demonstrate better outcomes on all the measures. (See Tables 14.1, 14.2, 14.3, and 14.4.) Teachers became more competent and forged powerful professional alliances. Resources were allocated more efficiently. Time and activities previously devoted to staff development based on teacher interest and preference were reallocated to focus on topics pertinent to the inclusive initiative, such as best practices in heterogeneous grouping, curriculum modification, and instructional strategies. Perhaps most important was Meadow Rock's blossoming new belief that hard work and vision can produce powerful change.

CONCLUSION

Growing diversity in student population and increasing emphasis on accountability led one school to look at new ways to improve delivery of special education services.

ISLLC QUESTIONS

Standard 1

- What steps does the school administrator take to support the success of all students?
- How is the vision for learning established?

Standard 2

- How did the strategic planning process create a school culture that treated all individuals with dignity and respect?

Standard 3

- How were resources allocated to modify the learning environment?

Standard 4

- How did the leader collaborate with families and other stakeholders to implement this vision?

Standard 6

- How did the strategic planning process influence the larger social concern of inclusion?

REFERENCES

Billingsley, B. (Ed.). (1993). *Program leadership for serving students with disabilities.* Blacksburg: Virginia Tech.

Goor, M. (1995). *Leadership for special education administration: A case-based approach.* Fort Worth, TX: Harcourt Brace.

Rea, P. (1997). Creating inclusive schools: Tips for administrators. *ISEE Update,* 1-3.

Rea, P. (2001). Setting expectations and fulfilling responsibilities: An administrator's guide to fostering teacher collaboration. *Special Education Law Bulletin,* 7(10), 1-2.

Rea, P., McLaughlin, V., & Walther-Thomas, C. (2002). Outcomes for students with learning disabilities in inclusive and pullout programs. *Exceptional Children, 68*(2), 203-222.

Thousand, J., Villa, R., & Nevin, A. (Eds.). (1994). *Creativity and collaborative learning: A practical guide to empowering students and teachers.* Baltimore: Brookes.

15

Talent Development With English Language Learners

Nora G. Friedman

Overview

The Schoolwide Enrichment Model (SEM) provides a broadened concept of giftedness and an increased range of curricular and instructional practices that can help every principal successfully meet the diverse learning needs of all students. This model focuses on students' interests, abilities, and learning styles. It benefits more students than usually selected for traditional gifted programs and can be infused into a total school improvement plan. This means that students for whom English is a second language, sometimes called English language learners, whose talents may be unnoticed as they struggle with a new language and culture, can participate in talent development programs.

Our schools are welcoming children from faraway places in record numbers. Every principal grapples with how to successfully meet the

Table 15.1 Enrichment Learning and Teaching Principles

Each learner is unique. Therefore all learning experiences must take into account the abilities, interests, and learning styles of the individual.	Learning is more effective when students enjoy what they are doing. Therefore, learning experiences should be designed and assessed with as much concern for enjoyment as for other goals.
Learning is more meaningful and enjoyable when content and process are learned within the context of a real problem, when students use authentic methods to address the problem, and when they have an impact on a real audience.	Enrichment learning and teaching focuses on enhancing knowledge and acquiring thinking skills. *Applications* of knowledge and skills must supplement formal instruction.

SOURCE: *The Schoolwide Enrichment Model: A How-To Guide For Educational Excellence* (2nd ed.), by J. S. Renzulli and S. M. Reis, 1997. Adapted with permission from the authors.

diverse learning needs of all students; and for many principals, this includes students for whom English is a second language. English language learners, also known as ESL students, face particular challenges as they try to become comfortable in new communities and schools. They often struggle to adjust to their new surroundings while facing the extraordinary task of learning to understand and communicate in a different language and culture. As a result, their special gifts and talents may not be as easily recognized as those of their native English-speaking classmates.

For example, "Maria" came from a remote village in Mexico with her parents and baby sister. Her mother is a homemaker and her gardener father found work with a local landscaper. Maria, who spoke little English, spent countless hours in her new classroom doodling in the margins of her papers, sketching elaborate fashion designs while her classmates worked on their studies and acquired the skills to help them become successful in school and later in life. She had no idea that her new school's philosophy asserted that all children are entitled to an enriching education. Unlike many schools, the educators here sought any pathway possible to crystallize her interest to help her succeed and become engaged in school life. Talent development opportunities comprise an integral instructional component of the total school program.

Maria's school utilized the principles of enrichment learning and teaching inherent in the Schoolwide Enrichment Model (Renzulli & Reis, 1997) (see Table 15.1 and Figure 15.1). This model's implementation has helped to

Figure 15.1 The Schoolwide Enrichment Model

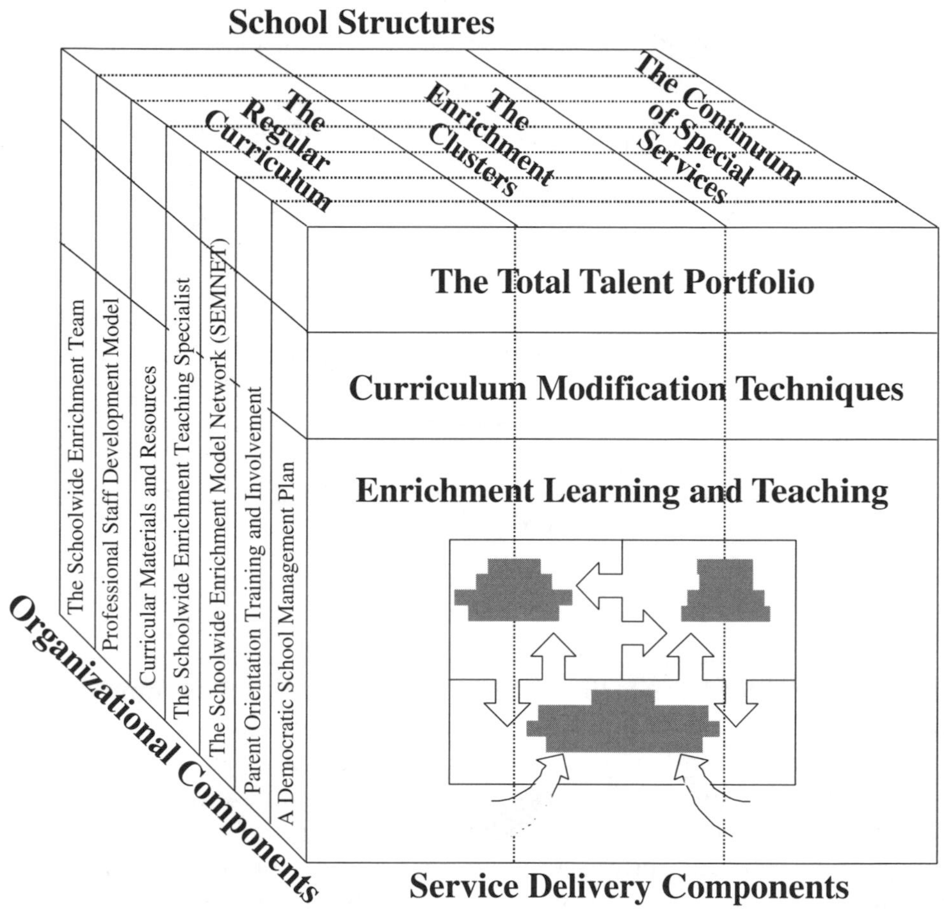

SOURCE: *The Schoolwide Enrichment Model: A How-To Guide For Educational Excellence* (2nd ed.), by J. S. Renzulli and S. M. Reis, 1997.

reduce the impact of the national trend toward standardized testing, with its emphasis on basic skills rather than students' creativity and interests. This standards-based and high-stakes testing environment might limit the children's talent development, and so in our school, developing the gifts that lie within each of our students became a focus of our work.

Before reaching this point, the newly assigned principal's task included understanding the history of the school and the perceptions of colleagues and the community at large regarding teaching and learning. The process of learning about what had brought them to the profession of education took place in many different forums: faculty meetings, grade level meetings, informal breakfasts and all-important discussions in the hallways. All helped a new principal understand the school's values and our collective hopes and dreams for our students.

Figure 15.2 The Three-Ring Conception of Giftedness

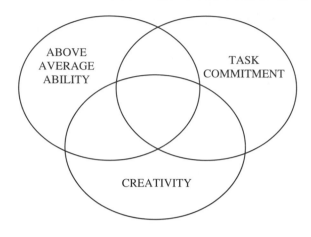

SOURCE: From *The Schoolwide Enrichment Model: A How-To Guide For Educational Excellence* (2nd Ed.), by J. S. Renzulli and S. M. Reis, 1997.

Numerous days and weeks of listening to voices in the school community helped create the best possible teaching and learning environment in our school. The resulting Schoolwide Enrichment Model (SEM) benefits more students than the small percentage usually selected for participation in traditional gifted programs, and it can be infused into a total school improvement plan. The model provides a framework that facilitates enrichment learning and teaching strategies in a school environment and can benefit school systems with increasingly diverse populations. The model is not intended to substitute for or decrease existing services to high-achieving students. The broadened conception of giftedness (Renzulli, 1978) depicted in Figure 15.2 reflects the belief that challenging and appropriate educational opportunities can only be achieved when students' individual differences are recognized and celebrated.

After engaging in a range of professional conversations with colleagues, the school leadership, faculty, staff, and parents designed a course of action that matched our image of what we hoped our school could be. Being a principal is not a role; it is a relationship—and the relationship formed with students, parents, and staff provides the impetus for moving a school in a given direction.

We soon agreed that enrichment is vital to all of our students, to bring relevance, excitement, and authenticity to learning. This was my colleagues' number one priority, and this emphasis remained critical for students to have any chance of reaching their potential. Students' interests, abilities, and learning styles, key elements of the Schoolwide Enrichment Model, help identify talent potential in more of our students, including our English language learners. Unlike their predominantly English-speaking classmates traditionally identified for participation in gifted programs, they often do not qualify for services because of their language and cultural differences. By using the Schoolwide Enrichment Model, however, our faculty began to discover this special group of youngsters' gifts and talents.

Together, we began applying the tenets of the model to help us capitalize upon on our students' interests and strengths to help them become more engaged in school. These tenets fell into three major categories: (1) identifying the students' strengths by analyzing their interests, learning styles, and types of projects they enjoy completing; (2) modifying curriculum to provide more appropriate learning opportunities through techniques such as curriculum compacting (Reis, Burns, & Renzulli, 1992); and (3) providing a number of enrichment opportunities as specified in the Enrichment Triad Model (Renzulli, 1977).

Some professional tension emerges whenever introducing change. Over time, the provocative issues associated with innovation lessened. We all examined the Schoolwide Enrichment Model from a professional development perspective and determined what the teachers needed to understand. Eventually, the teachers willingly agreed to pilot the distribution and analysis of student interest surveys (Renzulli, 1997) as a way of demonstrating our commitment to knowing students well and providing interest-based learning. Tapping students' interests is important to their overall academic success. Educators must then follow up by providing every student with the opportunities, resources, and encouragement necessary to pursue those interests and achieve his or her maximum potential.

The school we wanted for our students was the same school we would want for our own children. Teachers who saw Maria's intense interest in drawing and who took the time to review her interest survey soon realized that nurturing her budding talent could be one way to engage her in the learning process and the fabric of school life.

The integration of a rigorous curriculum, adept instruction, and a sound organization provided students with powerful learning, recognizing the diversity we face in today's schools as a positive element. Engaging our students and fostering motivation to learn and improve achievement are important because of the growing diversity of our student populations in a standards-based era.

The Schoolwide Enrichment Model provided a blueprint for infusing enrichment learning and teaching into our total school environment and was flexible enough for us to develop a program suited to our unique situation. It is critical to build relationships and capacity by sharing a common vision and then easing into new teaching practices together to meet the unique learning needs of all of our students.

Maria was provided with many outlets for her interest in drawing. She eventually presented her work to a variety of audiences and found encouragement to pursue her dream of becoming a fashion illustrator. Maria soon began to love school and had an outstanding year. It is the responsibility of all educators to offer opportunities for students to develop their talents. A schoolwide commitment to talent development and to providing enrichment learning and teaching can shift the emphasis many schools currently have on remediation to an emphasis on the development of the interests and talents of all children.

CONCLUSION

The Schoolwide Enrichment Model motivates students to master a challenging academic curriculum through emphasis on students' interests, abilities, and learning styles. This approach brings diverse students to a level of high achievement.

ISLLC QUESTIONS

Standard 1

- How does the educational leader promote the success of all students by facilitating the development, articulation, implementation, and stewardship of a vision of learning that is shared and supported by the school community?
- How does this educational leader recognize and celebrate all school community members' contributions?

Standard 2

- How does this educational leader treat all individuals with dignity and respect?
- How does this educational leader gather more information and data about the situation from all stakeholders before making decisions?
- How does this educational leader maintain a culture of high expectations?
- How does this educational leader show knowledge of measurement, evaluation, and assessment strategies?
- How does this educational leader value the team process and stakeholder involvement for making decisions?
- How does this educational leader show understanding of human growth and development?

Standard 4

- How does this educational leader promote the success of all students by responding to diverse community interests and needs?

Standard 5

- How does this educational leader, who promotes the success of all students, act with integrity, fairness, and in an ethical manner?

Standard 6

- How does this educational leader promote the success of all students by understanding, responding to, and influencing the larger political, social, economic, legal, and cultural context?

REFERENCES

Reis, S. M., Burns, D. E., & Renzulli, J. S. (1992). *Curriculum compacting: The complete guide to modifying the regular curriculum for high ability students.* Mansfield Center, CT: Creative Learning Press.

Renzulli, J. S. (1977). *The enrichment triad model: A guide for developing defensible programs for the gifted and talented.* Mansfield Center, CT: Creative Learning Press.

Renzulli, J. S. (1978). What makes giftedness? Reexamining a definition. *Phi Delta Kappan, 60,* 180-184.

Renzulli, J. S. (1997). *Interest-A-Lyzer family of instruments: A manual for teachers.* Mansfield Center, CT: Creative Learning Press.

Renzulli, J. S., & Reis, S. M. (1997). *The schoolwide enrichment model: A how-to approach for educational excellence* (2nd ed.). Mansfield Center, CT: Creative Learning Press.

Demographic information can best be accessed at www.emsc.nysed.gov/repcrd2001/cir/280502060007.pdf

16

Connecting Authentic Knowledge and Academic Accountability

Kelly Clark/Keefe
Patricia Morgan
Susan Brody Hasazi

*I believe in the idea that every student needs a connection, some-
one who has a sense of the whole person. . . . I needed a system in
my school to make this happen.*

—Charles Phillips, Montpelier High School Principal

AUTHORS' NOTE: This article was supported in part by funds received from the U.S.
Department of Education under federal grant #H158V70053/02. The opinions expressed do
not necessarily reflect the position or policies of this agency, and no official endorsement
should be inferred.

Overview

> Personalized Learning Plans (PLPs), and the process of developing
> them, is a systemic reform initiative that puts all students at the center
> of their own learning. This approach can help principals and teachers
> find a balance between the seemingly competing goals of personalizing
> learning and standardizing academic outcomes. Concerns about students'
> social and emotional well-being, along with their academic achieve-
> ment, drive this process. Every student in Montpelier High School
> (under 500 students) has his or her own PLP.

The Montpelier School System is one of the smallest districts in
Vermont. Situated in the state's capital, it serves about 1,200 students
from K–12 (fewer than 100 students per grade level). The small-town setting differs, however, from many Vermont communities in that many of
the state agencies and public service groups make the rural capital their
home. This gives the school system and surrounding community both a
large number of community-based resources and a population of children
and families who access many of the services.

We enter Montpelier High School (MHS) and see Abby moving
through the hallways clutching two large textbooks close to her chest, her
dark eyes peering nervously through her wire-rimmed glasses. Two other
students step aside, high-fiving Troy who deftly maneuvers his wheelchair
through the congested corridor. Manuela bounds into the office where we
are setting up our interview-taping equipment. Smiling, she announces
excitedly that she *must* find Joe to tell him the news. The scene, as we
settle into our task of interviewing Charlie and Anne[1] about their work at
MHS, is one where typical adolescents within a high school environment
are searching, each in a unique way, for meaning in their educational lives.

How do leaders and practitioners faced with increased pressure to
standardize curricula and assessments respond to the individual styles,
interests, and capacities of students like Abby, Troy, and Manuela? What
are the elements of a school system that can and should transcend the
boundaries of special and general education? What does it look and sound
like to put students at the center of their own learning? Taken as a whole,
these questions provided the catalyst to the development and implementation of the Personalized Learning Plan (PLP) process at MHS. The purpose of this chapter is to describe the motivation for initiating this unique
reform effort and, using one student's story, illustrate how practi-
tioner/leaders[2] dealt with implementation issues.

FINDING MIDDLE GROUND:
OVERVIEW OF THE ISSUE

When asked what his reasons were for helping to guide and support the implementation of the PLP program, Charles "Charlie" Phillips, the principal of MHS, responded, "I first started thinking of the need for a better system during the strategic planning process in late 1993." In earlier conversations, we learned that this districtwide strategic planning process provided a critical forum for responding to the new state standards and assessments, the rising costs of special education, and the perception of an increasingly complex population of students. As was so often the case in our interview, these broad contextual issues were swiftly grounded in Charlie's recollection of one parent's concerns:

> I remember a parent . . . whose daughter was in the seventh grade. [She] said, "I don't want my daughter to fall through the cracks. She's not brilliant in anything. She's not a great athlete, not a great scholar. But she loves to write. She's a good writer. I want *all* her strengths, what she's *all* about, to be known when she gets to the high school." For me that was really the first time I started to think about, *how could we do that?* . . . I needed a system in my school to make this happen. . . . That led to a broader discussion about how we personalize education for all kids.

In response to a similar line of questioning, Anne Friedrichs, the PLP Coordinator, mirrors Charlie in her focus on the PLP as a systemic reform initiative that puts students' voiced interests and strengths squarely at the center of their learning: "[The PLP] has been a way of talking to kids. It's been a way of listening to kids. . . . With PLPs, there doesn't have to be only *one* structure that helps. It's a very flexible *set* of structures. It has to be."

It is not hard to see that Charlie, Anne, and others at MHS care about students and about their learning. Trust and respect were reflected in the content and tone of random interactions observed between teachers and students in the hallways. Notes and pictures of students acknowledged for a variety of achievements spilled off bulletin boards. Clearly, the desire to make meaningful connections among students, and between students and adults, has been a driving force behind the PLP process. Surrounding Charlie and Anne's expressions are broader, more complicated concerns about how to balance what can seem like competing goals: personalizing students' learning and standardizing academic outcomes.

MHS is similar to most public schools across the country, facing unprecedented goals for student achievement levels, adherence to state and national standards, and overall accountability. Yet surrounding this emphasis on individual performance and competition are highly publicized concerns about the students' social and emotional well-being. During the past decades, school safety and students' self-defeating behaviors have been in the headlines (de Marrais & LeCompte, 1995; Goodlad, 1983; Gordon, 1999; Sarason, 1990; Sergiovanni, 1994). The leaders/practitioners like Charlie and Anne must find middle ground: defining and supporting reform initiatives that both empower students of all abilities to clarify and realize their personal learning goals *and* respond creatively to the increased desire for academic accountability. One form that this middle ground has taken at MHS is the PLP program.

PERSONAL LEARNING PLANS: A CASE STUDY OF MONTPELIER HIGH SCHOOL

Historically, the Montpelier school district has been recognized for its innovative approaches to school reform. Such efforts include the development of a shared leadership model, a professional development school partnership with the University of Vermont (UVM), and a variety of student-centered initiatives that have a community-based focus. Additionally, Montpelier has a strong commitment to total integration of its special education services. Students with disabilities are included in all aspects of the school. In 1996, a multiconstituent management team designed the PLP program as a systemic response to create individualized learning plans for every MHS student. During its inception, the school district added a full-time leadership position devoted to the PLP program's development and ongoing evaluation. Today, the goal of full implementation has been reached and every student in the high school has her/his own PLP.

MAIJA: ONE STUDENT'S STORY AS ANALYSIS OF WHAT WORKED AND WHAT DIDN'T

The following student story offers a composite[3] sketch of how the PLP process has worked for students who arrive at school with varying needs. In addition to introducing the practical steps of implementing a PLP, the case reflects how special and general education service delivery can be integrated through the PLP process.

Maija

Tenuous peer and adult relationships characterized Maija's story. Both Maija and her teachers viewed these relationships as disruptive to her learning. For her, the initial high school transition was made more difficult by a home life marked by discord between divorced parents and shifting residency. Since middle school, Maija received special education services as an Emotionally/Behaviorally Disabled (EBD) student. She had the extra burden of entering high school 2 years after her academically and socially successful older sister. This was made painfully clear at Maija's first PLP conference where her mother compared her daughters' different work ethics.

Along with Maija, members of her initial PLP conference included her new teacher advisor (TA), her special education case manager, and her parents. A modified version of the MAPS (McGill Action Planning System) process was used during Maija's first conference as a planning tool to articulate her history and to identify her hopes, dreams, fears, interests, and strengths (O'Brien, Forest, Snow, & Hasbury, 1989). Using this process, her TA assisted in identifying short- and long-term goals that integrated her PLP with her IEP/Transition Plan. For Maija, these goals included staying motivated for morning classes, building on her strengths in mathematics, getting into a spring session of Drivers' Education, and finding a way to engage with peers around common interests. Maija participated during this initial conference but relied heavily on the TA's leadership.

As Maija's PLP unfolded in her sophomore year, her team noticed that she was becoming increasingly withdrawn and isolated from her peers. She began reluctantly expressing concerns about finding ". . . friends that won't pressure me into any . . . not good things." Her request for avoiding early morning classes was not always possible and her grades began to slip. Additionally, Maija's home life began to involve more frequent changes in her parent's visitation schedules and weekly moves between their residences. When Maija's TA retired at the beginning of her sophomore year, Maija's teachers and parents grew concerned that this disruption in her high school education might further disengage her from her school and peers.

Highs and lows in her personal and academic life characterized her subsequent high school years. Teachers close to Maija recognized that identifying her new TA would require careful consideration to ensure continuity with trusted adults.

The new TA acknowledged Maija's interest in developing meaningful and safe relationships with her peers and helped her identify several steps toward validating her self-worth. With her TA's guidance, Maija became a peer tutor for students having difficulty in math as well as an active member of the Students Against Drunk Driving (SADD) taskforce. During her senior year, Maija had grown increasingly comfortable and confident in her school surroundings and began to take more leadership during PLP conferences. Rather than relying on the adult members of her team, Maija initiated conversations and actively problem-solved some of the challenges she was facing rather than assigning blame or responsibility to team members. She successfully completed her high school program and made plans to continue working in the field of computer technology.

BACK TO MIDDLE GROUND:
A RETROSPECTIVE OF THE PLP PROCESS

School leaders/practitioners have much to learn from Maija's and other students' PLP stories. With respect to special education, the PLP process allows learning relationships to transcend rigidly categorical approaches to meeting students' needs. Maija helps us understand that PLPs can provide an important forum for students, their families, and educators to process learning experiences, meaningfully integrate educational goals, and articulate future plans. Trusting relationships and continuous open dialogue become central to implementing reform.

An ongoing challenge for administrative leaders is supporting faculty to find their own middle ground. Leaders must encourage faculty to consider that academic accountability is not at odds with the students' personal learning interests and goals.

As we begin to gather up our tape-recording equipment, a tall young man stumbles into Anne's office, halted only momentarily by our unexpected presence in his advisor's space. As he effusively informs her about his recent acceptance into a juried art show, it becomes obvious that our time with Anne should come to a close. As we leave MHS, we are reminded of Anne's earlier message about what is at the heart of the PLP process: "It's a way of talking to kids. It's a way of listening to kids. . . . This is about *students* taking on the work of learning."

CONCLUSION

Personalized Learning Plans (PLPs) help educators face the increased pressure to standardize curricula and assessments by responding to students' individual styles, interests, and capacities. The PLP process transcends rigid categories to best meet students' needs.

ISLLC QUESTIONS

Standard 1

- Describe this school and community's vision for learning.

Standard 2

- How does this school provide an instructional program conducive to (all) students' learning?
- How does this school maintain a culture of high expectations for students and faculty?

- How does the Personal Learning Plans process reflect a deep understanding of human growth and development?

Standard 4

- How does this instructional program respond to diverse community needs?

Standard 5

- How does this school understand, respond to, and influence the larger social, economic, legal, and cultural context?

NOTES

1. The information for this chapter was derived from semi-structured interviews with Charles Phillips, the principal of MHS, and Anne Friedrichs, the PLP coordinator at MHS.

2. The term practitioner/leader is used here to reflect the fact that there is a shared leadership model in place at MHS, and that Charlie and Anne are both administrative leaders as well as faculty. Both are also in the role of teacher-advisor, guiding the PLP process for a cohort of students.

3. The term *composite* denotes a blending of several MHS students' stories.

REFERENCES

de Marrais, K. B., & LeCompte, M. D. (1995). *The way schools work: A sociological analysis of education* (2nd ed.). White Plains, NY: Longman.

Goodlad, J. (1983). *A place called school: Prospects for the future*. New York: McGraw-Hill.

Gordon, E. W. (1999). *Education and justice: A view from the back of the bus*. New York: Teachers College.

O'Brien, J., Forest, M., Snow, J., & Hasbury, D. (1989). *Action for inclusion*. Toronto: Frontier College.

Sarason, S. B. (1990). *The predictable failure of educational reform: Can we change course before it's too late?* San Francisco: Jossey-Bass.

Sergiovanni, T. J. (1994). *Building community in schools*. San Francisco: Jossey-Bass.

17

Severely and Profoundly Disabled Students in the School Community

Phyllis Milne

Overview

When an elementary school was designated as the site for a severely and profoundly disabled students' program, the principal began working with her teachers and school community to welcome the newcomers and to make them part of the school's educational family. By

---

AUTHORS' NOTES: Names of students have been changed to protect anonymity.

Tabb Elementary School is located in suburban York County, Virginia. Approximately 25% of the school's 600 students live in military housing, and another 33% of families are military or government employees. During the 2000-2001 school year, 125 students transferred in and approximately the same number moved to other locations. The ethnic makeup is 73%% Caucasian, 18% African American, and 9% Asian, Hispanic, and Others. Approximately one-fourth of Tabb's students participate in the free and reduced breakfast and lunch program. By December 2001, 137 of Tabb's 600 students were identified with special needs.

introducing the issue, inviting all stakeholders to contribute strategies to constructively address the situation, and listening carefully, the principal helped educators plan collaboratively. "How can we make this work?" was always the response to increased demands on educators. Teachers and students rose successfully to the many challenges they faced. More students with diverse learning needs followed and enrolled in regular education classes, so the school began an inclusion program with classes jointly taught by regular and special educators. Five years later, 21% of the student body held IEPs.

In August of 1996, Tabb Elementary became our school division's designated location for a growing population of severely and profoundly disabled students. Installing equipment and removing physical barriers took some forethought, but leadership energy also addressed resolving the staff and parents' fears and concerns. Predicted objections included, "Why are these children in a public school?" "What do we have to offer?" and "How will we meet their physical needs?"

Expectant parents speculate about their new offspring's gender and physical characteristics. Some parents-to-be confess that they would be delighted to birth and raise the first female president or the next Michael Jordan; but without exception, prospective parents hope and pray that their eagerly anticipated child will be healthy and "normal." Many parents are painfully aware, however, that the traditional journey to adulthood can be drastically altered or permanently interrupted by one catastrophic acicident, one dreaded disease, or one stray gene.

In one instance, an adolescent son's survival of a life-threatening automobile crash was followed by 2 years of agonizing surgeries and painful therapy. The family never considered a reclusive recovery away from friends and relatively "normal" teen life. Instead, they traded a bulky metal chair for the "speedy sports model" and transformed both plaster-casted legs to painted-on Nike hightops. Stares from curious passersby and small children's fearful glances met grins and greetings from a wired mouth and an arm with extruding metal pins. Memories of physical obstacles and of equally painful invisible barriers remained with child and parent long after removing the pins and plaster and abandoning the wheel chair. Ramps, curb cuts, and reserved parking for the handicapped would be forever appreciated and respected. "Short-term" physical handicaps, however, offer only a glimpse into the constant challenges and suffering of the families whose children experience a lifelong physical, mental, or medical impairment.

As principal, I met staff members' concerns by patiently explaining the students' and families' legal rights and with reminders that these children could be their own children or grandchildren. Teacher by teacher, in faculty meetings, and in small, informal groups, I offered reassurance, positive talk, and group problem solving. In response, staff members slowly began revealing personal information about disabled family members or friends. As teachers shared personal accounts of experiences with disabled individuals, their colleagues' objections softened. Carefully listening, I invited all stakeholders to contribute strategies to overcome the objections they had raised or predicted.

We planned strategies for the success of the new class collaboratively. We would locate the special students near the nurse, but in the midst of other classes, not in a separate wing. We needed space for standing frames, walkers, and a changing table. The special needs classroom would be noisy and busy all day, so the room had to have some sound protection.

On the other hand, some decisions were not negotiable. The students would be included in all assemblies and school events, and individual students would be mainstreamed whenever possible. Time was short, but the Tabb Elementary "moving company" rallied to create an attractive and inviting environment. We set the tone. We would embrace our new children!

By the first day of school, faculty and staff determination replaced concerns. Secretaries greeted our new students by name, and staff members made conversation while wheeling students to their classes. A fourth-grade teacher trained her students to be adaptive physical education buddies, and a second-grade teacher encouraged her students to be official greeters. The custodian assisted with minor tune-ups to classroom equipment. Parent advisors and PTA members stepped forward to welcome our new students. Volunteers offered to assist in the classroom and scheduled days to assist at mealtime. In every possible way, the students were special, and they were ours.

Curious stares became friendly greetings as students in the regular education classes reached out. It was encouraging to see aggressive fourth graders demonstrate patience and kindness with our special kids. Some students improved their behavior or increased their productivity to earn time in the special class. Teachers admired the special education staff and nominated the severe and profound team for Apple Achievement Awards. The division superintendent presented Apple Awards to the four team members for outstanding service to students. The families of our disabled students became comfortable with their children's placement. One father commented that it was reassuring that students from the school were excited to see and to greet Tommy by name at the Food Lion or at the 7-11. One mother expressed hope that her daughter could stay in this class indefinitely because "Lillian is safe and accepted here."

Problem solving continued as we encountered new obstacles. Strategies focused on increasing students' independence and communication skills, but we faced daily challenges to success. We redirected traffic and additional staff monitors helped to load and unload five buses with elevator lifts. Teachers and teacher assistants learned to reposition and to diaper students. Even with two-person lifts, staff members battled back strain and injury. Once, a single ambulatory student in the class of eight ran away from adults and posed an unintentional danger to the less mobile students. One blind and deaf student cried constantly and could be comforted only by holding, stroking, and rocking. Although we reached out to ease her pain, the student's health worsened. Finally, her mother called to tell us Marion had died in her sleep.

A child's death is unsettling for both the adults and the students in a school. The school counselor supported families and students, and students created cards and letters to remember their friend. Before the year was over, a second child in the class had died. The ceremony that followed Deja's passing offered an opportunity to understand and to respect the church of Islam. Before the service, a helpful sister explained expectations. Women and men were separated in the mosque. Guests were welcomed but reminded that noise or crying during the service would interrupt the child's journey to peace. We had joined in song during the celebration of Marion's life, and with the same respect; we sat quietly during Deja's union with Allah. We hoped that the time these girls had spent with us offered some comfort for both families.

In addition to the program for severely and profoundly disabled students, an increasing number of students with a wide variety of disabilities were enrolling in our regular classes. Classroom teachers volunteered to pilot the expanding inclusion program, and students with special needs were clustered into classes jointly taught by regular and special educators. We intentionally assigned the new classes three to five fewer students than other grade-level sections to provide maximum attention for each student in the room. We scheduled Friday morning "fireside chats," during which teachers met to discuss problems and to share strategies. Administrators provided coffee, doughnuts, and encouragement, and the school psychologist offered advice, strategies, and support. Both regular and special educators benefited from built-in peer coaching. The program ran smoothly the first year, and by the second year, a larger number of classroom teachers participated.

The adjustment to accommodate special needs students was not always easy or successful. As the numbers of special students grew, regular education teachers struggled to balance the needs of non-disabled students with those identified. Each child was unique, and many disabilities were perplexing. We attempted to make connections with students who had physical disabilities, emotional disorders, and mental retardation. We stretched to overcome the mysterious barriers of autism and Aspberger's syndrome. Some parents of special needs students enlisted advocates who demanded expensive equipment and extensive accommodations. Limited funds meant that special educators stretched to work with larger numbers of classroom teachers. Regular education teachers devoted more planning and instructional time to modify and deliver instruction to a wider range of students' learning needs. Students with emotional issues occasionally disrupted instruction and compromised students' safety. Parents of non-identified students frequently assumed that all children who acted out or disrupted class were special education students. As parents began to request non-inclusion classes for their children, classroom teachers became more apprehensive and less willing to accept disabled students.

By 2001, twenty-one percent of our student body held Individual Education Plans. Every class now included some students with special needs. Child study, eligibility, and individualized educational plan meetings consumed the calendar. Accountability, state standards, and achievement testing added to the challenge. Experienced special educators accepted more lucrative or less stressful assignments, and recent college graduates struggled to survive their first years in the demanding programs.

Our earlier experiences with severely and profoundly disabled youngsters laid the framework for our expanded inclusion program. We strove to confront each problem with the question, "How can we make this work?" rather than the list of reasons why "This can never work." To increase our understanding of how to best address our students' learning needs, we replaced "Fireside Chats" with afternoon "Teachers as Readers" sessions. Administrators purchased current professional books and encouraged experimentation. Teachers read about, attempted, and discussed innovative strategies. Participants shared appreciation for each other and common laughter while reflecting on colleagues' triumphs as well as ill-fated attempts. We revised strategies and rescheduled personnel. We offered "Parent Universities" and home visits to include reluctant parents in the learning process. Some students were not successfully included, and some parents were not satisfied. We learned from each new situation, and we brainstormed possible solutions for the next problem.

One staff member commented that good teaching means making connections and maintaining high expectations. It means relating academic content to students' background knowledge. Teachers connect with students by respecting their learning styles and personal interests. School personnel and families collaborate to support student success. Surely a third component of good teaching is overcoming barriers. Kindergarten children adapt to group dynamics and learn turn-taking. First-grade students transform into beginning readers as they break the printed word's code. Teachers guide older students to multiplying fractions, interpreting text, and accepting responsibility for one's actions.

Special needs students have the right to attend public schools, and public school personnel have the responsibility to remove the physical as well as the invisible barriers to students' success. Working together, school communities will learn to embrace and include different learners, to maintain high expectations for staff as well as for students, and to connect with all types of families.

CONCLUSION

Principals set the tone for successful problem solving with information sharing, collaborative discussions, and sensitive listening to colleagues' concerns. Schools can meet the needs of diverse learners when all stakeholders work together to address learning needs. School divisions must remain mindful, however, of the limits and supports that administrators and teachers need in order to effectively accommodate the demands of educating special needs students.

ISLLC QUESTIONS

Standard 1

- How does the school administrator promote the success of all students with a vision for learning that is shared and supported by the school community?
- How does the school administrator identify and remove barriers to learning?

Standard 2

- How does the school administrator create a school culture that treats all individuals with dignity and respect?
- How does the school administrator value conflict resolution and consensus building?
- How does the school administrator help teachers redesign, implement, assess, and refine the curricular program?

Standard 3

- How does the school administrator ensure management of the organization by addressing health and safety issues first?
- How does the school administrator use school support systems flexibly and effectively?

Standard 4

- How does the school administrator build family partnerships to support students' learning needs?

- How does the school administrator respond to diverse community interests?

Standard 5

- How does the school administrator promote the success of all students by acting with integrity, fairness, and in an ethical manner?

Standard 6

- How does the school administrator respond to and influence the larger political, social, economic, legal, and cultural context?

18

Working With Special Education Advocates

Marguerite A. Pittman

Overview

Principals need certain skills and information to work professionally and effectively with special education advocates to support student achievement. Having a calm, professional attitude, knowing the law and your school division's procedures and practices, knowing the student completely as a person and as a learner, and understanding the advocate's purpose are all important considerations.

"Advocates" and "advocacy" are words that we as educators promote. Yet when the words "special education" precede them, our thoughts are often negative.

Educators frequently become anxious as they prepare for meetings that involve special needs parents and their advocates. We want to do what is right for each student, but we sometimes feel uncomfortable that an "outsider" might challenge our experiences, ideas, and practices. We appreciate working in a multidisciplinary team, valuing the varied insights, perspectives, and solutions that a caring and knowledgeable group might bring to problem solving. Nevertheless, many educators dislike working collaboratively with legal or informal advocates who may be unfamiliar with our practices. At the same time, parents and advocates may actually be more knowledgeable than we are about the individual student, special education law and procedures, and educational alternatives.

Principals want to provide an encouraging and effective learning environment in which each student can learn. Our teachers are ready to individualize, differentiate, and modify instruction to assure that each student learns to his or her maximum capacity. We welcome resources that help us successfully address students' special learning needs. To this end, educators need certain skills and information to work professionally with special education advocates to support student achievement. The following case study and recommendations address this issue.

A CASE STUDY

I work in an urban school division of single- and multiple-family homes with approximately 34,000 students of which 45% receive free or reduced lunches. A highly diverse community, our total elementary school population is about 57% African American, 36% White, 4% Hispanic, and 3% Other. Eleven percent of our elementary students receive special education services, and 5% are involved in Talented and Gifted programs. Our school has 750 students, 34% on free or reduced lunch, with 52% White students, 37% African American, and 5% Hispanic. Seven percent of our students receive special education services, while 17% of our students participate in Talented and Gifted programs.

The school day had begun, and things were settling into their normal routine after the morning's hustle and bustle. The phone rings and the call is for me; it's one of my student's parents. She says she wants her child's IEP amended, and she wants her advocate to attend the meeting. Chills rise and my heart pounds more vigorously because the advocate is known for an adversarial approach. He has informed her that we must meet within 5 days, and his schedule is quite crowded. I am to call his assistant and work out a time to meet.

This parent and I have previously enjoyed a very good and open relationship, so I'm a bit perplexed. I explain that the meeting must be held within 30 days, but since she has concerns, we'll certainly schedule it sooner. I'll have the teacher contact her with several possible meeting dates so she as the parent can invite anyone she would want to come, but it would be inappropriate for me to go around her and schedule a meeting with someone who is not the child's guardian.

On the day of our meeting, I was pleased to find that the advocate did not deem it necessary to tape-record our deliberations, since he had previously worked with me and determined that I was reasonable. As principal, I facilitated the meeting, ensuring that we kept the focus on our common purpose and that each individual had the chance to contribute. Several times during the meeting, I had to redirect the conversation because the advocate began talking when someone asked the mother a question, or he interjected information about the law that didn't always apply to the points we were making. We kept bringing the conversation back to the mother's concerns and the ways in which we either were presently addressing them or might do so in the future.

It came to light that the advocate had actually contacted the mother about the collaboration model we were currently using to serve her child. He was looking for people with special needs children who had previously been served in self-contained settings but who were now receiving special education assistance in the regular education classroom. It seemed that he was building a legal case against the school division for changing the service delivery model for a specific classification of children.

The advocate lost his credibility with the parent when he repeatedly referred to the child by the incorrect name. He probably lost her confidence completely when he kept referencing her child's disability with the wrong label. It became evident that this advocate was not concerned about her child but with making a legal case. The problem was that this child had nothing to do with his case.

The parent was able to revisit the data and look at current examples of the student's schoolwork to recognize that the delivery model was effective for her child. Trust was back in full force when it became clear to the parent that we knew her daughter, her abilities, and appropriate ways to help her learn. In addition, the advocate had been heard and allowed to express his opinion. He had some useful ideas that we were able to incorporate into our plan for the student's learning.

As educators concerned with the child's best interests, we welcomed the advocate to come and participate in the meeting. Some advocates can be very aggressive. In this case, the advocate took control of the meeting, although he was only a guest. The point is to keep the educator in charge, through active leadership and group facilitation. The school personnel set and professionally enforced the agenda to focus on what was needed for this child as an individual. We received all contributions respectfully and considered them in the best interests of the child.

RECOMMENDATIONS
FOR WORKING EFFECTIVELY
WITH SPECIAL EDUCATION ADVOCATES

Working with special education advocates can be difficult and call on our best leadership, communication, and group facilitation skills. Several factors that the educational leader brings to these meetings can make a real difference in handling the occasion constructively.

Frame of mind is important. Our overall objective is the same; we all want the child to benefit from the designed program and to be better than he or she would be without it. It is important to recognize that discrimination against special needs students is a reality. Acknowledging this and approaching the meeting from a partnership perspective can help to lessen tension and open doors for productive discussions.

Knowing the law and your school division's procedures and practices are important. It is vital to know special education law, regulations, and procedures. Advocates make it their business to know, select, and espouse those laws that benefit their clients. Some may not be forthcoming with decisions connected to the law that they do not see as helpful to their case. Using official language, citing federal and state codes, and talking as an expert are tactics that advocates can use convincingly. Expressed forcefully and confidently, the advocate's statements can make an uncertain principal doubt his or her own information and judgment. To do the job well, educational leaders need to be equally knowledgeable and convincing.

Knowing the student is important. The parents or guardians bring the advocate because of uncertainty that the school is serving their child's best interest. They do not feel secure in their own ability to be advocates. More often than not, educational personnel know the student better than the advocate. The more completely you know the student as a person and as a learner, the more credibility you will have with the parents, and the greater the parents' confidence in your and the school's ability to successfully meet their child's learning needs.

Frequently, advocates speak in generalities about the student's needs based on the labeled disability and on education law. The educational leader's expertise is based on knowledge of the law and on knowing the child firsthand from daily interactions in a variety of settings and what his or her individual needs are as a learner.

Understanding the advocate's purpose is important. Keep in mind that the advocate's job is to ask for as many services and as much attention and support for the student as he or she can. The advocate's key focus is to *maximize.* The educator's focus, on the other hand, is not one of minimization but one of stewardship, equity, and educational access. There is common ground: meeting the student's learning needs.

CONCLUSION

Working with special education advocates brings unique opportunities for school leaders. A calm, professional approach can focus the meeting on helping students benefit from school. It is vital to prepare for meetings. Reviewing special education law, local policies, guidelines and procedures, best instructional practices, and familiarity with the individual student helps educators work effectively with advocates.

ISLLC QUESTIONS

Standard 1

- How does the educational leader recognize and celebrate the contributions of all members of the school community?

Standard 2

- How does the educational leader treat all individuals with dignity and respect?
- How does the educational leader value the team process and stakeholder involvement in decision making?
- How does the educational leader value conflict resolution and consensus building?

Standard 4

- How does the educational leader build family partnerships to support learning and address instructional issues?
- How does the educational leader respect diverse needs?

Standard 5

- How does the educational leader promote the success of all students by acting with integrity, fairness, and in an ethical manner?

19

Technology and Gifted Learners

Sandra L. Berger

Some things are so unexpected that no one is prepared for them.

—Leo Rosten in *Rome Wasn't Burned in a Day*

Overview

The Internet and World Wide Web have reformulated how we work, play, go to school, think, learn, and teach. Teachers have discovered new ways to meet gifted and intellectually advanced students' needs using technology when differentiating curricula within mixed-ability classrooms. Studies show that student achievement is higher when teachers organize instruction around assignments that connect to students' lives beyond school, demand higher-order thinking, in-depth understanding, and elaborated communication. This technology-integrated learning process allows gifted students to pursue their individual interests within the curriculum to a direction, depth, and subtlety which they find highly motivating. As a result, students produce more intellectually complex work and perform at a higher level on standardized tests. Unfortunately, less than 10% of teachers have the technology facility to actively use computers to advance student learning and only 23% report feeling well prepared to use computers or the Internet in the classroom. Staff development for technology integration is a critical concern for classroom teachers.

The 20th century opened with a chain dry goods store and closed with a dot.com. And somewhere in between, a technological revolution took place. Technology has transformed teaching and learning, industry and commerce, the arts and media, and virtually every other field of human endeavor. In just 20 years, a technology revolution has grown faster than its capabilities can be harnessed in today's classrooms.

During the 1980s and 1990s, educators were first encouraged and then pushed to embrace computers. At first, computers sat in their boxes, buried in temporary "computer labs" that were often unused classrooms. The vision—groups of happy students busily learning to use software applications—lacked a plan. It seemed as though computers were expected to change education just by their presence.

The Internet's emergence in the late 1980s and early 1990s was a key event that brought the computers out of their boxes and into the classrooms. The U. S. Department of Defense conceived the Internet in the 1960s as an electronic network for sharing computer power and as part of our national defense strategy. Soon university researchers joined the network and the Internet was poised to become a government-created and -funded infrastructure called the National Information Infrastructure (NII) (http://nii.nist.gov/), run by a volunteer coalition of engineers, programmers, and educators. For technical or political reasons, NII oversight was to be shared among several federal agencies, but no one would "own" the system; it would exist through the altruistic efforts of all who participated in making it work.

It looked as though anything could be accomplished using the information superhighway, as it soon became known, and educators began to hypothesize that the system would be a great "leveler." If all schools and libraries were connected to the Internet, they said, the great divide between the "haves" and the "have-nots" would at last be narrowed. As America entered the 20th century's final decade, computers and technology had become inextricably linked with the educational reform movement (U. S. Department of Education, 1993).

As computer usage exploded, technology mainstreaming became the 1990s' defining trend (Blachere, 1999). The breakout year for the Internet was 1995. The major online service providers—America Online,

Compuserve, and Prodigy—added millions of new users to the World Wide Web, and quickly made "Internet" a household word. By the decade's end, more than 50% of American homes could boast of at least one computer. A system that had emerged only 15 years before as a scientific and engineering network suddenly became a major force in American business and communication. During the century's final decade, "e-mail" and "e-commerce" became part of our lexicon. E-mail developed into not only a major communication mode and marketing device, but also a way we identify ourselves—"My e-mail address is. . . ." The blending of e-mail and e-commerce and the introduction of "dot" and "com" to each other offered the world a new way to think about business and educational software. Children spoke of "e-pals and key-pals," and wrote digital letters to other children who lived in faraway countries and continents.

A second trend during the final decade was a dramatic decrease in educational services designed to meet the needs of gifted students. Education reform and dwindling school budgets had taken its toll on gifted education. Professional development had all but ceased to exist. Sixty-five percent of the children were sitting in regular education classrooms with teachers who meant well but were not trained to meet their needs (Archambault, Reis, & Westberg, 1990). Digital communication filled a decades-long sense of isolation experienced by gifted students, their families, and their teachers, who welcomed the opportunity to become acquainted, exchange ideas, and brainstorm about some of the educational problems they experienced. Given the opportunity to learn about other cultures through the eyes of e-pals, gifted children took to the airwaves using the few available classroom computers.

The 1996 Telecommunications Act created the E-Rate program, providing discounts of 20 to 90% to schools (depending upon the number of poor children in a district) to purchase Internet access for the school or library. In 2000, the United States invested $5.7 billion on educational technology (Cattagni & Farris, 2001), and there is no reason to believe that this spending level will drop anytime soon.

The Internet and the World Wide Web have reformulated how we work, play, tend to our health, go to school, think, learn, and teach. Teachers have discovered new ways to meet gifted children's needs using technology when differentiating curricula for their advanced students. At the same time, however, juxtaposed with our romance with technology, several concerns have emerged and continue to lurk: 1) the capacity of teachers to use technology in ways that will increase student achievement (Archer, 1998), and 2) the scarcity of reliable data linking computers, Web technology, and student achievement (Education Week on the Web, 1998a; Mendels, 2000; Schacter, 1999).

TEACHER USE OF COMPUTERS

The number of classroom computers has increased exponentially. The most recent federal research found that more than 99% of American public schools have some kind of Internet access for students, with a student computer ratio of 5 to 1 (Cattagni & Farris, 2001). Some 77% of instructional classrooms have Internet connections, although the number drops to 60% for schools with the highest concentrations of poverty (Williams, 2000). However, less than 10% of the teachers who have classroom computers are using them to access model lesson plans or research or to employ best classroom instructional practices that integrate curriculum, instruction, and technology. Only 23% reported feeling well prepared to use computers or the Internet in the classroom (Lenhart, Simon, & Graziano, 2001).

A National Center for Education Statistics (NCES) survey (Rowand, 2000) found that less than 40% of teachers were using computers to create instructional material. However, teachers who had received training in the use of computers and the Internet over the previous 3 years were more likely to assign students work involving computers or the Internet. For example, teachers with more than 32 hours of professional development were more likely to assign problem solving (41%), graphical presentations (31%), and demonstrations or simulations (29%) than teachers with 0 to 8 hours of training. Newer teachers, with greater exposure to technology, were more likely to use computers or the Internet to accomplish teaching objectives, communicate with colleagues, gather information for lessons, or create instructional materials (Becker, 1999; Milken Exchange & The International Society for Technology in Education [ISTE], 1999).

In *Getting America's Students Ready for the 21st Century*, the U. S. Department of Education (1996) recommended that 30% of a school district's technology budget be spent on professional development. In fact, the average tends to vary from 3% to 5%. Some researchers believe that inadequate teacher training is perhaps the biggest bottleneck limiting effective use of computer networking in many of the nation's classrooms (Conte, 2000).

In a telling study, students reported that less than one-third of their teachers used computers to help them understand new concepts (Education Week on the Web, 2001). Students surveyed by *Education Week* (1998b, 2001) indicated that they did not have the skills to effectively use Internet search engines to find relevant answers to their questions. They said that their teachers did not know, either. In addition, students say they use computers far more at home than at school (Lenhart, Simon, & Graziano, 2001; NCES, 2001).

Research studies conducted by the Consortium on Chicago Schools project (Newmann, Bryk, & Nagaoka, 2001) have shown that when teachers organized instruction around assignments that demanded higher-order thinking, in-depth understanding, and elaborated communication, and then made a connection to students' lives beyond school, students produced more intellectually complex work and performed at a higher level on standardized tests. Similar studies have shown that the more demanding an assignment, the better students applied themselves to it (Finnan, St. John, McCarthy, & Slovacek, 1996).

Yet researchers studying grades 3, 6, and 8 in 19 Chicago schools found that less than 30% of the assignments offered a significant degree of challenge. Using computers as a teaching tool, teachers could introduce complex concepts in mathematics and physics using simulations, demonstrate mathematical analysis by using applications that generate spreadsheets, and demonstrate new concepts using computer-generated graphics, if they were provided with professional inservice training in the use of technology and given the time to learn to effectively integrate technology and curriculum. Teachers lacking the facility to integrate technology with instruction have greater difficulty providing appropriate high-level learning activities for gifted—or any—students.

TECHNOLOGY AS A MEANS

There are several ways to differentiate curriculum for gifted students. The following examples illustrate the way that teachers use process, content, and product to individualize the curriculum in mixed-ability classes.

Robbie and Julia, two 7-year-olds brimming with energy and enthusiasm, led the school visitors down the hall, past the brightly colored murals that marked the grade levels, around the lines of children going to recess, and into their own classroom. Yanking on the visitors' arms, they giggled and drew the visitors closer to what looked like an ordinary pile of Lego blocks and a television monitor. But these were not ordinary Lego blocks. Robbie and Julia pressed a button and the monitor came to life, showing several icons. "Put your finger here on the screen," Robbie instructed. Following instructions, one of the visitors touched an icon on the screen and the Lego blocks came to life. The Lego steam shovel rolled forward, picked up several blocks, and, turning, dumped its cargo into a cart and then turned back to pick up another load. "We made it!" Robbie proclaimed loudly and with great pride. "We talked to a scientist by e-mail who helped us figure out how to work the electronic Lego and decide what we wanted to do! Then we drew it on paper and now it's finished!" Eager to show off, he asked, "Do you want to know about electronic circuits?"

Robbie and Julia are students in a classroom where the curriculum has been reconfigured to incorporate and integrate technology and where class projects make full use of the Internet and other technologies. Although they are gifted, they have not been formally identified. Their teacher knows how to differentiate curricula to account for their advanced abilities and intense curiosity. The robotics project described above was based on a science unit using the broad theme of change. Other classmates who have advanced verbal skills chose to use word processing to write about the project for the school newspaper. Students with advanced mathematics skills have learned how to construct and use a spreadsheet to keep track of progress. All the children involved in this project became authors and creators of knowledge, rather than just receivers. Technology was the means to an end. The children's activities are examples of differentiating process—*how children acquired information,* content—*the types of information collected,* and product—*the way children expressed what they learned.*

A variety of technologies and instructional strategies were used in the following example:

As part of a 10-school collaborative project, young gifted students were provided with an opportunity to use interactive, real-time magnetic resonance imaging (MRI) to view developing chicken embryos while simultaneously incubating eggs in their classrooms. The students were taught to manipulate the MRI scanner, housed at the National Center for Supercomputing Applications, to study different views of the developing embryos. Students communicated using e-mail. They celebrated the chicks' birth with a birthday party. Technology use combined with the science curriculum offered an interdisciplinary approach that met several goals simultaneously: technology literacy, mathematics, and science. Language arts goals were met when the students wrote an article about the project.

THE LINK TO STUDENT ACHIEVEMENT

According to the U. S. Department of Education Web-Based Education Commission (2000), research and evaluation studies demonstrate that under certain conditions, school improvement programs that employ (Web-based) technology for teaching and learning yield positive results for students and teachers (Bialo & Sivin-Kachala, 1996; U. S. Department of Education, 2000). Does this mean that students are using the various technologies in ways that deepen and improve learning and, if so, how shall we measure the improvement? Early studies did find improvements in student scores on tests closely related to material covered in computer-assisted instructional packages (Kulik & Kulik, 1987; Kulik, 1994). But these studies did nothing to help us understand how technologies might or might not help support the kinds of sustained and substantial inquiry and analysis that we all want our children to be capable of or understand how to assess the influence of technology on student achievement scores (Wall, 2000).

Research published by the National Assessment of Educational Progress (NAEP) indicates that student achievement is higher when teachers are proficient in the use of computers, and when those computers are used for teaching higher level skills, simulations, and applications (*The Nation's Report Card: 2000 Science Assessment*). A 1997 Educational Testing Service (ETS) study (Coley, Cradler, & Engel, 1997) found that eighth-grade students made significant gains when they used computers for simulation, but scores decreased when computers were primarily used for drills. ETS found that eighth-grade mathematics students whose teachers had received technology training were about 13 weeks ahead in their mathematics skills when compared with students whose teachers had not received such training (Coley et al., 1997; Wenglinsky, 1998).

Gifted students often accelerate themselves, particularly in mathematics, and then wait for the rest of the class to catch up. In technology-enriched mathematics classes, the instructional pacing can be individualized to allow acceleration, depth, complexity, and the upper levels of Bloom's taxonomy: analysis, synthesis, and evaluation (http://chiron.valdosta.edu/whuitt/col/cogsys/bloom.html). Simulating physical and real-world events is one of technology's more powerful uses. It allows teachers to meet curriculum objectives for all students and is a perfect match for gifted students' conceptual and abstract thinking abilities. For example, the study of parametric equations and trigonometry can be connected with the study of projectile motion in physics. Gifted mathematics students can develop a spreadsheet to dynamically simulate projectile motion. Simulations allow teachers and students to explore mathematical and physical concepts in an open-ended environment and use higher-order thinking skills (analysis, synthesis, and evaluation) to analyze relationships.

PRACTICAL CLASSROOM SOLUTIONS

Research studies indicate that students learn best when (1) new ideas are connected to what they have experienced; (2) they are actively engaged in applying their knowledge to real-world problems; (3) learning is organized around clear, high goals; and (4) they can use their own interests and strengths as springboards for learning (Campbell, 2000; Resnick, 1987).

The World Wide Web offers all of the above by providing (1) access to experiential learning through interactive demonstrations, (2) access to higher-order thinking in problem finding and problem solving of real-world problems with real-world audiences, (3) more individual freedom to define goals and less pre-defined structure in reaching them, and (4) a sense of ownership for one's own strengths and talents. These characteristics also describe technology integration—the key to effective computer use—and represent highly able and gifted students' intellectual needs. The ability to obtain, organize, evaluate, and use information—skills that students will

use throughout their entire lifetime—can be taught whenever students use the World Wide Web for research, communication, problem finding, and problem solving. For example, using the Web site maintained for grades 5 to 8 as part of the Teachers Lab of the Annenberg/CPB Channel Project (http://www.learner.org/teacherslab/science/light/), students can learn about light as it relates to color, shadows, and perspective. The goal of the Teachers' Lab is to provide teachers with a deeper understanding of commonly taught math and science concepts. Each project includes a list of subjects covered by the lesson so that teachers can align the project with curriculum goals and standards. Each activity provides a scientific explanation of the results, modifications for lower grade levels, ideas for gifted extension activities, and links to other hands-on activities.

A recent publication by the International Society for Technology in Education (ISTE) provides a road map for educators to connect curriculum and technology and develop a plan for their own school districts. The ISTE publication, *The National Educational Technology Standards for Students* (NETS) (2000), is the outcome of a collaboration by 10 organizations to develop standards that can be used to facilitate effective use of technology to support PreK-12 education. The NETS standards can be used in conjunction with any of the content standards. Integrated with the standards, educators will find user-friendly lessons, activities, and instructional units that teachers can implement or modify. The Web site (http://cnets.iste.org) allows the public to search their database for lessons or units by title, subject, or grade.

"Teacher quality is the factor that matters most for student learning," note Darling-Hammond and Berry (1998). Therefore, professional development for teachers becomes the key issue in using technology to improve the quality of classroom learning (Rodriguez & Knuth, 2000). Professional development should include a variety of ways to implement the technology plan as well as some of the best practices research in integrating technology and curriculum.

The work of Bernie Dodge, an originator of WebQuests (http://edweb.sdsu.edu/webquest/webquest.html), has contributed significantly to this body of research. WebQuests, an inquiry-oriented activity designed by Dodge with Tom March at San Diego State University, makes maximum use of Web technology. Each WebQuest lists relevant Web sites, so students will spend less time searching for information and have less chance of being exposed to inappropriate material. WebQuests are designed as part of the curriculum and offer opportunities for all students—including those who are gifted—to work at a level of challenge.

The pedagogical structure of a WebQuest is not limited to the use of the Web and may complement other forms of media and instruction that do not require computers. Dodge (2001) offers a wealth of practical advice as well as 5 rules for designing WebQuests. His easy-to-remember acronym is FOCUS:

1. Find great sites.

2. Orchestrate your learners and resources.

3. Challenge your learners to think.

4. Use the medium.

5. Scaffold high expectations.

WebQuests are an ideal vehicle for gifted students because they are inquiry-based, open-ended, and align easily with curriculum goals that allow students to show mastery. Bernie Dodge's Web site (http://webquest.sdsu.edu/webquest.html) offers thousands of WebQuests that can be differentiated for students of all abilities. "Build your Own Sumerian City-State," for example, requires students to think about the following:

> We are tired of hunting and gathering and living a nomadic life style. The year is 3,500 B.C. and it is about time we all find a location to settle down and build ourselves a little community. Create a detailed design for a city-state.

The assignment's interdisciplinary nature requires that students think mathematically, scientifically, historically, and use language arts combined with computer software applications to show what they know. They employ all six levels of Bloom's taxonomy: knowledge, comprehension, application, analysis, synthesis, and evaluation. Students who complete their assignments with time to spare are given permission to use the templates on Filamentality (http://www.kn.pacbell.com/wired/fil/) to create a WebQuest that extends one key idea in the original assignment.

CAN WE MEET THE CHALLENGE?

Technology has brought the great libraries and museums of the world closer to the classroom than the cafeteria. Colorful, interactive, and up-to-date information, instantly accessible with a click of a mouse, has replaced heavy encyclopedias and pull-down maps. Students in otherwise ordinary classrooms literally anywhere can take fabulous "field trips" to far-off places, interact with other students in a classroom as big as the world, and see and hear the greatest assembly of scientists or speakers imaginable. Technology also permits students to express what they know to the world. Modest computer literacy and the use of the Web and multimedia products allow almost anyone to "publish" or demonstrate content mastery. "CD-ROM" and "hypermedia" are as familiar as the quill pen was 200 years ago. Children challenged by technology are learning to experiment, and are often teaching their parents this new "language" and the related skills. Time and distance have ceased to be barriers to either teaching or learning. Gifted students, their families, and their teachers—once isolated—now have access to people and resources throughout the world.

A 21st-century classroom is likely to look very different than the classroom we experienced. Imagine the following scene: A child prepares to present her report on "Snail Mail No More." But instead of pulling out a sheaf of papers, the student pulls out a small laptop and opens a computer file. A multicolored image with graphics and illustrations pops up on a screen so the class can follow along. The students make comments using an editing tool, while the teacher walks among the students holding her wireless keyboard and stopping to offer technical or academic support. Impossible, you may say. But this is an actual scene, and constitutes our present as well as our future.

CONCLUSION

Teachers lacking the facility to integrate technology with instruction have difficulty providing appropriate high-level learning activities for gifted— or any—students. Teachers can use process, content, and product to individualize the curriculum in mixed-ability classes and meet all students' learning needs. Technology integration supports instructional differentiation and benefits all students, especially gifted and intellectually advanced learners, by allowing them acceleration, depth, complexity, and the upper levels of Bloom's taxonomy: analysis, synthesis, and evaluation.

ISLLC QUESTIONS

Standard 1

- How can educational leaders use Berger's perspective on using technology to help gifted students meet their learning needs as leaders identify and remove barriers to the school vision?
- How can this awareness of technology supporting higher level learning for intellectually advanced students help the educational leader recognize and celebrate the contributions of all members of the school community?

Standard 2

- How can technology help educators maintain a culture of high expectations for all students, including those at the upper end of the intellectual spectrum?

- How can teachers use—or learn how to use—technology integration with teaching and learning to improve the instructional program, reflect principles of effective instruction, and provide students with varying learning needs multiple opportunities to learn?

Standard 3

- What does Berger suggest are the fiscal concerns associated with preparing teachers for effective technology integration, and how might educational leaders address these?

Standard 4

- Using the insights that Berger provides, how might educational leaders view the academic success of gifted and intellectually advanced students as a response to diverse community interests and needs, and mobilize community resources to advance their learning needs?

Standard 5

- How can educational leaders address the fairness issue concerning fully educating gifted and intellectually advanced learners?

Standard 6

- How is the educational leaders' advocacy for gifted learners within the school's learning program a response to the larger political, social, economic, legal, and cultural context?

REFERENCES

Archambault, F. X., Jr., Reis, S. M., & Westberg, K. L. (1990). The classroom practices study: What instructional practices are currently in use with gifted students in heterogeneously grouped classes? *Communicator: The Journal of the California Association for the Gifted, 20*(5), 30-31.

Archer, J. (1998, Nov-Dec). Technology counts. *Teacher, 10*(3), 18-19.

Becker, H. J. (1999, February). Internet use by teachers: Conditions of professional use and teacher-directed student use. In *Teaching, learning, & computing, 1998. A national survey of schools and teachers.* University of California, Irvine: Center for Research on Information Technology & Organizations. [Online] Available: http://www.crito.uci.edu/tlc/html/tlc_home.html

Bialo, E. R., & Sivin-Kachala, J. (1996). *The effectiveness of technology in schools: A summary of recent research.* Washington, DC: Software Publishers Association.

Blachere, K. (1999, December 29). *The decade in computing: A CNET special report*. [Online] Available: http://www.cnet.com/specialreports/0-6014-7-1494819.html

Campbell, D. (2000, January). Authentic assessment and authentic standards. *Phi Delta Kappan, 81*(5), 405-07.

Cattagni, A., & Farris, E. (2001, May). *Internet access in U. S. public schools and classrooms: 1994-2000*. Washington, DC: National Center for Education Statistics.[Online] Available: http://nces.ed.gov/pubsearch/pubsinfo.asp?pubid=2001071

Coley, R. J., Cradler, J., & Engel, P. K. (1997). *Computers and classrooms: The status of technology in U. S. schools*. Princeton: Educational Testing Service Policy Information Center. [Online] Available: ftp://etsis1.ets.org/pub/res/comp-clss.pdf

Conte, C. (2000). *The learning connection: Schools in the information age*. Washington, DC: The Benton Foundation. [Online] Available: http://www.benton.org/Library/Schools/

Darling-Hammond, L., & Berry, B. (1998, May 27). Investing in teaching. *Education Week on the Web, 17*(37), 48, 34. [Online] Available: http://www.edweek.org/ew/vol-17/37darlin.h17

Dodge, B. (2001). *FOCUS: Five rules for writing a great WebQuest*. Eugene, OR: International Society for Technology in Education. [Online] Available: http://www.iste.org/L&L/archive/vol28/no8/featuredarticle/dodge/index.html

Education Week on the Web (1998a). *Technology counts '98. Putting school technology to the test*. [Online] Available: http://www.edweek.org/sreports/tc/

Education Week on the Web (1998b). *Technology counts '98. Preparing students for a digital world*. [Online] Available: http://www.edweek.org/sreports/tc98/cs/cs3.htm

Education Week on the Web (2001). Technology counts 2001: The new divides. *Education Week, 20*(35). [Online] Available: http://www.edweek.org/sreports/tc01/tc2001_default.html

Finnan, C., St. John, E., McCarthy, J., & Slovacek, S. P. (Eds.). (1996). *Accelerated schools in action: Lessons from the field*. Thousand Oaks, CA: Corwin.

Glenna, T. K., & Melmed, A. (1996). *Fostering the use of educational technology: Elements of a national strategy*. A RAND Report. Santa Monica, CA: RAND [Online] Available: http://www.rand.org/publications/MR/MR682/contents.html

Kulik, J. A. (1994). Meta-analytic studies of findings on computer-based instruction. In E. L. Baker and H. F. O'Neil, Jr. (Eds.), *Technology assessment in education and training*. Hillsdale, NJ: Lawrence Erlbaum.

Kulik, J. A., & Kulik, C. C. (1987, July). Review of recent research literature on computer-based instruction. *Contemporary Educational Psychology, 12*(3), 222-30.

Lenhart, A., Simon, M., & Graziano, M. (2001). *The Internet and education: Findings of the Pew Internet & American Life Project*. Washington, DC: Pew Internet and American Life Project. [Online] Available: http://www.pewinternet.org/reports/toc.asp?Report=39

Mendels, P. (2000, January 5). Predictions for the top tech issues in schools. *New York Times*. [Online] Available: http://www.nytimes.com/library/tech/00/01/cyber/education/05education.html

The Milken Exchange & The International Society for Technology in Education. (1999, February 3). *Will new teachers be prepared to teach in a digital age? A national survey on information technology in teacher education.* [Online] Available: http://www.mff.org/publications/publications.taf?page=154

The national educational technology standards for students (2000). Eugene, OR: International Society for Technology in Education. (http://cnets.iste.org/).

The nation's report card: 2000 science assessment. Washington, DC: National Center for Education Statistics, National Assessment of Educational Progress. [Online] Available: http://nces.ed.gov/nationsreportcard/science/results/teachcomputer.asp

Newmann, F. M., Bryk, A. S., & Nagaoka, J. K., (2001, January). *Authentic intellectual work and standardized tests: Conflict or coexistence?* Chicago: Consortium on Chicago School Research. [Online] Available: http://www.consortium-chicago.org/publications/p0az2.html

Resnick, L. B. (1987). *Education and learning to think.* Washington, DC: National Academy.

Rodriguez, G., & Knuth, R. (2000). *Critical issue: Providing professional development for effective technology use.* Naperville, IL: North Central Regional Educational Laboratory. [Online] Available: http://www.ncrel.org/sdrs/areas/issues/methods/technlgy/te1000.htm

Rowand, C. (2000, April). *Teacher use of computers and the Internet in public schools.* [Stats in Brief.] Washington, DC: National Center for Education Statistics. [Online] Available: http://nces.ed.gov/pubs2000/2000090.pdf.

Schacter, J. (1999). *The impact of education technology on student achievement: What the most current research has to say.* Santa Monica, CA: Milken Exchange on Education Technology, Milken Family Foundation. (Web site: http://www.milkenexchange.org)

U. S. Department of Education. (1993). *Using technology to support education reform.* Washington, DC: U. S. Government Printing Office. [Online] Available: http://www.ed.gov/pubs/EdReformStudies/TechReforms/title.html

U. S. Department of Education. (1996). *Getting America's students ready for the 21st century: Meeting the technology literacy challenge.* A Report to the Nation on Technology and Education. [Online] Available: http://www.ed.gov/Technology/Plan/NatTechPlan/

U. S. Department of Education. (2000). *The secretary's conference on educational technology 2000 white papers.* [Proceedings]. [Online] Available: http://www.ed.gov/Technology/techconf/2000/white_papers.html.

U. S. Department of Education, Web-Based Education Commission. (2000, December). *The power of the Internet for learning: Moving from promise to practice.* Report of the Web-Based Education Commission to the President and the Congress of the United States. Washington, DC: Office of Policy, Planning, and Innovation. [Online] Available: http://interact.hpcnet.org/webcommission/index.htm

Wall, J. E. (2000). *Technology-delivered assessment: Guidelines for educators traveling the technology highway.* Greensboro, NC: ERIC Clearinghouse on Counseling and Student Services ERIC/CASS Document # ED446327. [Online] Available: http://www.ed.gov/databases/ERIC_Digests/ed446327.html

Wenglinsky, H. (1998). *Does it compute? The relationship between educational technology and student achievement in mathematics.* Princeton, NJ: Educational Testing Service. [Online] Available: http://www.ets.org/research/pic

Williams, C. (Feb. 15, 2000). *Internet access in U. S. public schools and classrooms: 1994-1999.* Washington, DC: National Center for Education Statistics. [Online] Available: http://nces.ed.gov/pubs2000/2000086.pdf

Yero, J. L. (2002). *Teaching in mind: How teacher thinking shapes education.* Hamilton, MT: MindFlight.

Lessons Learned

Over the past two decades, we have enacted a national set of academic reforms designed to ensure higher student performance and greater professional accountability. Strong political influences and high accountability also impact special education as federal legislation, monies, case law, and state and local guidelines clearly govern who becomes eligible for particular services and the types of supports available to aid student learning. In its broadest sense, this student population includes gifted, talented, special needs, English language learners, and every other student in the general education cohort who could benefit from additional, personalized help to maximize learning.

As instructional leaders, principals must focus on balancing both students' unique and individual learning needs while maintaining group accountability for achievement. Principals must reconcile the outwardly competing goals of individualizing learning while providing standardized outcomes. Whatever the formal label or identification, all students benefit from tailoring the academic program and instructional practices to fit their unique learning styles, interests, goals, and capacities. All must meet the academic expectations set by the state, community, and local school, yet each can accomplish this through personalized means if the school culture and practice support this.

To meet individual students' learning needs within whole-school accountability, principals must draw deeply on their roles as change agents and instructional leaders in their work with faculty, students, and parents. The school community must increase awareness and value for differentiated approaches to meeting high standards. The school community must create a welcoming place for students with very different learning approaches and even varying physical needs at all ends of the cognitive and talent spectrum. Leadership for meeting individual learners' needs involves collaborative problem solving and negotiating, careful listening, a full understanding of the law and local guidelines, and firsthand knowledge of each student as a person and as a learner. Moreover, working to best address students' unique educational styles means developing skills to work effectively with outside experts, agencies, and advocates.

The growing diversity in student populations and the increasing emphasis on accountability means that principals must lead their schools to new ways of improving instructional delivery. Even though all students are expected to master common high standards for content and skills, "one-size instruction or curriculum" does not fit all. Designing an effective meld of teaching, curriculum, and technology can help all children learn to high levels and this is *the* significant leadership challenge for principals.

Part V

Accountability

20

High-Stakes Testing

Ronald S. Brandt

Overview

Testing is an essential part of the educational process. Today's high-stakes testing, however, provides a political as well as educational environment that makes often contradictory demands on principals. As public confidence in public education eroded after World War II, politicians and taxpayers wanted better ways to document schools' accomplishments. Standardized tests came to be viewed as indicators of public school quality rather than as gauges for individual students' achievement. Leadership for standards-based education requires that principals' first priority is to assure that all students are learning what is required for test success. Next, principals need to remember—and to help the school community remember—that not all important educational ends can be measured in conventional ways, and standardized test results cannot be full measures of a school's quality.

TESTING

Of all the issues facing principals in today's political climate, one of the most demanding is testing. Just a few years ago, most tests were prepared by teachers who used them to make judgments about their own students.

Standardized tests were administered from time to time, but the results were intended mostly to help teachers and parents know how their students compared with a wider sample. In the last decade, that has changed dramatically. Now the tests that really matter are designed by anonymous outsiders, and the scores on those tests, published for all to see, affect the future not only of individual students but of the school itself and the educators who work there.

Regardless of personal views, principals *must* attend to external tests and their consequences, especially if their school serves large numbers of needy students. Advice will come from many sources. Parents and superiors will expect schools to do whatever it takes to raise scores. Principals should respond to these pressures in ways that may sometimes feel contradictory. The first responsibility is to make sure that all students are learning what is required. But school leaders also need to keep reminding all concerned—including teachers, parents, and political leaders—to keep their priorities straight.

Why Testing?

Today's emphasis on testing is understandable and probably unavoidable. Tests have been around as long as there has been formal schooling, but until recently, educators assumed that it was individual students, not teachers or schools, who were being evaluated. As public confidence in public education gradually eroded following World War II, observers began to use test results differently. For example, the College Board's SAT, originally designed to gauge individual students' "aptitude" for college-level work, was reinterpreted—however inaccurately—as an indicator of the secondary schools' quality.

Even if trust in public education had not been undermined by periodic reports of low achievement, current conditions would probably have led politicians and taxpayers to demand better documentation of school accomplishments. Technological developments in recent decades—especially machine scoring of multiple-choice tests and the capability to assemble and analyze data in various ways—give the impression that the complexity of schools can be captured in a few simple statistics. We monitor the numbers for almost everything—the stock market, sports, even the quality of wine—why not schools? So, like it or not, test scores will continue to be a part of our professional lives.

EFFECTS ON TEACHING AND LEARNING

Testing is an essential part of the educational process. Even relatively poor tests get people's attention and focus their efforts. If the tests are tied to standards, teachers know what they must teach and students know what they're supposed to learn. If the tests are "high-stakes"—if they have important consequences—students will be more likely to take them seriously and prepare for them. These side benefits apply even when the tests themselves are less than perfect. But, of course, tests that are truly valid are especially valuable because of the useful information they provide about student capabilities.

Despite these benefits, many leading educators criticize testing, not because they fail to appreciate these virtues, but because they understand how mistaken some current practices are. Specifically, when some goals of education are evaluated and others ignored, the result may be overemphasis on whatever is being tested. Many of today's state testing programs depend too much on machine-scored, "selected response" test items because they are efficient and economical. Such items are certainly useful for particular purposes, but they cannot accurately measure some of the most important aims of education. If scores on such tests are treated as a full measure of school quality, teachers may focus their efforts on whatever the tests cover. And if the tests are given undue importance, educators frantic to produce higher scores may be tempted to engage in unprofessional or even unethical behavior.

Mandatory tests may also contribute to undesirable standardization. Of course, some uniformity is necessary. Some goals of education should probably be the same everywhere: All students should learn to read and write; they need basic knowledge of mathematics, science, and history. But ask people *exactly* what every student should know and be able to do in even such basic subjects, and the answers are sure to be different. Some of the most heated school wars in recent years have been over how mathematics, reading, and history should be taught. When that is the case, officials can use tests to enforce conformity with their personal views.

Standards-Based Education

These issues are currently prominent in many state standards programs. As interpreted by states and school systems, standards-based education tends to take two forms. The approach I call *conventional* involves identifying a relatively large number of what were formerly known as *instructional objectives* but are now called *content standards*. After studying a body of content related to these objectives, students take a paper-and-pencil test composed of items sampling all the knowledge and skills that might have been assessed. Officials set a "cut score" that specifies the percentage of items students must get right to pass. Along with the nature of the items, the cut score determines the difficulty of passing the test, so the higher the cut score, the higher your school's standards. The problem is that no matter how high the cut score, students who pass the test have not shown mastery of any particular standards.

The approach I describe as more *performance-oriented* involves the use of performance tasks and scoring criteria commonly called *rubrics*. From this perspective, *standards* describe the ability to perform a fairly complex task. Referring to examples of excellent performance and specific scoring criteria (rubrics), students are expected to *do* what the standard calls for.

Both these approaches may be described as "standards-based," but they are very different. Whereas conventional assessment is like the multiple-choice test of basic knowledge a person must take to get a driver's license, performance assessment is like a behind-the-wheel test of actual driving ability. Moreover, the conventional approach uses practices inherited from systems designed historically for sorting and selecting students rather than for meeting individual differences.

LEADERSHIP FOR STANDARDS-BASED EDUCATION

At this point, the state where you work may be committed to the conventional approach. Unfortunately, most are. If that is the case, the major part of principals' efforts must be devoted to helping teachers and students meet the expectations placed on them. Naturally, the challenge is greatest in schools serving large numbers of students from low-income families, those who ordinarily have the most trouble learning. Researchers have repeatedly established what leaders of such schools do to achieve high scores. First, leaders must demonstrate high expectations and get others, especially teachers, to raise their sights as well. The motto must be "no excuses," and everyone has to mean it. Even though many factors make life difficult for students, educators must see students as capable nonetheless, and insist that obstacles be overcome.

Part of overcoming obstacles is doing whatever it takes to get students in condition to learn. It may seem "unprofessional," but some principals actually have a washing machine to clean students' clothes. They make sure that students who need glasses get them, and so on. Principals of successful schools also build a social climate that encourages learning. Genuine parent involvement is an essential part of such a long-term social development effort.

Along with taking steps to create desirable conditions for learning, principals also need to attend to more technical matters, one relatively simple and the other complex and demanding. The first is to make sure that students are familiar and reasonably comfortable with testing protocols, because the testing situation itself should not hamper students' ability to score well. In some schools, this suggestion is hardly necessary; students already spend too much time learning test-taking skills, time that could be used for more productive activities. If that is the case, staff members need to restrict such efforts to reasonable levels.

The more demanding responsibility is to strive continually for alignment of the school's curriculum, instruction, and assessment. While this, too, should be obvious, researchers have found that low-scoring schools often do not teach everything they are supposed to and that their tests do not always assess what they teach. Conversely, high-scoring schools are invariably found to have devoted a great deal of attention to alignment.

Teachers need to know as clearly as possible what will be covered on required tests. They need to review curriculum documents and student learning materials to see how well they match the test content. Most importantly, their day-to-day planning and instruction must focus on what will be tested, even if that isn't quite what official standards call for. The role of instructional leader requires continually consulting with teachers as they pursue the elusive goal of perfect alignment.

The Challenge of Professional Leadership

I hinted earlier that all this is not enough. The fact is that, demanding as these tasks are, professional leadership involves more than the heedless pursuit of whatever outside officials have decided will be tested. The leader's responsibility is to guide staff members, with appropriate involvement of parents and community, as they make decisions about how the children in their trust will be educated. The adults who work directly with children must think about what young people need to learn, what experiences might help them learn it, and how the adults will know whether it has been learned. These classic curriculum questions are central to the role of the professional educator, and though they are hard to answer, they are also intellectually exciting, especially at this time of great social change.

The principal's challenge, then, is to maintain an appropriate balance between two extremes, either of which would be unacceptable. On one hand, be sure teachers meet the demands inherent in required tests—but also exhibit courage and professional judgment by resisting pressures to equate learning with test scores. On the other hand, leaders must encourage teacher creativity and enthusiasm but courteously question activities whose educational purpose seems unclear. Because what is best for students may sometimes seem incompatible with what the state requires, finding the right balance will frequently be difficult. That, in brief, is also a test—a test of educational leadership.

CONCLUSION

High-stakes testing has both political and educational ramifications. The principal's challenge as the instructional leader is to balance the need to help teachers prepare each student to pass the high-stakes tests and also to resist the pressure to equate the test scores with learning. Principal leadership requires attention to what is the best learning for students along with helping all students meet the standard.

ISLLC QUESTIONS

Standard 1

- According to Brandt, what is the leadership role in promoting the success of all students by facilitating the development, articulation, implementation, and stewardship of a vision of learning (and testing that learning) that is shared and supported by the school community?

Standard 4

- How would Brandt suggest school leaders promote the success of all students by collaborating with families and community members, responding to diverse community interests and needs, and mobilizing community resources?

Standard 5

- How does Brandt suggest testing be approached by the educational leader who promotes the success of all students by acting with integrity, fairness, and in an ethical manner?

Standard 6

- How does Brandt suggest the educational leader promote the success of all students in testing by understanding, responding to, and influencing the larger political, social, economic, legal, and cultural contexts?

21

Are Standards the Answer?

Linda Nathan

Overview

In a standards-based era, educators ask, How much of a student's grade should reflect whether his or her work has met an objective standard and how much should indicate how far that student has developed? How do we avoid measuring and sorting students by standardized tests when performance measures may show a fuller and more accurate picture of the student's real achievement? Boston Arts Academy has built a culture of high expectation, maximum support, and tolerance for different ways of exhibiting knowledge. Defining standards for arts and academics has been a rigorous process involving many outsiders from higher education, other secondary schools, and professionals from other fields to review educators' work and students' work. They agreed that the specific curriculum design mattered less than whether students were learning how to analyze, synthesize, draw conclusions, and communicate effectively with evidence. As a result, educators here assign two grades to student work: one for content and another for process, grading students on their individual growth in addition to how well they meet a defined, baseline standard. Through both arts and academic classes, teachers and students use a "RICO" model (refine, invent, connect, own) to assess student work. At this school, students achieve high standards because defining and working toward these standards has become the learning process' central focus.

Working with Teddy in writing class was never easy or fun. We always tried to put Teddy into a small group of students or to work one-on-one with a teacher. Even so, he resisted writing. He resisted almost as sport, but with such passion that it was painful to watch. At times he would resort to banging his head on the desk, moaning in a way that distracted everyone, "I can't write. I have nothing to write. This is soooo boring!"

The sad part of all this is that Teddy is a fairly skilled student. He is excellent in math, memorizes easily, loves historical facts, but just hates writing. He is a devoted music student. No writing assignment all year engaged him. He hated writing about himself in our first-term autobiography assignment. The second-term assignment of writing a research paper on an artist of the student's choice was equally painful; and third term's compare-and-contrast essay was torture. Teddy was a difficult student to teach. I never felt that I could engage him—neither one-on-one, nor in a small group. He used all his energy to resist enjoying even the most enjoyable writing activities.

Sadly, as a veteran teacher, I had to admit that I wasn't going to make headway with Teddy that year. I couldn't sacrifice everyone else in the class to Teddy's refusal to participate. Although we tried as often as possible to have Teddy working one-on-one, many days we just let him be. We needed a break. We needed to teach the rest of the class. Some days, if his refusals to write became too boisterous and we couldn't isolate him one-on-one, we had to ask him to leave. It was far from the ideal arrangement.

There were family conferences; there were individual conferences; there were conferences with our counselor; there were learning contracts; there were behavioral contracts. Not much progress was made. Teddy hated to write. Writing class was about writing.

One day I watched him in his music class. It was a listening class; students wrote their observations about the music into their journals and then discussed their comments together. Teddy participated in the discussions. However, with some relief, I noticed that he didn't write in this class either. He participated in the discussions, but by the end of the class, he had only written a line or two in his journal.

In May, at Teddy's recital evening, I watched intently as he walked onto the stage with his ensemble of eight other guitarists. His hair was combed. He was dressed neatly. I couldn't be sure that this was the same boy I taught in writing class. Usually, Teddy donned the torn-and-patched jean look with the high boots, jean jacket, and chains, if the security personnel hadn't confiscated them. I wouldn't have described him as dirty, but he certainly was never trying to look clean or well-dressed. When Teddy entered the stage of the Berklee College of Music recital hall, he looked like a handsome grown man. I did a double take. Then, the music started. I was embarrassed at the way I kept staring at Teddy. He seemed possessed by the music, transported to another place. He kept time beautifully with his ensemble. When he soloed, his fingers nimbly plucked the strings, and his chord changes seemed effortless. The piece ended, and I noticed that his entire family was there—grandparents, parents, sister—all clapping loudly. I wanted to give Teddy a standing ovation. I loved seeing him so engaged, seeing the music work its magic. I felt that Teddy had given me a great gift as a teacher. I would have another year to figure out how to engage him in writing. I had seen him engage. I knew it was possible—completely possible. Now, we would figure out together how to make writing flow like music.

Evaluating students is one of the hardest issues we face at Boston Arts Academy (BAA). How much should a student's grade reflect whether his or her work meets an objective standard? How much should it reflect how far that student has developed? Put another way, how de we balance content against process? How do we find the courage to keep the "richness" of teaching in the face of a national mania intent on measuring and sorting children by standardized tests? By any such test, Teddy would be marked a failure, "not worthy of a high school diploma." Our current high-stakes testing program in Massachusetts would probably have added Teddy to the dropout statistics. Nevertheless, at the Boston Arts Academy, Teddy is one of many such teaching challenges.

Our 400 urban high school students come from diverse academic backgrounds. Some come from rigorous elementary and middle schools where they were required to read extensively, take on complex projects, and comprehend challenging math problems and ideas. Others arrived with much more limited experience. They had been given basic math worksheets and been drilled on fractions, percentages, and decimals, but were never taught probability or statistics.

When our students present an exhibition, we take into account how their prior schooling prepared them. At the same time, we believe in high standards and holding all students to them. In our faculty discussions, we have considered that one possible solution is to give students two grades: one for process and one for content.

In some ways, balancing these two ideas is easier in our arts classrooms. Learning in the arts naturally integrates process with content. We understand that some students have had less experience than others in drawing, dancing, or acting. It is not so hard, for example, to combine students with differing levels of acting in one ninth-grade acting class. We observe students over the year and grade them on their individual growth as much as on meeting a defined standard. Some dance students have a more natural physical ability. We ask ourselves, Does the student with a more natural "turn out" receive a higher grade than a student who will never be so "turned out"? We seem to grapple with this kind of situation more easily in the arts classroom than in an academic arena, and we never think to have these students in different classes. They can learn from each other, and "turn out" isn't everything!

Making a heterogeneous classroom work is harder in math, Spanish, or science. Even when students are grouped by their level of skill and experience, there is a wide range of abilities in each class. We are very aware of our need as educators to learn more about teaching in such classrooms. Some students may be required to read more books, or write more papers; others may need to work on one theme and one text for the semester. Our goal is to tailor each student's work to his or her current capacity—to set the bar high, but not out of reach. Nevertheless, we must be clear with students, parents, and the public that there is a baseline or minimum standard in subject areas and that our students must reach that benchmark.

When the Boston Arts Academy opened its doors, our first step in defining benchmarks or standards was to understand what they were. Unfortunately, there is still a great deal of disagreement among national, state, and district-level organizations about what minimum competency looks like in the various arts and academic domains. If asked, 50 science educators deciding the essential areas to cover in high school biology, for example, would debate the issue. Nevertheless, we combed through the multitude of documents, and used our own strong backgrounds as educators as well as our knowledge of our local community and our students, to begin articulating what we thought our graduates should know and be able to do. Next, we had to communicate those standards to parents, students, and the public. This required us to spell out, in a readable way, our *outcomes*. What did we want students to know and be able to do after four, or sometimes five, years with us? What were the specific criteria that students needed to achieve? This is the language of rubrics. What were process outcomes, what were skill outcomes, and what were content outcomes? Most importantly, how would we communicate those criteria to our students and their parents? We knew that it was critical to develop many of our rubrics with the help of our students. If they didn't understand all the components that comprised an excellent research paper, then how could they ever strive to write one? Finally, did others, outside of BAA, agree with our thinking?

We invited a group of outsiders from higher education, other secondary schools, and other fields to review our work and the work of our students. Was what we were asking of students the "right" stuff? For example, in science, we were particularly interested in listening to college teachers respond to our curriculum design and sequence. They assured us that the most important thing to teach was critical thinking, and whether we did that through an integrated science curriculum or a more sequenced approach (biology, chemistry, physics) mattered less than whether students could analyze, synthesize, draw conclusions, and communicate effectively with evidence. Then, we asked if our grading criteria were rigorous enough. How did our students' work compare to the exemplars? Finally, what did it mean when we just couldn't teach a student? Where were we going wrong? Were we scaffolding our work enough for our most vulnerable students? Was it all right if over one-third of our students didn't pass our Humanities 3 benchmark? What did we need to do differently? These are just some of the questions we continue to ask. What if students weren't learning because of behavioral or attitudinal issues? Could we just say, "I'm a teacher. I don't deal with attitude"? Hopefully, students like Teddy helped us realize that the "I won't learn from you" attitude can be slowly and carefully challenged and changed.

I believe that we have been successful at BAA in helping students achieve high standards because we have made the centerpiece of our school be the process of defining those standards and working toward achieving them. How do we do this?

First of all, as educators we examine and grade student work together. We judge science projects together. We judge ballet skills together. We examine whether a student has true commitment to her character in a play. We use the Habits of the Graduate, or RICO (Refine, Invent, Connect, Own) as we call it, to assess whether our students truly "own" their work, can "connect" it to other areas, can "refine" their work, and, finally and most importantly, whether they are "inventive." Although these may sound like just words to the layperson's ears, it took 18 months of very arduous work to define what those terms meant in all of our classrooms. Our habits involve a series of questions. *Refine:* What tools do I need? Have I demonstrated good craftsmanship? What are the strengths and weaknesses? *Invent:* What is my passion and how do I use it in my work? Do I take risks and push myself? *Connect:* Who is the audience and how do I connect the work to the audience? How could I interpret or analyze this work? *Own:* How does this work affect others? How do I find the drive to go on?

Throughout our arts and academic classes, students demonstrate the habits of RICO. The capstone experience is the Senior Project. In this project, students write a proposal for a specific project that they will carry out, addressing a community need that has academic and artistic integrity. They must receive a Proficient score on their grant proposal in order to graduate, and some students are actually funded to enact their proposal. Like many working artists, we require our students to think critically about how to use their art, their gift, and their passion to improve our communities. Their work, like working artists, is judged by outside panelists in our Senior Project Big Night. All juniors are required to attend so that they begin to develop similar critical habits.

This is just one of our "benchmark" experiences. Do all students make the grade the first time? No. Is there shame about needing to continuously refine the work? No. Of course, some feel frustration. Nevertheless, we try to instill in our seniors that high school is not like a timed test or a race. Some skills may take longer to achieve. Not everyone works at the exact same pace.

This culture of high expectation, maximum support, and tolerance for different ways of exhibiting knowledge has paid off. In our first graduating class (2001) of 53 seniors, 49 graduated in June, and of those, 46 are going on to college and 3 are going on to a computer training program; 2 are graduating in August, and 2 are graduating next year. Slowly, we are convincing our urban young people that achievement at high levels is possible with appropriate support.

Teddy has taught me a great deal about how success generates success. High standards, a culture of high expectations, and tremendous teacher support are vital. It is sobering to realize that in an era of high-stakes testing, Teddy would be another dropout statistic. Boston Arts Academy has proved that despite tremendous odds, Teddy and countless others can succeed in school and society.

CONCLUSION

Standards need to include both content and process for a complete picture of student achievement. Critical thinking skills applied at high levels to a variety of contents are the primary goals. Clear high standards for content and performance, a culture of high expectations offered with maximum support for students' efforts, flexible time frames for meeting these, and acceptance of varied ways of demonstrating knowledge produces much student success.

ISLLC QUESTIONS

Standard 1

- How does this school promote a shared vision of learning where contributions of all school members are recognized and celebrated?
- How are the barriers to the school's vision identified and removed?

Standard 2

- How does this school maintain a culture of high expectations?
- How does this school practice its understanding of human growth and development?
- How did this school gather more data from stakeholders before making final decisions about its instructional program?

Standard 4

- How does the school community collaborate to promote student success?
- How does the school mobilize community resources to promote student learning?
- To what extent does the school build family partnerships to support learning and address instructional issues?

Standard 6

- How does this school understand, respond to, and influence the larger political, social, economic, legal, and cultural context?

22

Critical Issues in School Law

Jennifer A. Sughrue
M. David Alexander

Overview

Laws in various forums influence all aspects of public school setting. Principals must create an educational environment that collectively serves all students and staff while addressing their individual rights and needs. Often these dual goals conflict. School leaders best serve their schools' interests if they stay current with changes in the law, appropriately modify and follow written policies, and act with reasoned judgment. Emerging issues that impact school principals include search and seizure policies related to drugs and weapons in school; First Amendment decisions regarding prayer, minute of silence, and equal access in schools; and sexual harassment. The authors describe case law findings that can guide principals' actions in these areas.

Constitutional, statutory, and case law are dynamic forces that govern every aspect of public education. The variation in and the intensity of their impact often shift, requiring school boards and superintendents to actively seek to stay abreast of changes in the law or in their application to school districts.

At the school building level, legal issues tend to take on a personal tone. Principals are faced with creating an educational environment that collectively serves all students and staff while addressing their individual rights and needs. Often these dual goals come into conflict, sometimes resulting in costly litigation that is also time-consuming and may be perceived negatively by the community. Equally exasperating are the unanticipated events, both external and internal, that lead to reactive policies and practices. If not well conceived, these policies and practices too can generate court challenges.

School leaders best serve the interests of their schools if they stay current with changes in the law, appropriately modify and follow written policies, and act with reasoned judgment. To assist principals in that endeavor, the authors offer several current legal issues for review and suggestions for improving policy and practice. The topics were chosen because of the magnitude of recent case law on the subjects, because they are viewed as emerging issues of some interest, and because they have applicability to schools nationally. To be discussed are search and seizure policies; First Amendment decisions regarding prayer, minute of silence, and equal access in schools; and sexual harassment.

KEEPING DRUGS AND WEAPONS OUT OF SCHOOLS

Several state and federal statutes mandating drug-free and weapon-free schools have been enacted to focus educational administrators' attention on safety and security in the teaching and learning environment. However, in the implementation of these laws, usually through search and seizure protocols and drug testing policies, constitutional challenges arise under the Fourth Amendment.[1] Individuals claim their right to privacy is compromised by these practices and petition the courts to issue injunctions to stop them. There is a considerable volume of case law on the subject, giving substantial guidance to school leaders on the subject of search and seizure and drug testing.

Individual Student Searches

Generally, the courts have given wide latitude to state and school district efforts to thwart problems with drugs and violence in schools. Due to their "substantial interest . . . in maintaining discipline in the classroom and on school grounds,"[2] school officials need only reasonable suspicion to initiate a search of a particular student's locker, book bag, car, or even his or her person.[3]

Other parameters for searches of individual students exist, however. The search must be *justified at inception*; that is, there must be facts or circumstances that lead school officials to believe that a particular student has violated, is violating, or will violate school rules.

This requirement interfaces with another judicial standard, *individualized suspicion*. School officials cannot embark on schoolwide searches of students or their possessions to uncover evidence that leads to identifying someone guilty of a school infraction. Searching students must be tied to a reasonable suspicion that those students *specifically* are involved with breaking school rules.

Lastly, the *scope of the search* is of interest to courts. There must be a nexus between the intrusiveness of the search and the seriousness of the offense. A constitutional search is one in which "the measures adopted are reasonably related to the objectives of the search and not excessively intrusive in light of the age and sex of the student and the nature of the infraction."[4] In other words, searching the locker of a student who is suspected of stealing a wallet may be viewed as reasonable, whereas strip searching a student for a few missing dollars may not.

Random Searches

Random searches differ from individualized searches in that they do not require particularized suspicion. Rather, they involve large numbers of students selected randomly and subjected to searches, although the school officials have no reason to believe any of them is in possession of drugs or weapons. Periodic random searches are deemed appropriate where there is a real concern about safety in the school.

Metal detectors and sniffer dogs have become popular tools for random searches. Generally, the courts have looked favorably on metal detector and canine searches if the searches are related to safety concerns in the school and if the school follows procedures that provide notice, ensure random selection, and are not overly intrusive.

Metal detectors can be used to screen all students entering a school, if the administrators deem it necessary to maintaining a safe school. Such was the case in a high school in New York City.[5] Pursuant to a Board of Education policy, a special unit of police set up a scanning post in the lobby of the school. All students were subjected to scanning. However, if lines of students became too long, there were procedures for randomly selecting students. One such search produced a student carrying a switchblade for which she was then prosecuted. In turning down the student's petition to suppress the evidence, the court found the nature of the search reasonably related to the governmental objective of ridding the school of weapons without being unnecessarily intrusive.

Canine searches are more problematic, as reflected in the varying court opinions.[6] Using dogs to sniff lockers, book bags, and cars is usually viewed as constitutional under the standards of review for both random and individualized searches. However, some courts have judged canine searches of a student as more intrusive and not appropriate for random searches. As one court put it, "[T]he intrusion on dignity and personal security that goes with the type of canine inspection of the student's person . . . cannot be justified by the need to prevent abuse of drugs and alcohol when there is no individualized suspicion."[7] Principals would be wise not to engage dogs in random searches of students.

Strip Searches

There is little debate that strip searches are very intrusive and, therefore, require a high level of reasonable suspicion and a convincing government interest in the outcome. For this reason, strip searches of students have been upheld by the courts only when it was suspected that those students were concealing drugs, thereby creating a threat to the safety of other students.

Reasonable suspicion that a student is carrying drugs must come from reliable sources before school officials proceed with a strip search. Strip searches have been ruled constitutional in instances where reasonable suspicion was based on information from school staff and reliable students, on observable bulges in clothes, or on the suspicious behavior of students.

Dog alerts do not establish reasonable suspicion to strip search a student. Such was the conclusion of the Seventh Circuit Court of Appeals in a case involving junior high school students.[8] The primary plaintiff was a thirteen-year-old girl who was strip searched when, in the course of a schoolwide search, a drug-sniffing dog was alerted to her. In a scathing reprimand, the justices noted that it does not require a constitutional scholar to conclude that a nude search of a thirteen-year-old child is an invasion of constitutional rights of some magnitude. More than that, it is a violation of every known principle of human decency. Apart from any constitutional readings and rulings, simple common sense would indicate that the conduct of the school officials in permitting such a nude search was not only unlawful but outrageous under "settled indisputable principles of law."[9]

Likewise, the courts do not look favorably upon the use of strip searches to recover stolen money or insignificant contraband. For example, in *Oliver v. McClung*[10] and more recently, *Thomas ex rel. Thomas v. Roberts*,[11] groups of students were strip searched for small amounts of missing money. In both cases, the courts held that there was no strong government interest, such as recovering drugs, to conclude the searches were reasonable.

Drug Testing Students

There is increasing use of drug testing (urinalysis) as a means of detecting and deterring drug use in schools. The U.S. Supreme Court has said that the state has a "special responsibility of care and direction"[12] for their students and, in the current environment of school violence and drug use, "special needs . . . exist in the public school context"[13] that require flexibility in how school officials choose to combat these problems. This reasoning, coupled with the Court's belief that students have a diminished expectation of privacy, has supported the constitutionality of drug testing policies, depending on the population under scrutiny and the procedures followed.

The right to randomly drug test student athletes was upheld by the U.S. Supreme Court in 1995.[14] Among the reasons given for upholding the testing policy, it was argued that students who participate in sports have a lesser expectation of privacy due to the nature of the activities associated with athletics. It was also noted that sports are extracurricular activities, and students can choose not to participate if they disagree with the policy.

Since that ruling, some school districts have expanded their random drug testing programs to include students in all extracurricular activities and, in a few instances, to include all students, period. Circuit courts have differed in their rulings on the subject. However, certiorari was recently granted to a defendant school district in Oklahoma whose suspicionless drug-testing program covering all extracurricular activities was struck down by the Tenth Circuit.[15] The U.S. Supreme heard the case and ruled in *Board of Education v. Early* that drug testing could be expanded to students in all extracurricular activities.

Drug Testing School Employees

Teachers, administrators, and other school personnel can be subjected to drug and alcohol screening, too. Such was the conclusion in a 1998 case in the Sixth Circuit.[16] Relying on the judicial logic in *Skinner*,[17] *Von Raab*,[18] *Chandler*,[19] and *Vernonia*,[20] the justices agreed with the school district that teachers and administrators hold "safety-sensitive" positions in schools and therefore can be subjected to urinalysis or blood tests under certain circumstances.

The policy under the court's review had two categories of testing: *suspicionless testing* for persons who had been offered a job but had not yet begun to work, and *reasonable suspicion drug and alcohol testing* for all school employees. The first part of the testing program required individuals who accepted new positions or who asked for transfers to submit to drug tests. By policy definition, these individuals included principals, assistant principals, teachers (including substitutes and aides), school secretaries, and school bus drivers. The second component of the testing program required individual school employees who were reasonably suspected of being under the influence of illegal drugs or alcohol to submit to screening. Employees refusing to do so were charged with insubordination and were subject to disciplinary action.

Both sections of the policy were held to be constitutional under the Fourth Amendment. The court justified its findings by noting that school employees work in a heavily regulated industry and, like students, have a diminished expectation of privacy. The justices believed the reasoning of the school district to be sound, the policy to be sufficiently narrow in scope, and the procedures properly structured to give an accurate result and to protect confidentiality.[21]

Policy and Practice

Review of the case law on school search and seizure policies offers several lessons to school leaders. In the case of individual student searches, school officials can operate under the lesser standard of reasonable suspicion rather than probable cause. However, reasonable suspicion must come from reliable information, such as dependable teachers and students or observed bulges in clothing or student behavior. In the event that school officials do proceed, the scope of the search must be appropriate to the nature of the infraction and the age and sex of the child. For example, when a female student is involved, it is appropriate that a female police officer conduct the search.

A strip search is considered highly intrusive. Its use should be limited to reasonable suspicion that a particular student is carrying drugs and therefore creating a safety threat in the school. Strip searches cannot be used for nonthreatening situations such as missing money. A dog alert does not indicate sufficient reasonable suspicion to strip search a student.

Random searches using school personnel, metal detectors, and dogs are considered reasonable if the searches are related to safety concerns in the school and if the school follows procedures that provide notice, ensure random selection, and are not overly intrusive. Canine searches should be limited to lockers, book bags, and cars.

Suspicionless drug testing (urinalysis) of students involved in extracurricular sports is constitutional. However, procedures for collecting urine samples must ensure minimal intrusion on the students' privacy. The testing protocols must be narrowly focused and standardized: they must test only for the presence of certain illegal drugs and must not vary with individual students. Whether such a program can be expanded to other extracurricular activities is currently under review by the U.S. Supreme Court.

School personnel can be subject to drug and alcohol testing if there is a well-tailored policy that clearly defines the circumstances under which such testing can be required and specifies the procedures to be followed. Those circumstances include drug testing candidates for certain positions after they have been offered a job but prior to assuming it, and include drug and alcohol screening of any school employee based on reasonable suspicion. Drug screening procedures must provide for retesting in the case of a positive result and must contain safeguards to ensure confidentiality of personnel records, test results, and treatment.

Principals know their schools and their communities and what is required to maintain a school climate that supports teaching and learning. Accordingly, principals must weigh the benefits of employing policies that may invade the privacy of individual students or teachers against real concerns for the safety and security of the school population as a whole. What principals can strive for are reasonable policies that will yield reasonable results.

PRAYER, MINUTE OF SILENCE, AND EQUAL ACCESS IN SCHOOLS

There are centuries of conflict that demonstrate that government and religion do not mix. That is why it is particularly important in pluralistic societies like the United States that separation between church and state be maintained. However, religious freedom and prohibition against government support of religion are American constitutional guarantees that seem to generate a great deal of tension in public schools. As a result, principals find themselves pulled by community sentiment, personal beliefs, and threats of litigation as they implement policies that may or may not accommodate religious freedom and may or may not prevent government endorsement of particular religions or religious practices.

There is a plethora of case law that involves the establishment clause of the First Amendment and public education. However, prayer, a minute of silence, and equal access in schools are three issues that receive substantial media attention and create the most confusion for both school leaders and the public. For these reasons, they are addressed here.

Prayer

First and foremost, all children and school employees have a right to pray privately. The problem comes when an employee or representative of the school organizes or leads the prayer, or communicates religious conviction through dress or other forms of speech.

The U.S. Supreme Court has been fairly clear on the distinction between genuine free exercise by students and implied or explicit government sponsorship of religion through the actions of school employees. Students can talk about religion, associate themselves with other students who share their beliefs, and can participate in religious activities that are student-led. Nevertheless, even genuine student-initiated religious speech, including prayer, is like other forms of student speech and is subject to reasonable restrictions on time, place, and manner. Statutes permitting student-led religious speech at school events can be challenged if the state, through its representatives in the school, participates in or supervises such activity to a degree that exceeds custodial care.

Questions of permissible religious speech have come up when prayer is offered at school events. In 1992, the U.S. Supreme Court struck down the practice of clergy leading prayer at high school graduation, even though the principal attempted to minimize the constitutional conflict by encouraging a "nonsectarian prayer."[22] Some school districts responded to that ruling by crafting policies that were attempts to overcome constitutional prohibitions of state-sponsored religious activity.

On one hand, there was the Santa Fe Independent School District policy in which high school students could choose to hold an invocation at football games, then elect a student to lead prayer over the public address system.[23] When challenged in court, the defendant school district argued that the policy simply allowed students to decide if they wanted to engage in religious speech. In truth, the policy had the effect of furthering the district's intent to promote majoritarian religious beliefs. The invocation only existed because the school board allowed it, and the selection process would guarantee that representatives from other smaller religious groups would never be chosen. The policy was ruled unconstitutional.

On the other hand, there are school district policies that developed mechanisms for truly unrestricted student-led religious speech at graduation. Graduating seniors can determine if they want one of their own to offer a religious message or prayer at graduation. Such a policy was challenged in a Florida school district, but the Fifth Circuit ruled the policy constitutional.[24] The policy was constructed to support genuine, student-initiated religious speech by a student volunteer who was elected by the graduating class. More importantly, school officials did not supervise or otherwise engage in the preparation or editing of the speech.

Minute of Silence

Some states have passed legislation encouraging or requiring school districts to adopt policies implementing a minute of silence at the start of the school day. In the past, federal courts have struck down such efforts as failing the *Lemon* test.[25] However, recent high-profile violence in schools has given legislators new arguments. They assert that such violence and other evidence of a breakdown in discipline require actions that encourage students to reflect and to become more introspective. This is creating a re-emergence of "minute of silence" legislation.

In 2000, Virginia amended a 1976 statute[26] that established a minute of silence "for the expressly stated purpose of allowing students to meditate, pray, or engage in any other silent activity."[27] Prior to 2000, school districts had the option of adopting such a practice. The new amendment requires all districts to comply.

The State argued that its intent was to create an opportunity for students to absorb themselves in quiet activity, including prayer if they wished, and "be subject to the least possible pressure from the Commonwealth either to engage in, or to refrain from, religious observation."[28] The guidelines provided by the Virginia State Board of Education instructed teachers not to air their opinion on how the students should use their time and, likewise, that they must not allow students to coerce each other into religious activity or to engage in praying aloud. The Fourth Circuit upheld the statute.

Equal Access

In 1984, the Equal Access Act[29] was passed by the U.S. Congress. Under this legislation, public high schools that receive federal money cannot deny use of school facilities to any student group if other noncurricular groups are allowed to meet on campus. This also applies to religious groups or religious activities. Under the law, allowing student groups, whose existence or purpose has no direct connection to the high school curriculum, to use the high school as a place to meet and hold their activities creates a limited open forum. Once a limited open forum is established, then no student group, regardless of the religious, philosophical, or political nature of the group or activity, can be denied access to the school.

Allowing access to all student groups has generated some philosophical and political conflict and has drawn media attention when groups, whose beliefs or goals are contrary to those generally embraced by the school community, petition to use the high schools for their meetings. For instance, a student group, the Gay Straight Alliance Club, had to sue to gain access to a high school in California.[30] The high school had a limited open forum campus, but the school board voted to deny club status to the student group. The board argued that the group would create a substantial disruption to the educational activities of the school. The court disagreed and required the school to grant access. Some schools have chosen to avoid such conflict by simply denying access to all student groups.

Policy and Practice

While the lower courts are still struggling to create distinctions between genuine, student-led religious speech and district policies that promote religious practices through student speech, case law has made a few things clear. First, students can engage in religious speech at graduation ceremonies. Having a religious message must be at the discretion of the graduating class and must be given by a student volunteer or by one who is selected by the seniors. Most importantly, it should be genuine, student-initiated, unrestricted religious speech. That is, school officials may not contribute to, edit, or comment on the content of the speech.

Policies permitting student-led religious speech at other types of school events, such as extracurricular activities, are less likely to survive court scrutiny. Frequent, ongoing extracurricular activities differ from graduation ceremonies in scope and purpose and are not limited student forums that foster private speech.

There is an emerging judicial tolerance for "minute of silence" legislation that is secular in purpose, neither prohibits nor promotes religion, and avoids excessive government entanglement with religion. For example, Virginia legislation requires all schools to start the day with a quiet moment that can to be used by students to reflect, organize their thoughts, meditate, or pray, as long as it does not disturb others. Students can be required to sit quietly at their desks and teachers must refrain from influencing the nature of the quiet reflection in any way. They also have a duty to prohibit students from coercing others into religious activity and from engaging in vocal prayer.

Application of the Equal Access Act requires principals to pay attention to several essential elements when allowing access to school facilities. First, if the school grants access to one noncurricular student group, it must permit access to all. However, the act does entitle schools to prohibit groups or activities that would "materially or substantially disrupt the orderly conduct of educational activities within the school."[31] It also charges the school with the authority to maintain discipline, to protect the well-being of the students, and to ensure that participation in the student groups is voluntary.

Principals cannot try to forgo creating a limited open forum by characterizing existing clubs and other student groups as necessary to and directly related components of the school's educational program. If group participation is voluntary and student-initiated, it will be difficult for a school to argue that these groups are required curricular components.

Principals have a duty to understand the free exercise rights of all their students and to resist efforts to create uncomfortable situations in which students are subjected to the religious beliefs and practices of others. Likewise, principals cannot deny access of student groups to schools based on their personal or philosophical beliefs. These duties are not solely in recognition of the diversity of the student body, but are models of the principles of the U.S. Constitution that protect religious freedom and free speech.

SEXUAL HARASSMENT

Sexual harassment is a form of sexual discrimination and therefore illegal in educational institutions through Title IX of the Education Amendments of 1972 and Title VII of the Civil Rights Act of 1964. The Civil Rights Act of 1991 provides damages to victims of intentional sexual discrimination. Both school employees and students are protected under these statutes.

Sexual Harassment of Employees

Courts and schools have long been aware of sexual harassment in the workplace. Legally speaking, there are two forms of sexual harassment: *quid pro quo* and *hostile work environment*. The first, *quid pro quo*, involves power relationships and the demand for reciprocation of sexual advances in exchange for employment opportunity. Supervisors or administrators who use their position to coerce sexual favors from a subordinate in return for a promise of job opportunity or advancement, or under threat of job security, can be prosecuted for sexual harassment.

The second form, *hostile work environment*, refers to the conditions under which an employee works that foster tension and abusiveness in the work environment. Sexual innuendo and inappropriate remarks, gestures, or touching by an employee toward a co-worker are examples of factors that create a hostile work environment. An employee choosing to leave her or his position due to such conditions at work constitutes constructive discharge and is forbidden by Title VII. The Supreme Court has characterized a hostile environment in terms of the severity of the offending conduct, whether the conduct is threatening or humiliating, and if it effectively impedes the victim from doing her or his job.[32] The Court further ruled that the harassing behavior need not be so severe as to seriously affect the victim's psychological or physical well-being; it is enough that the environment "would reasonably be perceived, and is perceived, as hostile or abusive."[33]

If a school administrator has constructive knowledge that an employee is being subjected to sexual harassment by a supervisor or by a co-worker and does not act, the administrator can be prosecuted for vicarious liability. However, if the employer proactively seeks to prevent sexual harassment in the workplace through employee education and training and acts in a reasonable manner to investigate the complaint and to take corrective action, the employer can offer an affirmative defense against liability.

The harassment of a student by a teacher or other employee of the school is perhaps one of the most coercive and harmful of offenses. The teacher holds a power position over a student that could affect grades and other factors that have an impact on a student's standing in school. Worse yet, it could have tremendous psychological and emotional consequences for the student.

There are two important U.S. Supreme Court cases that speak to a school district's liability in such instances. The first, *Franklin v. Gwinnett County Public Schools*,[34] determined that damages are available to the victim under Title IX. A female high school student was sexually harassed by a teacher/athletic coach, starting in her tenth-grade year in a Georgia high school. Although other teachers and school administrators knew of the problem, they did not intervene on Franklin's behalf and in fact discouraged her from filing a complaint with the police. The district court dismissed her suit, saying that Title IX did not allow damages, and the court of appeals agreed. The Supreme Court reversed the decision.

The second case, *Gebser v. Lago Vista Independent School District*,[35] set the standard for *deliberate indifference* regarding school district liability. The case involved a female ninth-grade student who was coerced into a sexual relationship by a male teacher. The student did not report the teacher, saying she was unsure of how to proceed. The principal became aware that the teacher was making inappropriate remarks to students in his class when parents of two other students reported his behavior. However, he was unaware of the teacher's intimate relationship with Gebser until the police caught the two of them engaged in sexual intercourse. Up to the time the police became involved, the principal had never advised the superintendent of any problem. The Court ruled that in order for a school district to be held liable under Title IX, a person in a position to act on the behalf of the district must have constructive knowledge of the harassment yet take no action to bring a halt to it.

Peer-to-peer harassment received attention from the Supreme Court in 1999 in *Davis v. Monroe County Board of Education*.[36] An elementary school girl was subjected to continuous sexual harassment by a male classmate. The victim reported each incident to her mother and to her teacher. Her mother, in turn, spoke with the teacher who assured her that the principal had been informed. Nonetheless, the principal did not intervene and the male student, though his harassing behavior spanned many months, was never disciplined by the school for his actions. In its decision, the Court reiterated its previous ruling that private suit for money damages is available under Title IX. It also noted that substantial case law established school district liability for failure to protect students from harmful acts or behavior of other students. Applying its standard for liability, deliberate indifference, the Court ruled in favor of the girl.

Policy and Practice

Sexual harassment case law has resulted in substantial guidance from government agencies, such as the Equal Employment Opportunity Commission, and from professional associations, such as the NSBA, on developing meaningful policies that define and function to prevent sexual harassment, and delineate clear procedures for reporting, investigating, and remedying incidents of sexual harassment.

These policies describe clearly the prohibited behaviors and should make a strong statement that sexual harassment will not be tolerated. It should be well understood by employees and students that those reporting such behavior will enjoy confidentiality to the degree possible under the circumstances and will be protected from retaliatory action. All investigative and corrective action taken should be reported, while protecting confidentiality when appropriate.

Policy alone will not protect school districts and principals if these policies are not properly communicated and training is not provided. All employees should receive instruction on how to recognize and deal with incidents of sexual harassment through periodic training sessions. This is particularly crucial for new employees and any who come into the school system during the school year. Written policies should be included in faculty, staff, and student handbooks and distributed accordingly. Most importantly, principals and others in leadership positions must take prompt and deliberate action to investigate complaints and must notify their supervisors of the problem.

Meaningful policies that are widely communicated will serve many purposes. They will discourage sexual harassment at all levels and among all groups and, in the event of private suit, will demonstrate to the court a proactive and constructive effort to prevent such injury.

CONCLUSION

Principals are encouraged to stay current with the law through their professional associations and through professional development opportunities. If the situation permits, school leaders should seek advice when confronted with a problem in which the correct solution and legal obligation are not clear. Lastly, principals should be guided by their experience, good sense, and moral judgment. They are, after all, the best models to demonstrate respect for the individual's rights to protection, appropriate behaviors, and good decision making from staff and students.

ISLLC QUESTIONS

Standard 1

- How can a principal's understanding of school law issues identify and remove barriers to the school's vision?
- Describe several current issues affecting student learning and school climate and how understanding of current school law decisions can help principals remove barriers to students' success and staff safety and well-being.

Standard 2

- How do principals' understanding and practice of "justified at its inception," "individualized suspicion," and "scope of search" help them treat all individuals with dignity and respect while protecting the safety and security of all in the school?
- Give two examples of how a full understanding of current school law decisions requires principals to obtain more data and information about situations from all stakeholders before making decisions.

- In what ways do current school law decisions impact faculty and staff's safety and dignity?

Standard 3

- How can knowledge of current school law decisions help principals design and use school protocols regarding search and seizure, First Amendment rights, and sexual harassment to protect students and faculty and maximize student learning?
- Explain how principals can flexibly apply the Court's view of the obligation to provide school safety to the individual's right to dignity with regard to metal detectors, canine searches, strip searches, and random drug testing?
- Describe how principals can prevent and remedy sexual harassment and hostile environments in schools as it affects both students and employees.

Standard 4

- How does a principal's understanding of his or her community contribute to decisions about what expectations and practices are required to maintain a school climate that supports teaching and learning?
- What does school law say about a principal's responsibilities regarding school prayer and respecting that parents and students have civil and religious rights?

Standard 5

- How can a principal use case law and written policies to assure fairness and balance of community sentiment in the use of resources with regard to students' political, religious, or sexual-identity (i.e., gay or lesbian) clubs meeting at the school?

Standard 6

- How does an educational leader's full awareness of current school law promote the success of all students by understanding, responding to, and influencing the larger political, social, economic, legal, and cultural context?

NOTES

1. The Fourth Amendment of the U.S. Constitution reads: "The right of the people to be secure in their persons, houses, papers, and effects, against

unreasonable searches and seizures, shall not be violated, and no Warrants shall issue, but upon probable cause, supported by Oath or affirmation, and particularly describing the place to be searched, and the persons or things to be seized."

2.   *New Jersey v. T.L.O.*, 469 U.S. 325, 339 (1985).

3.   Id. Police officers must meet the higher standard of probable cause before they can conduct a search. The lesser standard of reasonable suspicion for school officials was adopted by the U.S. Supreme Court in *New Jersey v. T.L.O.*

4.   Id. at 342.

5.   *People v. Dukes*, 580 N.Y.S.2d 850 (N.Y. Crim. Ct. 1992).

6.   E.g., see *Zamora v. Pomeroy*, 639 f.2d 662 (10th Cir. 1981); *Doe v. Renfrow*, 475 F.Supp. 1012 (N.D. Ind. 1979), opinion adopted on this issue and reversed on another issue, 631 F.2d 91 (7th Cir. 1980); *Jones v. Latexo Independent School Dist.*, 499 F.Supp. 223 (E.D. Tex. 1980); and *Horton Goose Creek Independent School Dist.*, 690 F.2d 470 (5th Cir. 1982).

7.   Id. *Horton* at 481-482.

8.   *Doe v. Renfrow*, 631 F.2d 91 (7th Cir. 1980).

9.   Id. at 92-93.

10.   919 F.Supp. 1206 (N.D. Ind. 1995).

11.   261 F.3d. 1160 (11th Cir. 2001).

12.   *Vernonia School District 47J v. Acton*, 515 U.S. 646, 662 (1995).

13.   The *special needs doctrine* was set out in two non-school related cases, *Skinner v. Railway Labor Executives' Assn.*, 489 U.S. 602 (1989), and *National Treasury Employees Union v. Von Raab*, 489 U.S. 656 (1989). The U.S. Supreme Court held that government employees in safety-sensitive positions could be subject to suspicionless drug testing. Id. at 653.

14.   Supra note 18.

15.   *Earls v. Board of Education of Tecumseh Public School Dist.*, 242 F.3d 1264 (10th Cir. 2001); *Board of Education v. Earls*, no. 01–332, decided June 27, 2002.

16.   *Knox County Education Assn. v. Knox County Bd. of Education*, 158 F.3d 361 (1998).

17.   Supra note 13.

18.   Supra note 13.

19.   *Chandler v. Miller*, 403 U.S. 207 (1971).

20.   Supra note 12.

21.   Id. The court observed that the suspicionless testing was a one-time requirement as opposed to ongoing random testing and that requiring any school employee to undergo screening based on individualized suspicion was reasonable under the Fourth Amendment.

22.   505 U.S. 577 (1992). While the Court acknowledged the benefit of encouraging moral and ethical behavior among students, it noted that government promulgation of "civic religion" was equally infirm under the Constitution.

23.   *Santa Fe Indep. School Dist. v. Doe*, 530 U.S. 290, 120 S.Ct. 2266 (2000).

24.   *Adler v. Duval County School Board*, 250 F.3d 1330 (5th Cir. 2001). Certiorari denied, 122 S.Ct. 664, (U.S. Dec 10, 2001).

25.   The *Lemon* test is a tripartite standard established in *Lemon et al. v. Kurtzman, Sup't. of Public Instruction of Pennsylvania, et al.*, 403 U.S. 602 (1971). The legislation has to be secular in purpose, has to neither advance nor hinder religion, and can not create excessive government entanglement with religion.

26.   § 22.1-203.

27.   *Brown v. Gilmore*, 258 F.3d 265, 270 (4th Cir. 2001). Certiorari denied, 122 S.Ct. 465 (U.S. Oct 29, 2001).

28.   Id. at 271.

29.   20 U.S.C. §§4071-4074 (1984).

30.   *Colin v. Orange Unified School District*, 83 F.Supp. 1135 (C.D.Cal. 2000).

31.   Supra note 29.

32.   *Harris v. Forklift Systems, Inc.*, 510 US. 17, 114 S.Ct. 367 (1993).

33.   Id. at 367.

34.   503 U.S. 60, 112 S.Ct. 1028 (1992).

35.   524 U.S. 274, 118 S.Ct. 1989 (1998).

36.   526 U.S. 629, 119 S.Ct. 1662 (1999).

23

Emerging Issues in Special Education Law

Kathleen S. Mehfoud

Overview

The 1997 Individuals with Disabilities Education Act (IDEA) brought important changes in focus and practice for educators. Before, the law emphasized providing disabled students with access to educational services. Now, IDEA asserts higher expectations and outcomes for disabled students' achievement. Disabled students are expected, to the greatest extent possible, to learn in the general curriculum, participate in high-stakes testing, and score well enough in classes and on local and state-mandated assessments (traditional, with accommodations, or using alternative assessments) to earn standard diplomas. Only an IEP committee can make an exception to this testing. In addition, parents' role in the special education process has increased and strengthened, and educators must document their efforts to involve parents in identifying their children for special services and for educating them by developing the IEP. Moreover, principals and teachers must respond knowledgeably to language and bias issues to limited English speakers and minority students to avoid their overidentification for special education services. All these changes in law and practice have significant implications for principals and all educators in the education of disabled students.

The Individuals with Disabilities Education Act[1] (IDEA), first enacted in 1975 as the Education for All Handicapped Children Act[2] (EAHCA), offers guidance to special education's future. EAHCA's initial emphasis provided disabled students access to special education services and established a comprehensive set of procedural protections for them. The EAHCA accomplished this goal by providing a free appropriate public education through an individualized education plan (IEP). In return for granting this access and for providing appropriate educational services, the states would receive federal funding to support the education services for children with disabilities. The original law acknowledged that prior to the legislation's enactment, about one-half of the disabled children were not being served in an appropriate educational program, and a large number of these children received no service at all.[3]

The 1997 IDEA's "Purposes" section detailed special education's future direction, acknowledging a Congressional change in focus.[4] The emphasis was no longer on students' access to educational services, as that goal had been attained. Instead, Congress placed new importance on achievement outcomes and higher expectations for children with disabilities.[5] Disabled students would meet increased expectations of outcomes by providing them access to the general curriculum, when appropriate, strengthening the parents' role, and addressing the special needs of limited English proficient students and minority students.[6] Issues such as dropout rates, overidentification of minorities, and the inclusion of students with disabilities in state and districtwide assessments were also discussed.[7]

Extensive provisions dealing with the discipline of disabled students were also included in the 1997 IDEA language.[8] These provisions discussed for the first time the procedural protections available to identified students with disabilities if disciplined, as well as the protections available to those not yet eligible but suspected of having a disability at the time they were referred for discipline.

Changes in the IDEA over the past decade have been extensive. It can be anticipated that these past changes and the recitations in the law itself will provide the basis for future revisions to the IDEA.

PARTICIPATION IN THE GENERAL CURRICULUM AND TESTING

Children with disabilities will have greater access to the general curriculum and specialized regular education classes in the future. The IDEA has emphasized that students with disabilities have a right to participate in the general curriculum to the maximum extent appropriate.[9] The inclusion of a regular education teacher and a local educational agency (LEA) representative who is usually the principal or assistant principal, on the IEP team underscores this provision's importance.[10] The LEA representative is required to be knowledgeable about the general curriculum.[11] This access to the general curriculum does not necessarily mean that students with disabilities will be educated totally in the regular classroom. They must have access to the general curriculum to the extent appropriate. The IDEA continues to provide for a range of placement options and, as a result, no legal endorsement of total inclusion for all students with disabilities exists.[12]

Access to the general curriculum is consistent with another stated intent in the 1997 IDEA, that the outcome of the educational services for students with disabilities be assessed.[13] An improvement in outcomes could only be realized if students with disabilities received the same curriculum as students without disabilities, whenever appropriate for the individual student. Teaching both disabled and nondisabled students the same curriculum increases the likelihood of disabled students graduating with a standard diploma.

To further underscore the importance of access to the general curriculum, Congress mandated that students with disabilities participate in state and districtwide assessment programs.[14] Under the newest IDEA provisions, there can be no blanket exclusion of students with disabilities from testing programs in an effort to obtain improvement in a school's overall test scores. The IDEA requires that all students with disabilities participate in the state and districtwide testing programs in which regular education students participate.[15] The only exception to this requirement is that the IEP committee can determine that an individual special education student should not participate.[16] Administrators, individually, cannot make this decision; the entire IEP team must make it. Congress anticipated that only a few students with disabilities would ever be excluded from participating in routine testing programs. If excluded by IEP team determination, the student would have to participate in some alternate assessment program.[17]

PRACTICAL APPLICATIONS

For the majority of students with disabilities who will participate in the statewide and districtwide assessment programs, IEP teams and administrators have a strong incentive to ensure that these special students receive instruction in the general curriculum. Teaching the general curriculum would be necessary to ensure that the students with disabilities are familiar with all of the same information as the regular education students so that they might score well on the tests. It is of note that students with disabilities will be permitted to receive accommodations on the tests so that they can demonstrate their knowledge rather than the effects of their disabilities.[18] The IEP team determines which accommodations will be provided.

To meet this requirement, schools must develop effective ways to teach the general curriculum to students with disabilities, whether they are educated in special education or regular education classes. One method to meet this need is through co-taught classes, that is, regular education classes that are taught by a regular education and a special education teacher. Special education teachers will need to learn more about the standard curriculum during their teacher preparation coursework and will need to teach curriculum in their classes. Likewise, regular education teachers will need to be attuned and responsive to their disabled students' individual learning needs.

Another future consideration may be the teaching of the general curriculum at a slower pace in specified regular education classes to accommodate learning difficulties. This approach may already be used in some classes such as mathematics and other classes that cover the curriculum in two years rather than one. Whatever method is developed to provide access to the general curriculum for special education students, it is clear that these students should have access to the general curriculum whenever appropriate so they will achieve at higher levels and earn better scores on state and districtwide assessments. Where graduation requires successful completion of an assessment program, the access to the general curriculum is essential to permit students with disabilities to obtain a successful outcome from school, namely, graduation with a standard diploma. As more states adopt high-stakes tests, teaching the general curriculum to all students becomes crucial.

STRENGTHENING THE PARENTS' ROLE IN SPECIAL EDUCATION

The 1997 IDEA strengthened the role of parents of disabled students in the special education process. Previously, the parents were part of the IEP team. Now their strengthened role includes participation in all stages of the process, from identification through placement.[19] Parents are now required to help decide the evaluation components used to conduct assessments to determine eligibility for special education services.[20] In addition, parents must also take part in the eligibility determination.[21] Parents continue to be required participants in the IEP process and are listed first in the identification of IEP team members.[22] Congress believed that parents' inclusion in every aspect of the identification, eligibility, and IEP process would help ensure the child's receipt of a free appropriate public education.

Parents must be given enough advance notice of meetings to allow them to take part.[23] The IDEA defined specific mandatory steps school officials must take to encourage parents to participate in IEP meetings.[24] These efforts include telephone calls to the parents, visits to the home or place of employment, and documentation of efforts to convince the parents to participate.[25] Only if school officials cannot convince the parents to participate in the IEP meeting can schools hold it without them. Finally, the parents are required to be part of any meeting that determines their child's placement.

Practical Steps Regarding Parental Involvement

As discussed, the IDEA places great emphasis on involving parents in all aspects of special education. It is critical to show that parents have been permitted to participate in the various stages of the process, or any resulting IEP may be invalidated. Documentation of efforts to involve the parents is key for showing that the requirement to include parents in IDEA decision making has been met. An administrator must be able to show that the school consulted the parents about evaluation components, that the school invited the parents to participate in eligibility determinations, and that the parents received notice of IEP meetings and encouragement to attend. Too frequently, the meeting notice is sent too close to the scheduled dates to allow parents' participation. Schools must be able to show that parents are given notice of the time, date, place, purpose, and any participants in any IEP meeting before the meeting can be held. If the parents choose not to participate, schools are required to document their extensive efforts to include the parents. This documentation should reflect who has called a parent, the time and nature of the call, and any message. Documentation should show whether the call was completed or whether a message was left. Copies of mailings to the parents should be maintained in a file. Only if the school district has documented that it made reasonable efforts to involve the parents in accordance with the IDEA can the meeting be held without the parents and without fear of non-compliance with the IDEA.

These types of procedural matters receive close scrutiny under the IDEA and form the basis for complaints of noncompliance with IDEA procedures.[26] Parents file these complaints with the state's Department of Education and they can form the basis for compensatory education services or for monetary reimbursement in appropriate cases. Thus, an administrator must follow the IDEA procedures rigorously in order to successfully defend against any complaints.

MINORITIES AND THE LIMITED ENGLISH PROFICIENT UNDER THE IDEA

The 1997 IDEA singled out two groups for specific recognition: limited English proficient (LEP) students and minority students. Issues concerning the overidentification of minorities and LEP students as disabled will be an expected focus of special education programs in the years to come.

Turning first to the issue of the LEP student, the concerns expressed in the 1997 IDEA amendments began with an acknowledgement that this population was increasing rapidly.[27] The U.S. Department of Education noted that educational services provided to these students did not respond to their academic needs, and that there was a tendency toward overidentification of this population as disabled. Referral, assessment, and educational services were listed among the problems associated with the LEP student and special education services.[28] These concerns appear to be based on the belief that improper assessment techniques that do not account for the student's language difficulties can lower assessment scores and result in overidentification of the student as disabled. Obviously, if the LEP student is improperly identified as disabled, the student may be removed from the mainstream of regular education classes and educated in an overly restrictive placement. To solve this potential problem, Congress directed that the determination of eligibility for special education services must not be attributed to limited English proficiency.[29] Carrying the concept further, Congress directed that the IEP team consider, as a special factor in IEP development, the child's language needs.[30] Mandating consideration of these items requires the eligibility and IEP team to take steps to ensure that LEP students are not improperly identified as disabled and are not placed in special education services without the existence of a genuine disability.

Congress also responded to the unique issues involving minority students and their participation in special education. It acknowledged that the needs of a diverse society must be responded to in an equitable manner.[31] Congress suggested that schools were not responding appropriately to minorities' needs. As a result, schools overidentified these students as disabled, and disproportionately identified them as having mental retardation.[32] It was further noted that these students had higher dropout rates.[33] Congress acknowledged the need for appropriate role models in the teaching profession in order to prevent this result.[34]

To address the overidentification of minorities, Congress made provisions similar to those for LEP students. The evaluations administered to determine eligibility must not be culturally or racially biased.[35] Congress also wrote a requirement to track progress toward the goal of proper assessment and identification. Schools became obligated to track performance on assessments and dropout rates, and the states were required to report on these criteria.[36] Presumably, these provisions would allow monitoring so that the special needs of minority students would be taken into consideration and that correct educational decisions would follow.

Practical Considerations for LEP and Minority Students

The major issue with LEP and minority students and special education programs is overidentification and improper classification. To respond to this concern, careful attention should be paid to selecting test instruments. Test instruments should be ones that are widely utilized and accepted as valid by teachers or other professionals. The tests cannot be racially or culturally biased. The tests must also be administered in the student's native language.

If necessary, schools should give a preliminary test to assess a student's English proficiency. If proficiency is a problem for the student, the student should be tested with instruments administered in his or her native language. Giving a preliminary screening test for English proficiency may prevent invalid test results and the mistaken identification that may result from the incorrect selection of an otherwise appropriate test.

CONCLUSION

As discussed in the preceding sections, some current issues in special education are likely to be forerunners of future ones. The main theme for the future is that children with disabilities must receive a quality special education program. The program's success can be assured if the student has access to the general curriculum. Instruction in the general curriculum can be delivered in either special education or regular education settings. Measurement of success in reaching this goal can be determined from test scores, if the students participate in state and districtwide assessment programs. Accordingly, it is assumed that students with disabilities will participate in these assessment programs.

The parent remains the champion for the disabled student. The parents will likely pursue the best outcome for their child. As a result, the increase in parental involvement throughout the special education process provides a means of ensuring student access to the general curriculum and success of any special education services provided.

The theme of high expectations for all students with disabilities carries over to the treatment of minorities and limited English proficient students under the IDEA. These students are entitled to special consideration in test selection, identification of a disability, and IEP development. These special considerations are needed so that only those students who truly have disabilities are identified as disabled. The tests that are administered to these students should not have cultural, racial, or language bias that results in an incorrect determination of a disability. These varied considerations should result in correct determinations and the receipt of proper educational services in an environment most likely to help students experience success.

ISLLC QUESTIONS

Standard 1

- How does the author's discussion of the new federal special education focus on higher expectations and outcomes for disabled students help educational leaders identify and remove barriers to the school's vision?
- How does the author see the new federal special education focus on outcomes and higher expectations contributing to the recognition and celebration of all members of the school community?

Standard 2

- In what ways does the author advise principals to use the new special education laws to maintain a culture of high expectations?
- How do the new special education laws increase expectations for educational leaders' knowledge of measurement, evaluation, and assessment strategies both for special education program admission and traditional school outcomes, such as disabled students' graduation with a standard diploma?
- How do the new requirements for parent involvement help principals value the team process and increase stakeholder involvement for making decisions?

Standard 3

- In what areas does the author reference the new issues in special education to encourage principals to show flexibility in dealing with students' learning needs?
- What are the cautions to principals as the new special education laws address the needs of students with limited English proficiency and minority students?

Standard 4

- How can principals use the special education law to build family partnerships to support learning and address instructional issues?

Standard 5

- What are the expectations for documentation in the special education law that ensure that school leaders act with fairness, integrity, and in an ethical manner?

Standard 6

- How does the special education law help principals understand, respond to, and influence the larger political, social, economic, legal, and cultural context?

NOTES

1. 20 U.S.C. §§1400, *et seq.*

2. Public Law 94-142.

3. *Board of Education v. Rowley*, 458 U.S. 176 (1982).

4. 20 U.S.C. §1400(c).

5. 20 U.S.C. §1400(d).

6. 20 U.S.C. §1400 (c) & (d).

7. *Id.*

8. 20 U.S.C. §1415(k).

9. 20 U.S.C. §§1400(c)(5)(A); 1414(d)(1)(A)(i)-(iv).

10. 20 U.S.C. §1414(d)(1)(B)(ii) & (iv)(II).

11. 20 U.S.C. §1414(d)(1)(B)(iv)(II).

12. 20 U.S.C. §§ 1412(a)(5)(A) & 1413(d)(1).

13. 20 U.S.C. §1412(a)(17).

14. 20 U.S.C. §1412(a)(17)(A).

15. 20 U.S.C. §1412(a)(17)(A).

16. *Id.*

17. 20 U.S.C. §1414(d)(1)(A)(v).

18. 20 U.S.C. §1414(d)(1)(A)(v)(I).

19. 34 C.F.R. §300.501(a)(2).

20. 20 U.S.C. § 1414(c)(1).

21. 20 U.S.C. § 1414(b)(4)(A).

22. 20 U.S.C. § 1414(d)(1)(B)(i).

23. 34 C.F.R. § 300.501(b).

24. 34 C.F.R. § 345(c) & (d).

25. *Id.*

26. 34 C.F.R. § 300.660.

27. 20 U.S.C. § 1400(c)(7).

28. 20 U.S.C. § 1400(c)(7)(F).

29. 20 U.S.C. § 1414(b)(5); 34 C.F.R. §§ 300.532(a)(2) & -534(b)(1)(ii).

30. 20 U.S.C. § 1414(d)(3)(B)(ii).

31. 20 U.S.C. § 1400(c)(7).

32. 20 U.S.C. § 1400(c)(8).

33. *Id.*

34. 20 U.S.C. § 1400(c)(9).

35. 20 U.S.C. § 1414(b)(3)(A)(i) 34 C.F.R. § 300.532(a)(1)(i).

36. 20 U.S.C. § 1412(a)(16)(B).

24

Sustaining The Investment: Technology or Teachers?

Kenneth A. Engebretson

Overview

Education is using technology to support student learning to a degree and expense never seen before. Sustaining the effort brings many challenges. As technology costs increase, the author asks whether school divisions' technical support staff and infrastructure can leverage their considerable investment in technology for administrative and educational purposes and also pay for the other public education costs, such as rebuilding schools, and adjusting teachers' salaries to appropriate levels. The author gives examples from one school division about the exploding costs of providing a computer infrastructure to support administrative and instructional operations.

"You've got mail!" chimes the computer; "Error—not enough memory" pops up on the screen; a student copies and pastes photos off the

Internet to use in his school project. Public education uses technology to support student learning to an extent never before seen, making it possible for classes to communicate through words, pictures, video, and voice with peers halfway around the world. What an impact in providing authentic learning experiences! Various computer technologies also support the school system's business operations: student information management systems, budget, purchasing, payroll, transportation, food services, plant management, work order processing, workmen compensation tracking, to name a few. Effectively using these resources to reach educational objectives in the classroom is a controversial topic being discussed today by many others.

This section addresses the challenge school districts face to ensure that technical support staff and infrastructure can leverage that investment. The prime question is, "Can we afford to do this *and* pay the other costs of public education, such as rebuilding schools, adjusting teacher salaries to an appropriate level, and providing incentives to draw students into becoming teachers?"

BACKGROUND

After 5 years, $30 million, multiple contractors, and staff growing from 10 people to nearly 100, our school district is within months of completing the build-out of infrastructure called for in its first Five-Year Technology Plan. Eight thousand five hundred computers, large TV monitors, networked monochrome and color laser printers, digital cameras, scanners, and LCD projectors are in place at 37 of our 45 schools. Every teacher has a laptop computer that is on the network and can be projected onto the TV monitor in the classroom. Student computers are installed at the ratio of 3 per classroom and in 25 station labs: 1 lab per elementary school, at least 3 per middle school, and at least 7 per high school. The elementary and middle schools include wireless iBook student computers that effectively provide "mobile labs" for appropriate project-based instructional situations. All the district's administrative support buildings are wired to the same degree. A large number of application servers have also been installed in the past 2 years, with over 100 handling various math, reading, and other content area programs. Some servers are dedicated to providing user account authentication, e-mail services, and Internet content filtering. There are also database servers and other systems that handle such functions as bus scheduling, central student records imaging, work order processing, and worker's compensation. Switches, routers, servers, and telecommunications facilities are housed in racks, usually in controlled areas, and provide electricity through uninterruptible power supplies.

All employees who use computers have received extensive training in basic office productivity software (we are standardized on Microsoft's Office Suite), and teachers have received additional courses on integrating technology into the classroom. Most content area or grade-level specific professional development offerings now include appropriate technology components. In addition, experienced, computer-savvy teachers are working in each of our elementary schools as Technology Curriculum Integration Specialists (full-time positions for the 15 largest elementary schools and half-time for the remainder); half-time positions will also be added to the middle schools' staff in the next school year. High schools will provide the mentoring, modeling, research, and direct support to each content area by using a regular staff teacher for 1 or 2 periods per day to work with content area peers. These teachers will use their planning period and possibly their other noninstructional period (teachers in our high schools teach 5 out of 7 instructional periods over 2 days in an A/B block schedule) to do this and will receive a salary supplement comparable to a lead teacher.

School-based technical hardware and network/system operation/ administration support has grown to two persons per high school, at least one person per middle school, and one person per each of our nine elementary schools. A central technical pool of six people, who also support the library system and handle most trouble-shooting and help-desk calls, provide secondary-level, depot-type hardware maintenance. Three people now give central network engineering and daily operations support. A central staff of seven people provides database development and traditional management information systems support. Local area network cabling design and implementation management is provided by one person and will be augmented with another in 2002.

SUSTAINING THE EFFORT

Similar to many other school divisions, our municipality government's initial funding plan covered the tremendous cost to install networks, electricity, furniture, and the first wave of computers and associated electronics; but it did not project expenses to cover a reasonable technology "refreshing" cycle. The yardstick used in the early to mid-1990s was to replace computers in 5 to 6 years. Of course, computer technology advances continue to increase in pace and capabilities at a rate that makes the 1997 computers quite ancient, prior to any projected 2002-03 turnover. One bright spot: the price-to-performance ratio is bringing the relative cost down for the buyer, as long as the software doesn't require the absolute top in computing or video processing speed. The computer capability required in 1997 for adequate classroom operation ran about $1,200 per unit. A $900 unit today can fulfill the requirement. The money "saved" from this can be directly applied to the other computing aspect, software. Software programs are usually purchased with a licensing agreement that provides Web-based referential information (e.g., current updates for world history textbooks), maintenance updates, and other support for a year. Continuing to use the product in this manner requires an additional fee that can be up to 30% of the purchase price, which may have been as high as $30,000 for a schoolwide license.

As teachers and administrators attend more conferences, they see an ever-increasing supply of programs marketed as the way to increase achievement and test scores while engaging students in a multimedia package that is hard to resist. Even if the money were available to purchase "good" programs, training and technical support issues add to the overall implementation cost. In addition, there is the challenge of ensuring that any students with special needs are also able to utilize all programs. Imagine a blind student interacting with an image-intensive Web site. Will he or she be at an unfair disadvantage if the material is potentially testable?

Keeping all licenses current and the hardware up-to-date is a multi-million dollar endeavor every year for our district, even when based on using hardware leasing and centrally reviewing every program request prior to authorizing its purchase. Never evident in the operational budgets 5 years ago, these costs now amount to 3 to 5 million dollars annually. The personnel expenditures to support this operation are a similar figure. Although gains will be made with internally developed lessons that cost relatively nothing and have no annual licensing fee, they will not supplant the professional, commercially developed software packages benefiting from years of research and experience. Expectations from students, parents, *and* teachers are that the computer resources are up-to-date, especially when the advertising and marketing literature "prove that product A has been shown to increase achievement by 20% within some short period of use" or other such hype that laypersons rarely question. Marketing glitz and promises tend to sway the public, regardless of the product, and education is no exception.

CULTURAL CHANGE

Even more challenging than finding revenue sufficient to support the ever-growing technology integration within the school division is finding a methodology to address the significant cultural change that must occur in the instructional classroom and throughout the business/administrative support areas in order to make effective use of this new "tool."

The business/administrative support areas at schools as well as in district central offices quite closely parallel the experiences of non-educational business environments, as technology tools became instruments to perform tasks with greater efficiency and effectiveness. From the first electric typewriters, to fax machines and high-speed copiers, personnel met the transition with initial resistance as the "new" equipment forced changes in the way they handled and distributed information. When terminals connected to mainframe systems made their way into the office, a new nomenclature came into being and technical training gained a foothold in staff development efforts. As the personal computer began to replace character-based mainframe programs, a skill carryover occurred because home computer use was also growing more prevalent. As new software programs were introduced, sufficient training and local functional experts provided the means to quickly gain proficiency with any new features or looks.

However, the instructional classroom has been a far different culture to change. Teacher-centered discussions or lectures tend to relegate the computer to a role no different than using transparencies or other projected media. The real value in classroom computers is the vast amount of information that is immediately available and transferable to various display modes to emphasize a concept or point (graphs, charts, text, pictures, 3-D rotational models, etc.). Moving an instructional culture from drill and practice learning (e.g., how to use word processing or fill in a spreadsheet) to one where the students research topics that are relevant to a project and then analyze, re-form, and present them to their classmates, moves the responsibility for learning from the teacher to the student. That paradigm shift is not easily accomplished, especially if the technology is not reliable, fast, easy to use, and affordable. Overcoming those challenges *may* encourage a teacher to more effectively and frequently use technology, but one huge obstacle remains: how to ensure that content is covered and understood in an educational system that is becoming more engaged with high-stakes testing required by state and federal education departments.

One key element can make technology integration successful (or at least more likely to be successful): engaging leadership in "staying the course" by committing to a plan of action and support for 3 to 5 years *after* the required elements have been in place (wiring, computers, software, Internet access, training, and technical support). That is the minimum time for educators to recognize that this is not a passing fad; it is supported from the top; and technology integration engages students and produces desired results in fostering teamwork, learning the material, and being able to see the connections to real-world problem solving.

THE PROVERBIAL BOTTOM LINE

In order to achieve long-term value from the huge investment in technology, local community and state funding must commit dollars not only to the technical component, but more importantly, to adequately compensate teachers for shaping the next generation's abilities to confront and successfully address issues and challenges in a world totally unlike the one when "we" were in school. Funding these two elements is not mutually exclusive; the two are inextricably linked. Nearly every aspect of life has become increasingly dependent on technology. To omit from our educational process the use of technology in relevant, well-connected ways would be to prepare our children to fail as they enter the workplace or college. To not simultaneously provide teachers with adequate supports and financial compensation will all but ensure that classrooms will be well stocked with children—without an instructional leader. We cannot allow either of these scenarios to occur.

Educational leaders must sustain the investment with technology *and* teachers if students are to benefit.

CONCLUSION

Technology has become an integral and increasingly expensive part of the schooling process, impacting all areas from instructional practices to business operations. Computer infrastructure, however, must be continually maintained and upgraded and takes an ever larger share of educational dollars. State and local policymakers and educators need to carefully weigh benefits against costs as they consider what important needs are funded or unfunded. Educators and communities have difficult choices ahead.

ISLLC QUESTIONS

Standard 1

- How does the author view technology in instructional and administrative domains as both identifying and removing as well as inadvertently creating barriers to the school's vision?

Standard 2

- What plans does the author describe to increase technology integration and use within the school culture?

Standard 3

- What are the ways that the author sees technology use and costs as a critical issue of fiscal management?

- What demands does technology make on budget planning and a school division's values?

Standard 6

- How does the author's argument respond to the larger political, social, economic, legal, and cultural context?

Lessons Learned

Accountability comes with the job. Principals have always been responsible for keeping students safe and learning within an efficiently managed school environment. Accountability as an emerging and critical issue for principals, however, refocuses attention from competent administration of the school rules, operations, and finances to instructional and change leadership. Today's principals have a more immediate and direct responsibility for assuring that all students make *sufficient* academic gains. Ensuring that *all* students achieve at high levels on standardized tests is nonnegotiable. Public, and sometimes professional, consequences result for schools, principals, and students if this does not happen.

As Ronald Brandt advises, principals must make certain that all students are learning what is required, that they are able to demonstrate mastery when assessed by high-stakes tests. At the same time, principals as educational leaders must look beyond the "narrow" tested curriculum and discuss with major stakeholders what it means to be an educated person in the 21st century. Principals must sensitively remind stressed teachers that a full education is more than remembering testable facts. Regardless of the specific content, leaders must encourage teachers (and, if necessary, show teachers how) to present learning activities that involve students in critical thinking about important content: reading with comprehension; reasoning, understanding the big ideas and concepts that link information together; comparing and contrasting the information studied; interpreting data presented in varied formats; analyzing and synthesizing key aspects under study; assessing and evaluating an idea's merit; and communicating findings effectively using many types of media.

Moreover, principals should encourage teachers to provide students with a variety of means—including standardized testing—to demonstrate their mastery. Making the time to learn curricula in these ways increases students' retention of information and their ability to recall and use it later. While assuring that all students successfully meet the high-stakes standards, school leaders must help teachers, students, and the community see that well-designed, high-stakes tests are a "floor" rather than a "ceiling" of educational attainment.

As instruction leaders, principals must help all stakeholders keep their eyes on the "big picture." Hiring and keeping teachers, and developing them to enhance their classroom effectiveness, is of paramount importance. Addressing the curriculum in meaningful ways in addition to successfully meeting state expectations for achievement are also essential. Both are critical and emerging leadership challenges.

Principals must create an educational environment that addresses both the group's and the individual's needs. Teachers and students as groups and as distinct individuals have certain legal rights. Sometimes, these dual goals conflict. School law is continually evolving and affecting schoolhouse practices. Principals must stay current with changes in the law, appropriately modify written policies and practices, and always act with reasoned judgment based on specific and reliable information related to school and individual safety.

Part VI

Future Trends in Education

25

Changes in Educational Practice

Gene R. Carter

There is nothing permanent except change.

—Heraclitus

Overview

Trends indicate directions of change and suggest what the future may look like. The increasingly diverse U.S. population, the impact of technology, new understandings of how students learn, and heightened public accountability for student achievement call for different approaches to teaching and learning. Society will continue to demand increased teacher quality. Increased challenges for educators occur concurrently with anticipated turnover in classroom and school leadership.

The world has a new look in the 21st century. It is changing dramatically, and the rate of change is increasing at an astounding pace. Yet even in the face of tumultuous and unprecedented challenges, it is possible to discern future trends in education. Rather than predicting what the future will be, trends indicate directions of change and suggest what the future may look like.

Over the last several decades, society in the United States has been changing in fundamental ways. These include racial trends, demographic and economic trends, broadening conceptions of intelligence, technological advances in the classroom, and the academic standards movement.

RACIAL TRENDS

Between the years 2001 and 2015, all but two states—Arkansas and Mississippi—are projected to see an increase in their minority population. Many school districts will have student enrollments that are markedly different than they are now, with the largest growth occurring in the Hispanic population.

These minority-group growth statistics affirm this demographic shift:

- Today, about 65% of U.S. school-age children are non-Hispanic whites. That figure is projected to drop to 56% by 2020 and below 50% by 2040.
- The Hispanic school-age population is predicted to increase by about 60% in the next 20 years. By 2065, nearly one in four school-age children will be Hispanic.
- The school-age Asian and Pacific Islander population is expected to increase from 4% in 2000 to 6.6% in 2025.
- African American and Native American school-age populations are predicted to remain relatively stable. (Olson, 2000a, p. 34)

These patterns will present schools with cultural challenges in addressing the needs of all learners. Moreover, a disproportionate percentage of the teaching force represents the white middle class (Brandt, 2000). Bilingual education will take on increasing significance, and providing a personalized education for each learner will become more complex than ever before. In addition, findings that children from these racial groups are more likely to be from low-income families than non-Hispanic white children will reinforce the national need to address equity in our schools.

Few issues in U.S. education have drawn more intense attention and controversy than school segregation (Laosa, 2001). Current trends point to a return to widespread segregated schooling in America. According to a study by the Civil Rights Project at Harvard University, black and Latino students have become more segregated in impoverished school districts than at any time in the last 30 years. The segregation of white students is so pronounced, the study says, that it occurs even within majority black and Latino school districts (Fears, 2001). These findings are especially significant, said Harvard professor Gary Orfield, chief author of the study, because research has shown that segregated minority schools are located on islands of poverty and offer very limited opportunities. Clearly, these realities will create a test for schools that are already struggling to weave greater diversity into their social fabric.

DEMOGRAPHIC AND ECONOMIC TRENDS

Demographics are reshaping the United States in profound ways. Fewer students live in traditional nuclear families. Recent trends reported by the 2000 U.S. Census indicate that an increasing percentage of U.S. families are not cast in the traditional two-parent mold (Trotter, 2001).

Household trends indicate the following:

- Less than one-fourth of U.S. households are made up of married couples with children under age 18—a slight decline from 1990, when just over 25% of households were composed of married couples with children.
- The proportion of households led by single mothers with children of school age or younger has edged up from 6.6% in 1990 to 7.2% in 2000.
- Single parents, married parents, and remarried parents are joining the work force in ever-increasing numbers. Few children have a caregiver at home who does not have a full- or part-time job. (Trotter, 2001)

In addition to changes in family structure, a large number of children are also growing up in working-poor families. Approximately 1 in 5 U.S. children live in poverty. Childhood poverty has a detrimental effect on students' readiness to learn, and concentrated poverty in schools is associated with lower achievement for both poor and nonpoor students who attend such schools (Olson, 2000b). A recent analysis from the Washington-based Brookings Institution suggests that while poverty rates have fallen, extreme poverty is becoming more concentrated in a handful of neighborhoods, particularly in U.S. inner cities (Olson, 2000b).

The combined effect of these trends—increasing numbers of children without a nonworking caregiver in the home and more children living in working-poor families—overextends school facilities and requires that schools provide more services to compensate for the lack of learning readiness.

BROADENING CONCEPTIONS OF INTELLIGENCE

Knowledge creation and breakthrough thinking will stir a new era of enlightenment.

Current and projected trends favor a broadening of the concept of intelligence. Cognitive psychologists and others continue to investigate the nature of intelligence. Howard Gardner, who has identified eight distinct intelligences—linguistic, logical-mathematical, spatial, bodily-kinesthetic, musical, interpersonal, intrapersonal, and naturalist—has made discoveries in this field that have significant implications for learning (Brandt, 2000).

Traditionally, our schools have focused on the linguistic and logical-mathematical intelligences, but there is a need to develop other areas as well. Recent cultural trends also call for students to develop *understanding*, as opposed to merely memorizing information; and there is an increased reliance on thoughtful, open-minded questions and group activities. This shift means that teachers can be involved less in disseminating information and more in fostering students' critical-thinking skills and ability to synthesize information. More than ever before, students need to develop information-gathering and analytical skills.

Research on how the brain processes information, or brain-based learning, enhances our understanding of how to nurture intelligence. "We are on the verge of a revolution: the application of important new brain research to teaching and learning. This revolution will change school start times, discipline policies, assessment methods, teaching strategies, budget priorities, classroom environments, use of technology, and even the way we think of the arts and physical education" (Jensen, 1998, p. 1). Educators will come to apply brain-based learning practices to foster greater student achievement in an increasingly diverse population.

The importance of critical thinking raises the issue of what some see as a shift from education's traditional focus on instructional delivery to the concept of learning-centered education (American Association of Colleges for Teacher Education [AACTE], 2000). Flexible and adaptable teachers will be able to recognize different learning styles and make use of various technological advances to assist them in creating a learning-centered classroom. Ongoing professional development will be imperative to keep teachers informed of new developments.

TECHNOLOGICAL ADVANCES IN THE CLASSROOM

In the global digital economy, technology is rapidly changing how people live and work. Now we need to harness technology to benefit our nation's schools, communities, and most importantly, students. In the classroom, technology can create a more engaging learning environment and address the individual needs of students, including breaking down language and cultural barriers. Furthermore, it increases students' access to information, shifting the teacher's role from keeper of information to that of facilitator who assists students in accessing and analyzing information. Ensuring that all learners have access to both technology and training to use that technology is critical (AACTE, 2000).

THE STANDARDS MOVEMENT

Across the United States, policymakers and education leaders are implementing accountability and assessment measures in response to increasing calls for improved student performance (Goertz & Duffy, 2001).

As testing increases and the standards movement grows, educators face the challenge of balancing students' learning needs with professional accountability. The benefits of testing include motivating students, increasing equity in achievement, focusing teaching, and increasing the diagnosis of learning problems. The ongoing national discussion, however, must include using the test-aligned curriculum as the "floor" for achievement and avoiding "teaching to the test."

The research organization Public Agenda and *Education Week* (2001) noted these testing statistics:

- Increasing numbers of parents report that their children are required to take tests at various points in their schooling to ensure that they are acquiring necessary skills, a practice many standards advocates favor. Over half of grade-school parents (55%) report that their children must pass a basic-skills test before being promoted to middle or junior high school, up from 48% in 1999. Almost 6 in 10 middle school parents (59%) also say that this is true for their children to be promoted to high school.
- Teachers say standardized tests can motivate students and diagnose problems, and most say that "real learning" is not suffering in their own classrooms. But large majorities of teachers also say that districts are putting too much emphasis on tests, and that schools themselves are not chiefly to blame when students do poorly.
- Public Agenda's research suggests that most teachers have thought long and hard about the benefits and drawbacks of standardized testing—and they undoubtedly see benefits. Currently, just 20% say they themselves focus so much on test preparation that real learning is neglected—more than three-quarters (79%) say this is not the case in their classrooms.
- Nevertheless, teachers are also clearly worried. Large majorities fear that "teachers will end up teaching to the tests instead of making sure real learning takes place" (83%), and that "schools today place

far too much emphasis on standardized tests" (82%). Almost half—47%—fear that schools will be overwhelmed because too many students will fail.

The standards movement requires increased focus on learning and professional development, including realizing technology's potential to further learning, promoting teacher leadership, creating a stronger knowledge base for all learners, and involving the broader community. These needs must be considered in conjunction with the shifting paradigm from knowledge dissemination to the fostering of understanding. Increased knowledge about childhood development and how children learn will impact both curriculum development and teaching methods.

CONCLUSION

These trends—the increasingly diverse U.S. population, the impact of technology, and new understanding of how children learn—call for different approaches to teaching and learning. A number of conflicting factors will shape education and educators' needs. A record number of teachers and administrators will be retiring, creating a significant turnover in educational and classroom leadership. The student population will continue to grow and become increasingly diverse. Society will continue to demand improved teacher quality, increased student performance, and high-quality schools. In response, education leaders must incorporate the best of the old and the best of the new to create a more responsive and nurturing education system. The stakes are too high to ignore.

ISLLC QUESTIONS

Standard 1

- Given Carter's projected trends, how will an educational leader promote the success of all students by facilitating the development, articulation, implementation, and stewardship of a vision of learning that is shared and supported by an increasingly diverse school community?

Standard 2

- According to Carter, how would an educational leader promote the success of all students by advocating, nurturing, and sustaining a school culture and instructional program conducive to student learning and staff professional growth with changing demographic and economic trends, broadening conceptions of intelligence, technological advances in the classroom, and the standards movement?

Standard 4

- According to Carter's projected trends, how would an educational leader mobilize community resources with an increasingly diverse racial and economic population?

REFERENCES

American Association of Colleges for Teacher Education. (2000). *Log on or lose out: technology in 21st century teacher education, an Executive Summary.* Washington, DC: Author.

Brandt, R. (Ed.). (2000). Education in a new era. *ASCD Yearbook 2000.* Alexandria, VA: ASCD.

Fears, D. (2001, July 18). Schools' racial isolation growing. *The Washington Post,* p. A3.

Goertz, M., & Duffy, M. (2001, May). Assessment and accountability across the 50 states. *CPRE Policy Briefs,* 33, 1.

Good, D. G. (1999, January). *Future trends affecting education.* Denver, CO: Education Commission of the States.

Jensen, E. (1998). *Teaching with the brain in mind.* Alexandria, VA: Association for Supervision and Curriculum Development.

Laosa, L. (2001, Spring). The new segregation. *ETS Policy Notes, 10*(1), 1.

Olson, L. (2000a, September 27). Minority groups to emerge as a majority in U.S. schools. *Education Week, 20*(4): 34-35.

Olson, L. (2000b, September 27). High poverty among young makes schools' jobs harder. *Education Week, 20*(4): 40-41.

Public Agenda and Education Week. (2001, February 21). Public agenda: Reality check 2001. *Education Week, 20*(23): 51-58.

Trotter, A. (2001, May 23). Census shows the changing face of U.S. households. *Education Week,* 5.

26

Changes in the Educational Landscape

Paul D. Houston

Overview

The future of education is an amalgam of peril and possibility. The challenge for American education is not that it has declined but that its improvements have failed to keep pace with the world around it. The real failure of education is that we are teaching for tomorrow with yesterday's methods and programs. Educational leaders can make an important difference in the next few decades. Future challenges include providing equal and adequate supports for low-income students, viewing educational quality beyond the limits of standardized tests, addressing the increasing privatization of education, broadening the definition of schooling, and finding ways to connect us as similar yet diverse humans.

Educators often find themselves in that twilight zone between knowing what the dying day has wrought and sensing the gathering darkness of an unknown tomorrow. It is too easy to point out that educators are living in perilous times and that tomorrow will likely be even more difficult. It is also disingenuous to assert that tomorrow will be bright with the promise of new discoveries. It is doubtful that education will sink from sight under the weight of criticism and disinterest, and it is equally unlikely that things will be tremendously better. We should expect neither a lynch mob nor a pep rally.

The Chinese symbol for crisis has a dual meaning—great danger and great opportunity. That is true of education and of the leaders who serve it. The future of education is an amalgam of peril and possibility, and those toiling in its vineyards will be dealing with both. The last several decades have been a white-water ride for educational leaders. But turbulence is a given. It has been true of virtually every decade of the last century. The early 1900s saw the schools struggling to keep up with the teeming waves of immigrants searching for a new beginning in America. The booming twenties saw an America trying to find its moral center between fundamentalism and fun-seeking. The depression years of scarcity were quickly followed by the uncertainty of the war years. The innocence of the fifties was tempered by the need to adapt to the crush of the post-war baby boom. The sixties and seventies saw civil rights, integration, and equity in education, economics, and employment vying for a seat at the table. The eighties were a time when the schools put the "Nation at Risk." Never mind that the overblown rhetoric of that report and the dozens that followed were not born out by the reality in schools. America had been told it was caught in the undertow of a "rising tide of mediocrity" and that there would be hell to pay if something weren't done. That led to the modern reform movement exemplified by standards, testing, and accountability. America would improve its schools by bludgeoning them to greatness.

Part of the great irony of the reform movement of the latter part of the 20th century is that it was based on very shaky assumptions, and a sounder basis has not yet emerged. Perhaps never in the history of American education had more been done based upon such little evidence. The very premise of the *A Nation at Risk* report was that poor school quality led to our failing economy and the fears that we would not win the Cold War. This was a foolish assumption. The sluggish economy of the eighties turned into the booming one of the nineties without credit going to the schools. The walls of tyranny fell as the economy rose. So the very premise of the current reform movement was based upon twin fears that were short-lived.

Further "evidence" used to build the case of failing schools was equally flawed. Declining test scores in the seventies had already started turning up before the ink was dry on the first doomsday report. Much of the so-called "decline" was created because of the widely expanded pool of test takers. A much wider cross section of America was aspiring to college and taking the entrance tests—a tribute to America's schools, not the indictment it was made out to be.

Common sense would dictate that when you lean your ladder against the wrong wall, you paint the wrong house; and when you build a reform based upon poor assumptions, you might have a poor reform. The challenge of American education is not that it has declined but that its improvements have failed to keep pace with the social setting. The deterioration of the American family and the disintegration of the supportive social fabric meant that fewer children have the social capital behind them to learn properly. Furthermore, the economic setting that demands all its workers have a higher level of skills has raised the bar. It is an issue of incremental improvement in an exponential environment. The schools have gradually improved but have not kept pace with the world around them.

But the real failure of current education is much more a failure of motivation. Schools are trying to educate children wrapped in 21st-century interests in 19th-century classrooms. We are teaching for tomorrow with yesterday's methods and programs. We are teaching children in a sterile school environment only to see them leave school in the afternoon to go into a world rich in stimulation. Current reforms, which tend to narrow the curriculum to what can be easily tested, and which communicate to students that learning and doing well on tests are synonymous, will likely move the system further away from educational excellence rather than toward it. They are also squeezing the juice out of what might motivate children to learn. School must be a place where children want to be, and for that to happen, education must be meaningful and engaging.

It must be assumed that the schools will be buffeted by other, not-yet-defined "crises" that America must face. Schools will be blamed when things don't work, and ignored when they do. It is a fine American tradition to beat up its central institutions in times of difficulty but to celebrate success as an individual achievement. All this would lead to the thought that anyone considering a career in educational leadership should get a psychological workup before proceeding.

But that would be only part of the story. Just as fire tempers steel, challenges create leaders. If someone were considering a leadership role, the next few decades will be a prime time to step up and make a difference. What areas of challenge will the next generation find?

The first is one left over from our past—equity. Almost all the failures of American education can be found in the failure to address the issue of equity and adequacy. The children in America who need education the most are the ones who tend to receive the least support. Of course, that leads to problems of achievement and lower outcomes. For equity to occur, the system must deal with providing an education that is adequate to the test. Children living in poverty without adequate social capital must not be given the same resources as other children; they must be given greater resources. This will test the courage and the creativity of tomorrow's leaders.

This naturally leads to the next issue—quality. Education's mission is shifting from sifting individuals to raising the expectations for all. That is the driving force behind the standards movement and will likely permeate the educational landscape for some time to come. Issues around accountability and performance will shape much of the work. The challenge will be to move from a fixation on tests to a broader view of what education can and should entail. It will no longer be tolerable to allow some students to fail while others succeed.

The irony is that much of the current practice could well lead to more failure in the future if we continue on our current course. High-stakes tests and the elimination of social promotion are designed to raise the bar. However, in doing so, they may lower the ground. Retention in grades leads to overage students who already feel they have failed. The "one strike and you're out" mentality of high-stakes tests shuffles off children from their potential prematurely. School leaders will have to find ways to balance the legitimate desire for raising standards with a humane approach that gives students the resources and opportunities to be successful.

The third major issue facing school leaders will be the overall deregulation of the industry and the increased emphasis on privatization. A number of factors are driving this. First, many formerly public industries have been restructured and deregulated. From the U.S. Post Office to the airline and utilities industries, former highly regulated industries are doing work in a looser and more wide-open environment. The drumbeat of public criticism of schools and the legitimate disillusionment of some has also led the private sector into looking at education as a possible income source. Inside the schools, private companies are vying for a piece of the business. Outside, the pressure for vouchers, charter schools, and home schooling are reshaping the educational landscape. School leaders in the 21st century will need to be nimble and entrepreneurial to compete in this new environment.

The fourth major challenge to schools will go to the very definition of what schooling means. Technology is rapidly opening up the classroom doors. Not only does it provide a way for students and teachers to escape the classroom confines but also gives students and parents the opportunity to find learning in places other than school. Donald Tapscott has coined the term "disintermediation" to describe what happens when new technologies come into play. When Gutenberg invented the printing press, he disintermediated the church. The average man no longer had to ask the priest to tell him God's intentions; he could read the Bible and make his own conclusions. This disintermediated the church and led to the reformation. The power of computers, CDs, and the Internet now allows parents and children to find learning in a totally open environment. This has staggering implications for schools, because no longer will students need to go to that place to be educated. School leaders will need to find a way to ride this tidal wave of change and still help students connect to each other. This leads to the final, and perhaps greatest challenge to educational leaders.

Leaders in this century will be grappling with the very essence of what it means to be human and what it means to stay connected as humans in a technological environment. We will have to find ways to sustain a democracy in that setting. Educational leaders will come back to their core mission. Education has always been and will always be about the human condition. With cloning, unraveling the mysteries of DNA, and man's constant search for new ways to destroy himself, educational leaders will need to find ways of helping students, teachers, parents, and the broader community wind their way through fields littered with new technology and outworn ethics to safely rest at the other side. We will have to help humans remember what it means to be humane. As the world continues to separate and go in a thousand different directions, and as we "demassify" our ways of relating to each other—whether it is finding companionship in a "chat room" or our entertainment through some narrow niche cable channel, we will have to find ways to reinvent our relationships to each other as human beings. Tolerance and learning to accept and embrace differences will be a core skill in our increasingly diverse world.

Like Alice in Wonderland, we have eaten pills that make us larger and smaller simultaneously. The world is at our doorstep, but we don't know quite how to live in it. We have specialized our interests to the point where we no longer have to read or hear anything that doesn't interest us, but we have fewer bonds holding us together. This raises serious questions for how a democratic society is to survive. Democracy depends on civic engagement, and civic engagement hangs on the ability to rub up against those who are different. A peaceful world depends on understanding and accepting differences. Technology allows people to "cocoon" themselves into pockets of isolation every bit as elitist as gated communities. Educational leaders will have to find a way to use technology and the other social advances coming online to create a new sense of community and common purpose.

CONCLUSION

We are truly entering a twilight period, and like the old "Twilight Zone" series of the mid-twentieth century, we are "traveling through another dimension: a dimension not only of sight and sound but of mind; a journey into a wondrous land whose boundaries are that of imagination." That is the danger and the opportunity for educational leaders.

American education has always faced challenges. Tomorrow's school leaders will have to find enterprising and innovative ways to balance the legitimate desire for raising standards with a humane approach that gives all students the resources and opportunities to be successful. A democratic and peaceful world depends on it.

ISLLC QUESTIONS

Standard 1

- According to Houston, how does the educational leader promote the success of all students by facilitating the development, articulation, implementation, and stewardship of a vision of learning that is shared and supported by the school community?

Standard 4

- According to Houston, how does an educational leader promote the success of all students by responding to diverse community interests and needs?

Standard 5

- According to Houston, how does an educational leader promote the success of all students by acting with integrity, fairness, and in an ethical matter when responding to the following issues: equity and adequacy, educational quality and high-stakes testing, privatization of educational services, a new definition of "schooling", and what it means to be human?

Standard 6

- According to Houston, what influences have falsely characterized the cultural context of education?

Lessons Learned

Although American education has never been more effective than it is today, public schools' challenge is to keep pace with the world around it. As Paul Houston comments, the real failure of education is that we are teaching for tomorrow with yesterday's methods and programs.

Principals are working within a dynamic societal and political context that greatly impacts what happens in schools. The increasingly diverse student population, heightened public accountability for all students' achievement, more demands for teacher quality, new understandings about how students learn, and increasingly available technology require different approaches to teaching and learning. Competition from private and charter schools for students, tax dollars, and vouchers that will allow parents to enroll their children where they believe they can receive the best education, also mean public schools must design better ways to educate all students to high levels.

Today's schools must find successful and measurable ways to address equity and excellence. They must ensure that all students can meet the high standards set for each grade and for graduation. At the same time, public schools need to prepare students for a more complex, changing world than standardized test mastery can affirm. Principals must actively embrace their roles as change agents and instructional leaders to develop the school culture and classroom practices that value student and instructional diversity. Principals must help teachers develop and demonstrate confidence in their abilities to bring the highest quality teaching practices and meaningful curricula to *all* students. Ongoing, highest quality professional development must become regular features of schools; and schools must become true learning communities in which all—principals, teachers, and students—continue developing essential mastery in new areas. Principals as change agents and instructional leaders will have to keep the schools' focus on both ends of the educational continuum: the need to help all students meet world-class standards and the individualized learning approaches essential to help increasingly diverse learners reach them.

American education has always faced challenges. A democratic and peaceful United States and world depend on our success.

Epilogue

Leslie S. Kaplan
William A. Owings

While this text includes many chapters detailing new perspectives and approaches that keenly impact principals, critical and emerging issues in educational leadership can be viewed in three broad categories. First, principal leadership is crucial if schools are to accomplish their mission of educating all students to high levels. The various societal changes at work outside the school grounds play out in each classroom, and principals must help guide their communities to envision and enact new ways of schooling to ensure that both excellence and equity are well served.

Next, the principal's primary focus must be on teaching and learning. As more research becomes available about how people learn, and more strategies enter the classroom that can advance learning for diverse students, principals must focus attention on strengthening classroom practices and helping teachers learn and use approaches that bring all students to high achievement levels. These research findings raise important questions about the ways we practice instruction, curriculum, assessment, and technology. They also boost the dynamic tensions principals face, meeting individual learning needs within structures and practices intended for the entire student population.

Finally, principals now confront intense public scrutiny and accountability for all students' achievement to an extent not seen before, in addition to continued accountability for sound stewardship of public laws and finances. Principals must continue to upgrade their effective management practices that keep students safe and public policies and funds appropriately addressed, even as they commit their primary energies to the issues of teaching and learning.

PRINCIPAL LEADERSHIP IS CRUCIAL IF SCHOOLS ARE TO ACCOMPLISH THEIR MISSION

While American education has never been more effective than it is today, the challenge for public schools is to keep pace with the world around it. Paul Houston notes that we are teaching for tomorrow with yesterday's methods and programs. This, and not low student achievement, is education's real failure. Principal leadership is essential if schools are to bring quality education to each student. This is the time to make a difference.

Today's principals find themselves within a highly charged environment amid social, economic, political, and cultural changes. As Gene Carter describes, schools are welcoming increasing numbers of students from minority groups and other cultures. Fewer students arrive at school with educational support from traditional two-parent families. One in five children comes from poverty, a set of complex living conditions that harms children's readiness to learn. Immigration trends mean that more English language learners are enrolling. Schools with high levels of students from low-income homes are associated with lower school achievement. Nevertheless, principals are responsible for creating the conditions within their buildings and classrooms to help each student reach the highest achievement levels, regardless of family circumstances.

The principal's role has shifted from one primarily focusing on organizational management to one emphasizing leading change, bringing new approaches to teaching and learning to meet heightened public expectations for accountability. Michael Fullan and Gordon Cawelti provide us with models of how principal leadership can successfully address both excellence and equity concerns in student achievement. As Robert Marzano and Linda Darling-Hammond note, the cascade of research findings on teacher quality, teacher effectiveness, and how students learn is also fomenting the need for changes inside classrooms.

Leadership for school change involves both process and content. The process involves enacting a series of activities that mobilizes others in the professional learning community to act in concert with well-designed plans and practices to reach valued ends. Likewise, the content of school change includes a reliable knowledge base about improving teaching and learning that informs behaviors. Learning how to be a change leader requires more than formal coursework alone. Michael Fullan's five crucial mind and action sets for 21st-century leaders provide an insightful blueprint for principals as they become leaders of change: developing a deep sense of moral purpose; knowledge of the change process; capacity to develop relationships with diverse individuals; fostering knowledge creation and sharing; and the ability to work coherently with others while making many innovations at once. These vital components are as much matters of temperament, character, and cognitive dispositions as they are skills to be mastered in professional training programs.

The only changes that matter for students, however, are those that take place in their classroom. Principals, therefore, must become the "teachers of teachers," making change coherent and cohesive to faculty, parents, and students. Principals do this by being the central force for school change, articulating the ideas, mobilizing the people by developing a shared vision that prompts widespread commitment to acting on shared values, and monitoring their actions. Principals work with other educators to create a set of shared values, beliefs, and practices, building a school culture that supports their vision in all daily decisions and actions.

Leading change is not a one-season event. It requires more than gathering staff, parents, and community leaders for vision-setting or mission-statement writing activities. As change leaders, principals become culture leaders, continually nurturing the school ethos so that innovation can become an enduring practice. Teacher and parent "buy-in" and consensus are essential. Without the principals' *ongoing* investment of time, energy, and intellect in building a shared philosophy of values, belief, and practice, instructional changes become fads that shift and disappear when the classroom doors close rather than grow to become sustained habits that benefit teachers and students. As William Patterson notes from his experiences, the shared vision, beliefs, and practices must be continually reviewed, reinforced, clarified, and extended among both veteran educators and members new to the learning community. Accordingly, principals as cultural leaders need clear thought, high energy, people and intellectual skills, planning acumen, and time to monitor and adjust the process.

Change and *culture* are keywords for principal leadership. Making change work requires high degrees of both cognitive and affective skills. On the one hand, principals as leaders must ensure that all the school's educational policies and practices support quality teaching, learning, and leadership. On the other hand, principals must create an educational environment that engages others to enact their common vision in everyday decisions and behaviors. Successfully carrying out these important responsibilities successfully involves learning how to enact change in schools, involving others in these important tasks, and developing the personal qualities to put these ideas into action.

TEACHING AND LEARNING ARE PRINCIPALS' PRIMARY FOCUS

Principals must not only be leaders of change. They must be knowledgeable instructional leaders. Current and emerging research on how people learn and how effective teachers increase student achievement is significantly impacting teaching and learning. As instructional leaders, principals must not only stay abreast of our new understandings of intelligence, best instructional techniques, and how to promote student learning.

Principals must also help teachers translate these new approaches into classroom practices that enhance higher student achievement in diverse populations. Unless best practices enter each classroom, all students cannot benefit.

What students need most is an effective teacher. We know through theory and research what effective teaching is and the extent to which it shapes learning. Robert Marzano affirms that effective teaching accounts for two-thirds of the total effect of schooling on student learning. The influence of going to an effective school as opposed to an ineffective school is a 34-percentile point increase in measured achievement. Having an effective teacher accounts for about 26 percentile points. What specific teachers bring to the schooling process is the major influence on student achievement for students at all achievement levels. The impact of effective teaching on all students' achievement cannot be overstated.

Similarly, Linda Darling-Hammond says that, given the demonstrated influence of effective teaching on student learning and achievement, the increasingly diverse student population in our schools, and the required standards-based high-stakes testing as a barrier to promotion and graduation, principals' most important responsibility is providing each student with a successful teacher. In an era of teacher shortages, this challenge becomes greater and increases the strategies that principals and other educators must use to reach this goal. Principals must find innovative and proven ways to develop and support new teachers—both young first-careerists and mature midcareer entrants—as they enter the profession and induct them into the school culture. The press for ongoing professional development thoughtfully designed to change and sustain best teaching practices must include immediate classroom relevance, teacher choices within prescribed requirements, real-world practice and feedback, peer observations and mentoring, frequent classroom observations and conferencing. Teachers themselves must become professional learners as well as facilitators of others' learning.

While teaching is the process of facilitating learning, curriculum is what is taught. Curriculum reflects an organization's values; it is the school and community's "big picture." If, however, as Marzano suggests, the present standards-based curriculum is too large (and, some say, too inappropriate) for most students to learn in a single year, educators and the community must ask, What essentials do students need to know and be able to do to succeed in a *knowledge society* where they will be required to understand, analyze, synthesize, evaluate and use information for problem solving and communicating?

Instead of a curriculum that is too broad and too wide, one that lacks relevance for many students, or one that is tailored specifically for a certain standardized test, principals must help teachers and their communities understand that a prioritized curriculum focused on essential knowledge and skills that emphasize active information use for real-world problem solving will better prepare all students for economic viability in the 21st century, advanced education, and well-paying careers. To these ends, technology can be an engine that drives student learning with heightened relevance and meaning. Alan November sees technology not as a tool, but rather as an "environment" in which to teach real-world problem solving. Issues of relevance disappear and student engagement with learning heightens as they pursue topics of genuine interest within teacher-approved limits. What is more, learning how to read critically, think and reason with data for problem solving, and communicate these findings will likely increase what students remember, strengthen their ability to read and understand test questions and related materials, and thereby serve students well on paper-and-pencil assessments, too.

Moreover, as Carter observes, technology can also provide some of the differentiation needed to engage diverse learners for high levels of achievement. As a result of infusing technology into instruction, the teacher's role will change from information keeper to knowledge facilitator who assists students to access, analyze, and use information. Accordingly, the curriculum will become less rigid and text-driven, more individualized (within prescribed local and state content limits), and will increasingly enhance students' critical thinking and reasoning skills.

Along with teaching and curriculum, assessment is learning's third critical element. Assessment is a natural part of teaching and learning, informing both as part of the natural feedback loop. When most people think "assessment," they see high-stakes, multiple-choice tests that hold schools and students accountable for mastering a body of content. Serious consequences result for institutions and individuals if too low a proportion of students "pass" the test. Fortunately, assessment is broader than summative exams and can be a useful approach to increasing student learning. It depends on how educators and the public use it. Especially in this era of high-stakes testing, principals as instructional leaders need to understand assessment concepts and practices if they are to effectively support student achievement.

Assessment provides needed feedback about students' progress. Assessment can be *for* learning or *of* learning. The former practice actually increases achievement; the latter simply measures it. Assessments *of* learning provide evidence of student achievement for the newspapers. It happens at the end of a learning cycle, such as the end of a course or a school year. On the other hand, assessment *for* learning occurs throughout the learning process. It provides a continuous flow of information feedback about student achievement both to monitor and to advance student learning. When teachers and students can know moment to moment which areas the students are understanding and using fluently and which are still weak and need further explanation and practice, assessment is *for* learning. Assessment data are used for instructional planning and delivery to help more students succeed. These practices build students' self-confidence as well as achievement because they can correct small errors as they learn, without major penalty. Principals must help teachers understand and use assessment *for* learning to do their jobs better.

The emerging question for educational leaders is how assessment should be used to maximize student learning and growth. As Linda Nathan writes, principals need to view assessment as monitoring an individual's progress as well as his or her final standing relative to the standard. As Ronald Brandt also reminds us, not all judgments of educational or personal value can be determined with a pencil-and-paper tests. Educators need multiple measures to determine students' knowledge and skill mastery. This includes employing standardized tests as well as student performances, projects, and products matched against agreed-upon rubrics illustrating stages of quality from basic to mature. It includes monitoring the contents mastered as well as the processes used. Ideally, measurement should determine not only whether the student met standards but also the extent to which the individual has grown since the last assessment.

High-stakes tests *of* learning have enormous implications for instruction, curriculum, and assessment. Ironically, high-stakes testing has both narrowed and enlarged the curriculum to make it, for most teachers and students, unmanageable, unteachable, and unlearnable. A curriculum pumped up with information that politicians declare to be worth knowing has made what students are supposed to know at each grade level too broad to learn except superficially. At the same time, this inflated content size, coupled with high penalties to school and student for not mastering it, has the practical effect of narrowing what is taught to merely what is tested. This is much less—and much more—than what students need to be truly "educated."

Noting this dilemma, the principal as instructional leader has several important responses. First, as Brandt recommends, the principal must ensure that students are fully prepared for the formal assessments. This requires appropriate staffing, curriculum alignment, respect for instructional time, and opportunities for ongoing feedback and re-teaching of content to students who may not have learned it the first time, to keep all students moving forward. Next, principals must provide high quality professional development programs that tie best instructional practices to the taught and tested curriculum, offer collegiality, include shared study of student work, and incorporate ongoing classroom monitoring as teachers try out and refine these instructional practices.

In addition, even as they are preparing students to pass these tests, principals must educate teachers and the larger community that these standardized tests do not assess the full measure of what students need to be effective in a *knowledge society*. Moreover, principals must find ways to increase the range of quality learning experiences for students beyond that which will be measured by paper-and-pencil exams. Finally, as change leaders, principals can work with professional organizations and their coalitions to educate legislators and citizens about how to turn desirable standards into *realistic* amounts of *essential and appropriate* content for each grade level with proportionate and useful application of results for individuals and schools.

ACCOUNTABILITY IS REAL AND IMPORTANT

The principal's responsibility and accountability for student achievement is crucial. As Gerald Tirozzi reasonably concludes, public schools are public and must be accountable. Interested parents, communities, and legislators want and deserve evidence that students are learning. Taxpayers care about whether students are learning; student achievement is one indication that their monies are well spent. The taxpayers' concern expresses a logical civic issue about the quality of our national and neighborhood economies. As a result, we are seeing unprecedented and coordinated efforts from the statehouse to the schoolhouse to set high achievement standards for all students, transform the standards into rigorous assessments, and hold educators accountable for student achievement as reflected in their test scores. Similarly, policymakers have attached promised rewards for schools and students producing high scores and punishment for those who aren't.

To be accountable, principals must assure that all students are ready to perform well on standardized tests. Student scores and schools' pass rates on high-stakes tests provide a "report card" for a community to know how well their schools are succeeding. Principals know, however, that these test results measure only the educational "floor." Standardized testing represents a minimum acceptable education, only measuring student knowledge and thinking to the degree of complexity and depth that can fit a machine-scored, multiple-choice format. Real education that we want for our children is both less and more than state-mandated standards. Not all factors of educational value can be measured with standardized tests. Likewise, not all facts deemed significant enough to remember for a test are really useful or meaningful to an "educated person." To be fully accountable, principals must help their teachers and communities view standardized tests as one valid, important, and public means to assess learning. At the same time, educational leaders also need to help their communities keep a high and broad "ceiling" for different types of worthy achievement with varied means to demonstrate them.

Unfortunately, the push for accountability is influencing many educators to ignore best curriculum, instructional, and assessment practices as they rush to prepare students for high-stakes tests. Principals who understand teaching, learning, and assessment can remind teachers to use those very strategies that would increase student learning and achievement, recalling that good instructional, curricular, and assessment practices are time investments that pay off richly in student achievement, in class and on standardized tests.

In addition, principals face the dynamic tension of raising achievement of all students while addressing each individual's learning and growth needs. Principals must maintain high standards and common expectations for all students' high achievement, while respecting diversity of paths and means for each student meeting them. Fortunately, both federal and state laws and an increasing array of best practices provide direction and guidelines to help structure learning so diverse students can meet the common high standards set for each grade and for graduation. Special needs students have a civil right to an education that helps them successfully meet the bar set for all students, and must be given the opportunity to develop the competence and confidence to make them strong learners and economically viable citizens. As Chriss Walther-Thomas and Michael DiPaola write, while principals need not know every strategy to advance exceptional learners' achievement, principals do set the school climate and express the values that support vigorous and appropriate individual educational practices within the regular education program, to the greatest possible extent.

Finally, accountability also means effectively running the school facilities, operations, and resources for a safe, efficient, and effective learning environment. These are the traditional expectations for school principals as public stewards and managers. Teachers and students have legal rights, and school law continues to evolve. Principals must stay current with changes in legislative mandates and case law, and modify their policies and practices accordingly. While details will vary, principals have certain constants on which to base their behaviors. With attention to health and safety concerns the first priority, principals act within legal parameters when they act in good faith and use reasonable judgment based on specific, reliable information related to school and individuals' well-being. They must follow school procedures that tell the accused the nature of the charges against them, use practices that are not overly intrusive, and respect the individual's rights to protection. As professionals, principals must always treat others with dignity and respect, allegations of misdeeds notwithstanding.

CONCLUSION

As Paul Houston writes, "The future of education is an amalgam of peril and possibility, and those toiling in its vineyards will be dealing with both." Principals' focus is on teaching, learning, and leadership. They use all three aspects to create environments that place quality teachers in each classroom and assure that all students have the opportunity to—and do—reach high achievement standards. Teaching and learning are the focus; leadership is the process to enhance both.

Increasingly, principal leaders also have critical roles to play outside the schoolhouse. Our nation's economic and democratic health, our international standing, and our social environment are closely linked to the quality of our public schools. Rather than allow politicians to set the reform agenda, educational leaders must be active and vocal participants in the policy discussion, informing the national and local debate with their expertise and experience. This is another means for principals to address critical and emerging issues in educational leadership.

Index